THE
NO
CHOLESTEROL
(No Kidding!)
COOKBOOK

THE MEDICALLY PROVEN
KITCHEN CURE
FOR HIGH CHOLESTEROL

**By Mary Carroll
with Hal Straus**

Rodale Press, Emmaus, Pennsylvania

Printed in the United States of America on acid-free paper

Edited by Jean Rogers
Copyedited by Laura Stevens
Book design by Jerry O'Brien
Cover design by Denise M. Shade
Cover photography by Angelo Caggiano
Illustrations by Kathi Ember
Indexed by Andrea Chesman

If you have any questions or comments concerning this book, please write:

Rodale Press
Book Reader Service
33 East Minor Street
Emmaus, PA 18098

Library of Congress Cataloging-in-Publication Data

Carroll, Mary, 1954–
     The no cholesterol (no kidding!) cookbook : the medically proven kitchen
cure for high cholesterol / by Mary Carroll with Hal Straus.
          p.   cm.
     Includes bibliographical references and index.
     ISBN 0-87857-976-1   hardcover
     1. Low-cholesterol diet.   2. Hypercholesterolemia—Diet therapy—
Recipes.   I. Straus, Hal.   II. Title.
RM237.75.C37   1991
641.5′6311—dc20
                                                                                    91-16421
                                                                                          CIP

Distributed in the book trade by St. Martin's Press

2   4   6   8   10   9   7   5   3   1   hardcover

To my grandmother Hartzie for inspiring me at age 5 with my first cooking lesson. And to my mother, Betty, whose enthusiasm for cholesterol-free cooking inspired me all over again at 36.

—Mary Carroll

For Marilou, Matt, and Sarah, who are my inspiration for everything.

—Hal Straus

NOTICE

This book is intended as a reference volume only, not as a medical guide or manual for self-treatment. If you suspect that you have a medical problem, please seek competent medical care. Keep in mind that nutritional needs vary from person to person, depending upon age, sex, health status, and total diet. The foods discussed and recipes given here are designed to help you make informed decisions about your diet and health. They are not intended as a substitute for any treatment prescribed by your doctor.

About the Authors

Mary Carroll has been in the food business for over 16 years—teaching, catering, writing, and consulting. She previously owned and operated the Cuisine Naturelle Cooking School in Mill Valley, California. She has published two other cookbooks and writes a weekly syndicated food column on gourmet natural foods and vegetarian cooking. She currently lives in Minneapolis, Minnesota.

Hal Straus is a writer whose areas of expertise include health, food, psychology, and sports. He lives in Albany, California.

CONTENTS

ACKNOWLEDGMENTS   x

INTRODUCTION   xi

Chapter 1      Becoming
Heart Smart
1

Cholesterol Confusion   2
The Way to Any Heart Is through the Stomach   3
A Guide to the Players   4
Getting UninFATuated   8
How Much Risk?   10

Chapter 2      Countdown
to Zero
13

Starting the Journey to Health   15
Improvement Plus   17
The New Cuisine   18
Slow and Steady   18
Lose Weight Naturally   22
Almost Home   24

Chapter 3

Stocking the
No-Cholesterol
Kitchen
25

Beans Are Basic   26
Condiments to the Rescue   29
Oils: The Cook's Choice   31
Secret Seasonings   32
Thicken without Fat   34
Essential Whole Grains and Flours   35

Chapter 4

Techniques
and Tips
39

Making Your Life Easier   43

Chapter 5

Light Delights:
Appetizers, Hors d'Oeuvres,
and Snacks
47

Planning Ahead for Between-Meal Pangs   48
Making the Most of Leftovers   50
Turning Snacks into Special Occasions   51
First-Course Appetizers and Party Hors d'Oeuvres   54
On-the-Run Meals and Packable Lunches   61
Wholesome Movie and TV Snacks   65
Light Meals   68

Chapter 6

Salad
Symphonies
73

Take Salads to Heart   74
The Day-Round, Year-Round Salad Gourmet   75
Selecting Salad Ingredients   75
Presenting Your Salad   77
Creating Winning Salad Dressings   78
Quick Salads for Busy Cooks   83
Main-Dish Salads   88
Salads for Entertaining   94

Chapter 7

Soup
Sorcery
101

The Tricks of the Trade   103
Step 1: Preparing a Flavorful Cholesterol-Free Stock   104
Step 2: Sautéing Vegetables   105
Step 3: Seasoning Soups without Salt   107
Step 4: Combining the Vegetables and the Stock   111
Presenting Your Soup   111
Storing Soup   112
Basic Soup Stocks   113
Mock Cream Soups   114
Hot Soups for Cold Winter Nights   119
Cold Soups for Hot Summer Days   127
High-Protein Chowders and Full-Meal Soups   130

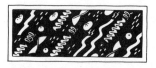

Chapter 8

Beans, Grains,
and Pasta
135

Legumes: Vegetarian Protein Plus   137
Basic Rules for Cooking Beans and Peas   138
Basic Rules for Cooking Whole Grains   139
A Word about Pressure Cookers   139
Family Entrées   142
On the Lighter Side   148
International Pasta Recipes   154
Easy Pasta Toppings   161

Chapter 9

The Joy of Soy:
Tofu, Tempeh, Miso,
and Tamari Dishes
165

Tofu's for You   167
Now, Now . . . Tempeh, Tempeh!   169
Miso and Tamari   169
Tofu Dishes   170
Tempting Tempeh   179
Cooking with Miso and Tamari   186

Chapter 10

Breads:
Oven-fresh
189

Yeast: Don't Leaven Bread without It   191
Sponging Off the Host   193
We All Knead the Dough   195
Getting a Rise out of Your Bread   196
Yeasted Breakfast Breads   197
Lunch Sandwich Breads   203
Family Dinner Breads   207
Sprouted and Sourdough Breads   213
Quick Breads   217

Chapter 11  Sweet
Treats
221

Sweet Choices   223
Flour   223
Sweeteners   224
Oils   224
Liquids and Thickeners   226
A Word to Experimentalists   229
Perfect Pies, Tarts, and Pastries   229
Fresh-Fruit Crisps   235
Ices and Parfaits   238
Mousses and Puddings   241
Easy Fruit Desserts   245
Poached-Fruit Desserts and Fruit Sauces   248
Low-Sugar Fruit Sauces   249

Appendix A  A Month's Worth
of No-Cholesterol
Meals
253

Appendix B  The Hidden
Cholesterol
in Your Diet
261

INDEX   267

ACKNOWLEDGMENTS

As most authors know, the most important contributions to a book often occur years before the book is actually written. In my case, Carol Flinders helped me get started as a food columnist years ago. Tony Moore offered encouragement—and editing talent—over many long and endless nights. Zanna Alexander provided inspiration and pep talks when the home team was ready to throw in the towel. My family and friends unknowingly provided (excuse the adjective) meaty material for the anecdotes that introduce these chapters.

More recently, Hal Straus injected my ideas with a voice and style. Debora Tkac and Jean Rogers and their staff at Rodale Press expertly polished the manuscript. And "special agent" Robert Briggs stuck by the project when others did not.

INTRODUCTION

One afternoon in 1985, I received an intriguing phone call from Dean Ornish, M.D., of the Preventive Medicine Research Institute in San Francisco. Would I be interested, he wanted to know, in designing recipes for a study on heart disease?

The goal of the study, he said, was to determine if certain lifestyle changes alone could reverse coronary artery blockages. No investigator had ever shown regression of arterial lesions before—not without surgery or drugs, that is. But Dr. Ornish felt that with the right diet, stress-management techniques, and exercise, the body could demonstrate powerful self-healing capacities.

Central to these changes, of course, was a strict dietary regimen—essentially a vegetarian, very low-cholesterol diet that got less than 10 percent of its calories from fat. That's where I came in. Dr. Ornish had heard of Cuisine Naturelle, my cooking school in Mill Valley, just a few miles from his institute. And Carol Flinders, coauthor of the classic vegetarian cookbook *Laurel's Kitchen,* had warmly recommended me.

The question was, Could I create recipes so tasty, so attractive, and so easy to prepare that heart patients in the study would enjoy eating them? Three meals a day, seven days a week, for an entire year? And all without using meat, eggs, butter, margarine, cheese, oils, or any other ingredients that normally give dishes a flavor boost?

Sure, I replied, and I can also leap tall buildings in a single bound.

Nevertheless, I took the job. What's life without a few challenges?

Weeks later, I was still in the kitchen, designing, creating, testing, and retesting. At that point, *I* couldn't eat my own dishes. How could I expect Dr. Ornish's patients to eat them? In essence, I was being forced to rethink every basic cooking technique—sautéing, baking, braising, and so on. In the early 1970s, I had been convinced that French cooking was the best in the world. The consequences of eating cream and butter sauces did not worry me. I was young and living in Paris.

But now, ten years later, my life had changed, and so had the culinary landscape. I had learned to cook a wide variety of cuisines. I had also discovered that "You are what you eat" was not just a clever epigram. It could also be an epitaph. Cream and butter sauces had to be about as distant to my culinary thinking as France itself.

Yet somehow I had to find a way to fit my beloved French methods into the limitations of my ingredients. And vice versa. Eventually, after a great deal more experimenting, I found some things that worked. I could now eat my own food.

And so could the patients. Meat and potato lovers their whole lives, they had expected something between hospital food and army grub. But when they actually got tasty meals, they were amazed and delighted.

The food did not hurt their arteries, either. Of the 22 people in the experimental group, 18 had reversals in their blockages after one year. By contrast, 19 people who didn't follow this new diet did not fare as well. In fact, the majority of them saw their blockages worsen during the same period.

Dr. Ornish's now well-known study has been hailed as a major break-through in the battle against heart disease. And it was, of course, the basis for his best-selling book, *Dr. Dean Ornish's Program for Reversing Heart Disease.*

Now after several years of honing and refining these recipes for other pursuits—cooking classes, two health-oriented cookbooks, friends and family—I think it's important to share them with you and the thousands of other people who want to improve their health and help their heart through a healthful diet.

I hope you'll find, as I did, that no-cholesterol cooking can be a rewarding experience—for the palate as well as the heart.

CHAPTER 1

BECOMING

Heart Smart

1

A few weeks ago, Andy, one of my neighbor's kids, was over for lunch, and I asked him why he wasn't drinking his milk. The four-year-old looked down at his sandwich and muttered, "Lester Ball."

"Who's Lester Ball?" I asked, puzzled.

"*Lester* Ball," he repeated, stressing the first syllable this time. "Lester Ball."

I shrugged finally with resignation. "I don't get it. This Lester Ball person told you not to drink milk?"

"He's not a person," said Andy. "He's a thing. Lester Ball. My mom said there's too much Lester Ball in milk."

Finally, of course, it dawned on me. "Lester Ball" was Andy's pronunciation of cholesterol.

Well, we certainly have become sophisticated in a very short time. It wasn't more than a decade or so ago that most adults had no idea what cholesterol was. Now four-year-old children are experts! In Andrew's case, the boy's family had a history of high cholesterol, so he knew that the substance was "bad" and had already been tested for it.

This kind of cholesterol awareness is being echoed in households across America. The most recent Food and Drug Administration survey on cholesterol awareness, conducted in 1988, found that almost 80 percent of adults felt that lowering their blood cholesterol would have a "large effect" in preventing heart disease. And from 1983 to 1989, visits to doctors for cholesterol testing increased ninefold, according to James Cleeman, M.D., of the National Heart, Lung, and Blood Institute.

Cholesterol Confusion

But cholesterol awareness doesn't always translate into dietary action. Although there's a mountain of evidence that high blood cholesterol can lead to heart disease, America's number one killer, many people refuse—or find it too difficult—to change their diet. One of the reasons is simple confusion. If the research has been relentlessly consistent in its portrayal of high cholesterol as a major villain in heart disease, it has sometimes been vague about how to reduce cholesterol levels.

If this weren't confusing enough, certain cholesterol-testing procedures—of both foods and people—have been problematic, if not downright unreliable. And last but certainly not least is the complexity of the subject itself. Do you know the difference between dietary cholesterol and blood cholesterol? What's "good" cholesterol and what's "bad" cholesterol? Do you understand the subtle interplay between dietary fats and blood cholesterol? Or the relationship between cholesterol and atherosclerosis? These are all complicated topics, jumbled even more by the ever-new discoveries linking diet and disease. Face it—you have a right to be confused.

And you're not alone. Doctors themselves are sometimes perplexed. Just the other day, my own doctor said offhandedly, "Vegetarians don't have to worry about cholesterol." This, of course, is not true. Many vegetarians eat eggs, cheese, butter, and other dairy products high in cholesterol and saturated fats. Even vegetarians who eat no animal products at all may consume the highly saturated tropical oils, such as palm, palm kernel, and coconut. These oils, found in many baked goods (read labels!), contain no dietary cholesterol but can raise blood cholesterol as surely as butter and animal fats.

The Way to Any Heart Is through the Stomach

What exactly is cholesterol, and what does it do in—and to—your body? Derived from the Greek words *chole* meaning bile and *stereos* meaning solid, cholesterol was originally the name given to a substance found in gallstones. Chemically it's a fatlike compound that in its pure form appears as pearly, waxy flakes.

Although the curse of cholesterol seems to have suddenly materialized in the last half of the twentieth century, it has probably always been a factor in human health. We're just more aware of it than our ancestors were. We're so aware of the dangers, in fact, that we often forget our bodies actually *need* a little cholesterol for proper functioning. Among other things, cholesterol helps build cell membranes, produce sex hormones, and make bile acids used in digestion. It also aids in the production of brain tissue, nerve coverings, and vitamin D.

The thing is, your liver and other organs produce quite enough cholesterol, thank you, to fulfill your body's requirements. Most people do not need more than very small amounts from food. Although this simple biological fact has been known for some time, millions of Americans continue to take in excess dietary cholesterol via fatty meats (especially organ meats), poultry skin, shellfish, whole milk, high-fat cheese, egg yolks, and other animal products.

Consider these figures: A serving of beef liver has about 389 milligrams of cholesterol; a large egg yolk, anywhere from 213 to 272 milligrams; and a quarter-pound burger, 82 milligrams. It's no surprise that the average American consumes between 400 and 500 milligrams of cholesterol per day, says Sonja Connor, associate professor of clinical nutrition at Oregon Health Sciences University, instead of the 300 milligrams or less recommended by the American Heart Association.

Once inside the body, dietary cholesterol is transformed into blood cholesterol. Because cholesterol does not dissolve in the water-based bloodstream, it is transported in the blood as lipoproteins—molecules composed of fat and protein that escort cholesterol to and from the cells. Any excess cholesterol risks being deposited in fatty streaks along the inner walls of your arteries.

These deposits build up over time and become a fibrous substance called plaque, which makes the artery walls less elastic and hampers the smooth flow of blood, just like rust in a pipe slows water flow. It's the first warning sign of atherosclerosis—hardening of the arteries. As arteries narrow, blood has a harder time getting through. Eventually, affected arteries may close completely. If this happens to an artery supplying blood to the heart muscle, a heart attack may occur. If it happens to an artery going to the brain, it can cause a stroke. Plaque formation may also lead to the formation of dangerous blood clots.

A Guide to the Players

The issue is compounded by the fact that there are actually three different types of blood cholesterol. And not all of them are bad! On the one hand, there's LDL cholesterol; doctors consider it the principal culprit in this drama. On the other hand, there's HDL cholesterol, which takes on hero status. Then there's VLDL cholesterol, and scientists are divided over how bad it is. Here are the roles each plays.

LDL cholesterol. Low-density lipoproteins (LDLs) are considered bad blood cholesterol. They're rich in lipids (or fats). LDLs are responsible for transporting about 70 percent of the body's cholesterol from the liver to the tissues. As they circulate in the bloodstream, some of them are picked up by LDL receptors in your cells.

Under ideal conditions, these receptors remove cholesterol from the blood. Unfortunately, when you eat too much cholesterol (or saturated fat) or when your body makes too much cholesterol, you end up with too many LDLs for the number of available receptors. The extra LDL stays in your bloodstream. And the higher your LDL level, research indicates, the higher your chances of suffering a heart attack or stroke.

It's the extra LDL particles that float around aimlessly in the blood, depositing cholesterol and other fats on artery walls. Eventually it hardens into dangerous plaque.

VLDL cholesterol. You can think of very low-density lipoproteins (VLDLs) as little 18-wheelers, carrying triglycerides and cholesterol through the bloodstream. Triglycerides, another type of fatty substance, are used by the body for energy. When found in excess, they're frequently linked with heart disease and may also lead to inflammation of the pancreas.

Like Batman and Robin, cholesterol and triglycerides often travel together in the bloodstream and on lab reports. A high triglyceride reading is not always cause for concern—consumption of fat-containing foods in the hours before a test will raise triglycerides. That's why triglyceride blood tests are usually given after an overnight fast. But a high triglyceride level after fasting is not good news, because it often indicates high cholesterol or low levels of beneficial HDL cholesterol.

As the little VLDL trucks travel through your blood, they unload triglycerides. Eventually, all that's left is cholesterol. At that point the VLDL-semis turn into LDL-mobiles, which are apt to deposit cholesterol on your artery walls. The longer VLDLs stay in the bloodstream, the more likely they are to turn into LDLs.

HDL cholesterol. Here come the good guys. HDLs transport cholesterol from the tissue cells to the liver to be used or excreted. Imagine HDLs as roving garbage trucks, scavenging the blood for stray cholesterol molecules, picking them up, and taking them to the city dump (better known to you as

WHAT DO THE NUMBERS MEAN?

The National Cholesterol Education Program (NCEP), a coalition of government and private groups led by the National Heart, Lung, and Blood Institute (NHLBI), has established these guidelines for total blood cholesterol levels in adults over age 20:

Less than 200	Desirable
200 to 239	Borderline high
240 and above	High

If your cholesterol level is desirable, keep up the good work and have your cholesterol tested every five years.

If you're in the borderline-high category and you have no other risk factors (see "Beyond Diet: Measuring Your Risk" on page 8), the NCEP recommends that you consider making dietary changes to reduce your cholesterol to the desirable range.

If your cholesterol level is borderline high and you have two or more additional risk factors or already have coronary heart disease, you would be treated as though your cholesterol level were high. You should consult your physician for further evaluation.

If your blood cholesterol falls within the high-risk category, the NCEP advises that you consult your physician.

For LDL cholesterol, counts of 130 or lower are desirable. Borderline levels are 130 to 159, and high risk is over 160.

Rating HDL levels is more problematic than evaluating either LDL or total cholesterol. According to several studies, people with high HDL counts are less prone to heart attacks. On the other hand, people with low HDL values are at an increased risk for a heart attack. But just what is a low HDL count? Some authorities, such as the NCEP, say it's a reading of 35 or less. Others, including the Fra-

your liver). Some researchers believe that HDLs also break up existing arterial plaque, thereby helping to reverse atherosclerosis.

In one study on men, Meir Stampfer, M.D., a Harvard University Medical School researcher, found that the risk of heart attack dropped 4 percent for each point that HDLs went up. Other studies suggest a more modest change: a 2 to 4 percent reduction in risk. In any case, studies suggest that people with very low HDL levels (below 35) have a much higher heart attack risk than those with very high HDLs.

The famous long-term Framingham Heart Study in Massachusetts recently confirmed these suspicions when it reported that over 15 percent of the patients in the study who died of heart attacks had HDL counts under 40.

Total blood cholesterol. This is the sum of all the types of cholesterol described above. It is this number—around 200—that is typically bandied

mingham Heart Study, intimate that readings of 40 or less are undesirable.

Many experts claim that it's the *ratio* of total cholesterol to HDL that's more important than a particular number. According to Framingham's William Castelli, M.D., if your ratio is below 4.5, you're at low risk—even with a high total cholesterol level. To find your ratio, divide your total cholesterol by your HDL reading. By way of example: If your total cholesterol is 225 and your HDL is 60, your ratio is a desirable 3.75 (225 divided by 60 equals 3.75).

The Search for Accuracy

The reliability of cholesterol tests is often called into question. Many people (including friends of mine) have discovered that their cholesterol counts vary significantly, depending on where they have the test done. Indeed, a 1990 University of Minnesota study found that the measurements gained from the type of cholesterol analyzers used at health fairs and mobile screening programs differed considerably from controlled laboratory tests done on the same individuals.

For the most accurate results, say doctors, be tested at your local hospital or by your doctor. If your test results are high, says Howard L. Lewis, director of the Health, Science, and News Division of the American Heart Association (AHA), don't jump into drug therapy. "The AHA recommends multiple cholesterol tests before someone is put on treatment with drugs. Don't base treatment on just one reading." California cholesterol expert Dean Ornish, M.D., concurs. He always recommends that his patients get two cholesterol tests done by the same lab, preferably about a week apart. Then he takes the average of the two tests.

about as your cholesterol count. But this number can sometimes be misleading because it includes the beneficial HDLs that you *want* to be high. Researchers believe that your LDL reading is a more accurate indicator of potential heart problems than your total cholesterol level.

So, the bottom line: Just how much will that cholesterol on your dinner plate raise your blood cholesterol? It's hard to say, because science hasn't determined a universally agreed-upon formula. But William Castelli, M.D., medical director of the Framingham Heart Study, has said that "For every 100 milligrams you change your cholesterol intake, you will change your serum cholesterol by about 5 points." That would mean, for example, that adding one egg yolk (at an average 250 milligrams) a day to your diet could add about 13 points to your cholesterol count; regular servings of chicken livers (at 631 milligrams) could elevate your cholesterol about 32 points.

Getting UninFATuated

Besides dietary cholesterol, another villain lurks in the foods we eat: *saturated fat.* Although saturated fat is not the same as cholesterol, it too tends to raise blood cholesterol levels—even more than dietary cholesterol. That may be because saturated fat helps the liver to manufacture cholesterol,

BEYOND DIET: MEASURING YOUR RISK

Diet, of course, is the focus of this book, but blood cholesterol is affected by more than just what you eat. Doctors say that the factors outlined below can increase your risk of heart disease. The more of these elements that you have working against you, the greater your risk. So they recommend that you take steps to eliminate any that are under your control. That might mean, for instance, stopping smoking and losing weight, says John C. LaRosa, M.D., dean for research at the George Washington University Medical Center.

Genetics. Medical professionals at Oregon Health Sciences University say that one of the strongest influences on cholesterol levels is heredity. Indeed, since two-thirds of the cholesterol in your body is manufactured by your cells, a family history of high cholesterol may explain some things—like why your best friend eats bacon and eggs every day and has no cholesterol problem, while your level seems to skyrocket if you merely *look* at an egg yolk.

People with family histories of high cholesterol should first try to lower their levels through diet, says Peter Kwiterovich Jr., M.D., of the Johns Hopkins University School of Medicine. If that fails, they

should consult their doctors about taking medication as well. Doctors recommend that in families prone to heart or vascular disease, cholesterol levels should be monitored from childhood.

Smoking. Heavy smoking doubles or even triples your chances of a heart attack, according to cholesterol researcher Scott Grundy, M.D., Ph.D., of the University of Texas Southwestern Medical Center at Dallas. And it has other bad effects upon the heart—not to mention the rest of your body.

One of the first studies to forge a direct link between smoking and high cholesterol was conducted by the American Health Foundation in 1989. More than 55,000 people were screened for this study. The findings: The more people smoked, the higher their cholesterol levels. Each cigarette smoked per day elevated cholesterol an average of half a point. So someone smoking 30 cigarettes a day would have a cholesterol level about 15 points higher than a nonsmoker.

The good news is that when you stop smoking, both your risk and your cholesterol level should soon come down. And it's estimated that within ten years after quitting, your chances of having a heart

or it may be that the fat interferes with the elimination of cholesterol from the bloodstream. The reason for the interaction between saturates and cholesterol is only partly understood.

Foods high in saturated fat are generally solid at room temperature. Common examples are butter, cheese, lard, many types of margarine, hydrogenated shortening, coconut oil, and the marbled fat in meats.

attack drop back to those of a nonsmoker. Much of the reduction in risk occurs within the first year after quitting.

Stress. One study done at Johns Hopkins University Medical School found that students who suffered heart attacks were "more vulnerable to stress" and also had higher cholesterol levels than their classmates.

Fortunately, other studies have shown that relaxation exercises, coupled with diet and moderate exercise, can improve cholesterol levels and even begin to reverse coronary blockages. At the University of California at San Francisco, Dr. Ornish put a group of heart patients on a strict low-fat diet and instructed them to practice yoga and meditation for an hour a day and to walk for half an hour each day. Most lowered their blood cholesterol levels by 50 percent or more in a year.

Gender. In general, men have lower levels of beneficial HDLs, which places them at greater risk than women for heart disease. The statistics bear this out: Under age 65, men have approximately three times as many heart attacks and heart bypass operations as women, says Dr. Kwiterovich. (Women are not in the clear, though; they just tend to develop heart disease 10 to 15 years after men do.)

Lack of exercise. Studies show that aerobic exercise can raise HDL levels and may even reduce undesirable LDLs, says Dr. Grundy. Aerobic exercise also helps you lose excess weight and reduce stress.

In a Stanford University study, sedentary men with normal blood cholesterol levels started walking three times a week and then gradually increased their exercise to running five times a week for 45 minutes. After nine months, they showed beneficial changes in both HDLs and LDLs.

Another study, this one at the University of Pittsburgh, found that exercise equivalent to a brisk amble helped women get their cholesterol levels in good shape. Those who burned an extra 1,000 calories a week exercising (a 30- to 45-minute walk three times a week) had significantly higher levels of HDLs than their sedentary sisters. Those who burned 2,000 calories a week had even higher HDLs, plus lower levels of total cholesterol, LDLs, and triglycerides.

Obesity. Thin people can certainly have high cholesterol levels, but the overweight are more likely to have elevated counts. The good news, says Dr. LaRosa, is that losing weight will raise HDLs and lower LDLs and total cholesterol counts.

The evils of saturated fat have been well documented by science. "The effect of saturated fat is about three times worse than that of dietary cholesterol," says Donald McNamara, Ph.D., a professor of nutrition and food science at the University of Arizona.

Just as there are good forms of cholesterol, there are good fats and oils, known as unsaturated fats. Researchers have found that these fats, usually liquid at room temperature, don't raise cholesterol as saturated fats do. Unsaturated fats can be further separated into categories of *polyunsaturated* and *monounsaturated,* according to their chemical makeup. Oils high in polyunsaturates include corn, soybean, and safflower. High-monounsaturate oils include olive, canola (also known as rapeseed), and peanut. Some foods, like avocados, contain plenty of both. (Although these foods also contain some saturates, the amounts are quite small.)

Both monounsaturates and polyunsaturates have been shown by several studies to lower total cholesterol levels. Some studies show that monos can selectively lower LDLs while leaving HDLs intact. Other studies have indicated that polyunsaturates decrease both LDLs and HDLs. So while the jury's still out on which of the unsaturates is superior, this verdict is clear: Neither is guilty of raising cholesterol levels. I'll talk more about unsaturated fats—and how to get just the right amount into your diet—in chapter 2.

How Much Risk?

Not all researchers believe that cholesterol poses a serious medical risk. In fact, the debate over the role of cholesterol in heart disease has been going on for years. Cholesterol was first found in arterial plaque more than a century ago. But it was not until the rate of heart disease began to skyrocket in the post–World War II era that scientists turned their attention toward plaque formation. During this period, investigators were able to raise the cholesterol levels of animals through diet, drugs, and other means.

Among the first scientists to link heart disease with too much cholesterol intake was Ancel Keys, Ph.D., at the University of Minnesota in 1948. A slew of studies generally supporting Dr. Keys's work followed over the next decade. Perhaps the most convincing one was the ongoing Framingham Heart Study, which first reported findings in the early 1960s. Begun in 1948

SEPARATING FATS FROM FICTION

Cholesterol ranks right up there with Madonna when it comes to attracting publicity. But it's probably more misunderstood. So let's try to dispel a few of the most persistent myths.

Myth #1: If you exercise and keep your weight down, you don't have to worry about cholesterol.

In general, your diet has more of an effect on your total blood cholesterol level than your weight or exercise regimen, says John C. LaRosa, M.D., dean for research at the George Washington University Medical Center. Obesity and lack of exercise are correlated with high cholesterol and heart disease, but anyone who eats a diet high in saturated fat or cholesterol is risking high blood cholesterol—whether that person is a slothful behemoth or an active bean pole.

Myth #2: As long as you eat oat bran, your cholesterol level will stay down.

Although some foods may help lower cholesterol levels (see chapter 2), don't depend on them to "neutralize" the effects of a diet high in saturated fat or dietary cholesterol, says Dr. LaRosa. Adding oat bran to a muffin recipe made with scads of butter is akin to shooting yourself with a bullet sprayed with antiseptic; the antiseptic is not going to be too effective. Oat bran will help, but the real key to lowering cholesterol is changing your overall approach to food.

Myth #3: If your doctor says your cholesterol levels are fine, you don't have to worry about your diet.

Not so long ago, most physicians believed that cholesterol levels between 220 and 300 were normal, Dr. LaRosa points out. It wasn't until the staggering heart disease statistics began commanding attention that the definition of "normal" shifted. The safest course is to work hard at keeping your levels down. And remember that your total cholesterol tells only part of the story. Find out what your HDLs and LDLs are to make sure your levels really are "fine," he says.

Myth #4: All you need to know to keep your cholesterol at a safe level is the cholesterol content of various foods, listed on all food packaging.

In other words, just make sure you're eating less than 300 milligrams per day and you'll be fine, right? Dead wrong. Blood cholesterol is much more complex than that, says Dr. LaRosa. One person could ingest 300 milligrams of cholesterol a day and maintain a reading of 160 her whole (long) life; another could eat the same amount and be pushing up the proverbial daisies way before his time. Many factors—including genetic ones—play a part in the cholesterol story.

What's more, neon-lit claims of "no cholesterol" on vegetable oils, margarines, and other foods can be very deceiving. Margarines and oils are still fats, and too much saturated fat can raise cholesterol levels. The safest course is to consult your doctor about monitoring your cholesterol level on a regular basis and to eat a steady diet of no-cholesterol, low-fat dishes—made with the kind of recipes, incidentally, that appear in this book.

with federal support, Framingham revealed that young and middle-aged men with high blood cholesterol (above 240) were three to four times more likely to have a heart attack than those with low cholesterol.

By 1964, the American Heart Association had seen enough evidence of cholesterol's dangers to officially recommend a daily intake of no more than 300 milligrams.

Despite some studies that have prompted criticism of cholesterol management, the vast majority of doctors are standing their ground on the dangers of cholesterol: We should all try to cut down our intake of eggs and high-fat meat and dairy products. In fact, the Surgeon General's "Report on Nutrition and Health" cites "strong and consistent evidence for the relationship between saturated fat intake, high blood cholesterol, and increased risk for coronary heart disease." The Surgeon General's advice: Reduce blood cholesterol and you could significantly reduce the risk of coronary heart disease.

CHAPTER 2

COUNTDOWN TO Zero

One day I picked up the phone and heard my friend Mollie on the other end. She was totally depressed. A hard-driving 58-year-old administrator at a midwestern university, she had just gotten back her first cholesterol test. And the results weren't good.

"My cholesterol is 265, and my doctor's concerned. He says my good cholesterol is too low, and my bad cholesterol is too high—whatever that means. He says I have to get my cholesterol down. I have to change my diet, and I need your help," Mollie said.

I understood my friend's concern. She thought she was heading for a heart attack. And she was miserable about the prospect of eating a diet of brown rice and vegetables.

"Don't worry," I told her. "I have a diet you can live with—and love. I can show you how to cook all the right foods. Someday you'll enjoy them even more than the foods that got you into this trouble in the first place. Honest!"

You might wonder why Mollie came to me for diet advice. It wasn't just because I've been a cooking teacher, caterer, and culinary consultant for a number of years. I also had experience creating very low-cholesterol recipes for people with severe heart disease.

A few years ago I was hired by Dean Ornish, M.D., director of the Preventive Medicine Research Institute in Sausalito, California, as part of a team to come up with heart-healthy recipes for his patients. Dr. Ornish believed that a very low-fat diet containing only very small amounts of cholesterol could benefit people with advanced heart disease. And he wanted me to design ten days' worth of recipes for a patient-education retreat.

At the time, I was a little overwhelmed. Although I had 12 years of restaurant work and teaching behind me, I knew that producing truly lean, but tasty, recipes would be a challenge. And I was right. In fact, during the first few months of the program, I'd prepare meals for the study participants, then I'd go out to eat elsewhere. It took a little while for me to create dishes that satisfied *me* as much as they did Dr. Ornish's heart patients, who were highly motivated to eat a low-fat, virtually cholesterol-free diet.

In the three years that followed, I worked closely with a medical nutritionist, learning which foods were high in fat and cholesterol and how to substitute deliciously healthy ingredients for them. I reached my goal to create recipes that the average meat-and-potatoes person would love—and that would keep his heart healthy, too. Soon I was catering for a local health club's heart program.

I think the turning point in my quest for delicious no-cholesterol recipes came when I discovered the wide world of international cuisines. Those from India, Southeast Asia, Africa, and South America, for example, rely on foods low in cholesterol and saturated fat as their primary protein sources. When I learned to use their ingredients and cooking methods, I started eating and enjoying my own food. And I began to look and feel better—just as Dr. Ornish's patients did. I'd noticed that on their new diet they traded their pasty-white complexions for rosy ones. And their fatigue and excess weight dropped away.

But most important of all, their cholesterol levels dropped. One man bragged about his drop from a high 305 to an amazingly healthy 135. Another joked that he couldn't decide which was better: his 100-point drop in cholesterol or his 40-pound weight loss. By following Dr. Ornish's no-cholesterol program, many patients even *reversed* their coronary blockages. In other words, their arteries lost some of the dangerous plaque buildup that can lead to a heart attack.

Starting the Journey to Health

My experiences with Dr. Ornish—and my later work as a dietary consultant —told me that Mollie would probably need a whole new approach to her diet to bring down her cholesterol. And to succeed, she'd need recipes that tasted great.

As a first step in helping Mollie, I took a close look at what she was eating on a daily basis to track down the hidden cholesterol and fat in her diet. I had her list her typical weekly menu, and then together we analyzed each dish for cholesterol and fat, including saturated fat. (You can do the same thing with your own diet using a comprehensive nutrient book such as *Bowes and Church's Food Values of Portions Commonly Used* by Jean Pennington, Ph.D., R.D. And you can get further help from *Dr. Dean Ornish's Program for Reversing Heart Disease.*)

Here, for example, is the kind of food Mollie often ate on a Saturday or Sunday. Admittedly, it's a little higher in fat and cholesterol than some of her weekday menus. But on the other hand, it is representative of the way she ate several times a week. She was very fond of ham and cheese sandwiches and had them for lunch frequently. She seldom ate a meatless dinner. And she made a daily habit of dessert after dinner—which often included a premium brand of ice cream.

Breakfast

1 egg, fried in butter
1 sausage link
Buttered toast
Coffee with cream

Lunch

Ham and cheese sandwich
Potato chips
Soda

Dinner

Pot roast
Potatoes au gratin
Cauliflower
Apple pie with ice cream

Calories: 1,960
Cholesterol: 539 milligrams
Fat: 97 grams (45 percent of calories)
Saturated fat: 44 grams (20 percent of calories)

The bottom line: Mollie was taking in way too much cholesterol and saturated fat. Considering Mollie's cholesterol count, you might say, "Obviously! It doesn't take a genius to figure that out!"

Knowing that diet isn't the only thing that can raise cholesterol, we also looked at some lifestyle and genetic factors (see "Beyond Diet: Measuring Your Risk" on page 8) to see if they might be be contributing to Mollie's problem. Fortunately, Mollie comes from a long line of pure-living folks whose life spans rival Methuselah's, so in all likelihood heredity was on her side. What's more, she didn't smoke, wasn't seriously overweight, and isn't a man—factors that often account for elevated cholesterol. Diet, indeed, seemed to be her biggest problem.

By the time we had finished evaluating her diet, Mollie was convinced she had to follow her doctor's advice. So she had set a goal to get her cholesterol count below 200—into the desirable range—within a year. And with her doctor's blessing, she set out to follow my no-cholesterol diet. (If you're in the same boat as Mollie, you, too, should follow your doctor's advice.)

Improvement Plus

Drawing on work I had seen Dr. Ornish do, I felt that a no-cholesterol, low-saturates diet would help Mollie get the fastest immediate results—and possibly prevent future problems. Dr. Ornish's studies showed that a near zero cholesterol diet may, when combined with other lifestyle changes, even reverse the progress of heart disease. In one study he did at the University of California, San Francisco, a select group of patients with severe heart disease consumed a very low fat diet (less than 10 percent of calories from fat), which included only nonfat milk, nonfat yogurt, and no added oils. They stopped smoking, exercised moderately, and practiced daily yoga and meditation. Results were dramatic, in terms of both cholesterol reduction and reversed arterial blockage.

Elsewhere, in a landmark study at the University of Southern California School of Medicine, people with atherosclerosis were placed on a low-fat diet. After two years, 36 percent had not worsened at all, and more than 2 percent had seen an improvement in their arterial plaque buildup.

Other studies have shown similarly encouraging results. In Japan, scientists reported halting and even reversing artery damage in 167 people who ate a diet with no animal fats, cheeses, or butter and only a small amount of milk and eggs. Dutch investigators found that arterial lesions in study participants were either unchanged or reduced by a vegetarian diet that contained twice as much polyunsaturated as saturated fat and no more than 100 milligrams of cholesterol daily.

The standard approach to cholesterol management is to keep daily cholesterol intake to no more than 300 milligrams, total fat under 30 percent of total calories, and saturated fat below 10 percent. That's what the American Heart Association (AHA) recommends. That level is geared for those who want a very gradual reduction of blood cholesterol. Those whose blood cholesterol does not respond to such a diet often drop to a maximum of 200 milligrams of cholesterol a day and less than 7 percent of their calories from saturated fat. The most aggressive approach, of course, is the no-cholesterol diet.

The New Cuisine

One of the features—and potential culinary drawbacks—of such a diet is that it's basically vegetarian (egg whites are the only animal product allowed). Many people regard vegetarian cooking as boring and flavorless. Mollie had the same fear. To win her over, I quickly invited her to stay for dinner. Serving a meal created exclusively from recipes I'd collected for this book, I showed her how tasty and exciting no-cholesterol cuisine can be.

To further help Mollie follow her new diet, I created four weeks' worth of menu plans for her (listed in Appendix A), again using recipes that you'll find in this book. If you prefer to make less radical changes in your diet than Mollie did, you can still use no-cholesterol recipes. Just mix them into your customary menus.

If your cholesterol level is high, a reasonable plan of action might be to prepare one or two meals a day using recipes from this book. After six weeks, have your cholesterol checked again. If your total has dropped by 10 percent or more, you're doing fine. Stick with the diet until you don't experience any more decreases or until you reach your target level, whichever comes first.

If your count has decreased by less than 10 percent, try upping the ante to two or three meals a day based on recipes from this book. Follow the new plan for eight weeks, then have your blood cholesterol level checked again.

Choose the approach that works best for you. Only you know your own capacity for adjustment. Don't underestimate the changes involved in moving from a standard cholesterol-containing diet to one that's essentially vegetarian. Go slowly.

Slow and Steady

Besides removing all the cholesterol from Mollie's diet, we made several other changes in the structure of her overall eating habits. For this we were guided by medical research, specifically by the general dietary guidelines from the National Heart, Lung, and Blood Institute and the AHA. Here's the first one we tackled.

Lower Your Total Fat Intake to Less than 30 Percent of Your Daily Calories

What does that mean in plain English? If you're like most Americans, your daily food intake runs somewhere around 2,000 calories, and close to 40 percent of those calories are in the form of fat—much of it saturated fat. This is an expensive way to travel—in more ways than one. Lowering this amount to 30 percent or less means eating fewer than 600 of those calories as fat and getting the rest of your calories from other sources, namely carbohydrates and protein.

Mollie was consuming about 1,900 calories a day. That was a little high for her height and ideal weight, so I recommended she cut back to 1,800. Her fat consumption should account for no more than 30 percent of that, or 540 calories. Each gram of fat has 9 calories, so Mollie should be eating no more than 60 grams of fat per day (540 divided by 9 equals 60).

As we saw above, Mollie's fat consumption hovered around 90 grams—50 percent more than what she should be eating. To reduce that intake to 30 percent, Mollie changed her diet in specific ways. First, she changed her normal breakfasts to a hearty bowl of oatmeal or one of the breakfasts outlined in the menu plans. By doing so, she was able to drop 15 grams of fat.

Second, she replaced her daily ham and cheese sandwich with a salad and an oil-free dressing (see "Ten Oil-Free Salad Dressings" on page 80 for some of Mollie's favorites). Voilà! Another 16 grams of fat out the window.

Mollie's biggest fat saving was omitting pie and ice cream and replacing them with cholesterol-free, low-saturates desserts like Summer Fruit Parfaits (page 239). She was able to cut about 17 grams with that maneuver! She made similar substitutions of low-fat dishes on other days in the week.

Then we moved to step two of the AHA plan.

Eat Less than 10 Percent of Your Calories as Saturated Fat

Saturated fat raises cholesterol, so you should keep your intake as low as possible. To continue with Mollie's example: Not more than 20 grams of her total fat intake should be saturated fat. (To get that figure: 10 percent times

1,800 calories equals 180 calories; 180 divided by 9 equals 20 grams of saturated fat.) For someone on a 2,000-calorie diet, the figure would be an upper limit of 22 grams of saturated fat a day—and less would definitely be better.

The recipes in this book all keep saturated fat to the minimum. If the menu plans or other combinations of recipes from this book comprise your *entire* diet, as they did in Mollie's case, you can rest assured that your saturated fat consumption will be well below the 10 percent limit. If you use these recipes to complement your existing meals, you can be sure that you are not adding significant amounts of saturated fat to your diet.

Next, we got even more particular.

Keep Polyunsaturated Fat to No More than 10 Percent of Total Calories

It has been known for many years that polyunsaturates (such as corn, safflower, sunflower, and many other vegetable oils) can lower blood cholesterol levels. So the astute reader might immediately pipe up: "If polyunsaturated fat lowers total cholesterol, why should we *limit* the amount? Why not drink 'til you're drunk?"

The answer is: There's a catch, namely that the "good guy" HDLs are also part of poly's cholesterol casualties. In other words, levels of beneficial HDL cholesterol decrease along with harmful LDL cholesterol. Then, too, all oils are made up of a combination of fats. Corn oil, just to give you an example, contains about 60 percent polys, 25 percent monos, and 15 percent saturates.

Also, oil is still 100 percent fat, meaning it's very high in calories. Just 1 tablespoon is 120 calories. A 1,800-calorie-a-day budget doesn't leave room for a lot of oil.

The general intent of this guideline is to keep *any* kind of fat low. Some people get so enthused when they hear about the wonders of unsaturated fats that they wind up eating more total fat in the bargain, just to get more of the unsaturated variety. Your real goal is to *reduce your total fat*. Then within a reduced total fat framework, try to eat more unsaturated than saturated.

Now for the good news. Here's what you can *add* to your diet.

Let Monounsaturated Fat Make Up the Remaining 10 Percent of Your Fat Calories

In 1986, a new gunslinger came to town—monounsaturated fat (predominant in olive oil, canola oil, and various nuts and seeds). Until then, scientists believed that only polyunsaturates could wipe out entire gangs of LDLs. But in that year, Scott Grundy, M.D., Ph.D., a leading cholesterol researcher, produced strong evidence that monounsaturated fats not only lowered bad cholesterol but also left good HDL levels intact, a heretofore unheard-of feat even for the powerful polys.

Dr. Grundy's landmark study was considered a logical explanation for the fact that heart disease is rare among the populations of the Mediterranean: These people consume large quantities of olive oil, which contains about 10 grams of monounsaturated fat per tablespoon.

Mollie was allowed 40 grams of total unsaturated fat a day. She made an effort to divide her daily allowance evenly between polyunsaturates (such as safflower oil) and monounsaturates (such as olive oil). How did she know how much of each fat she was actually getting? She could have purchased a computer software package or hired a nutritionist to figure it out for her. But she relied instead on the menu plans that I drew up for her. They take this factor into account by achieving the proper balance of polys and monos.

These plans make the next guideline easy.

Include in Your Diet as Many Cholesterol-Lowering Foods as Is Practical

Eating less cholesterol and fat will lower blood cholesterol, but medical research is gradually demonstrating that other foods and substances—when coupled with a low-fat, low-cholesterol diet—can also help to lower levels.

This was first illustrated in 1977, when James Anderson, M.D., the well-known cholesterol researcher from the University of Kentucky, placed men with high cholesterol on an oat bran diet and watched their cholesterol levels plummet.

Throughout the 1980s, Dr. Anderson continued his explorations into oat bran and other fiber-rich substances (such as pectin, the fiber found in many fruits and grains). In one study, he found that men who ate 1 cup of dry oat bran a day—in the form of hot cereal and five muffins (admittedly a *lot* of oat bran)—lowered their cholesterol levels 60 points in three weeks.

By the 1980s, oat bran became a household word. But it was not the last word. In 1990, a study reported in the *New England Journal of Medicine* showed that people who ate Cream of Wheat cereal regularly were as likely to show blood cholesterol drops as those who ate oat bran. While oat bran did lower cholesterol, a low-fat, low-cholesterol diet *without* oat bran did the trick equally well.

Rely on Complex Carbohydrates for Most of Your Calories

Complex carbohydrates should account for 50 to 60 percent of your calories, according to the National Cholesterol Education Program. How do you add carbohydrates to your diet quickly and easily? For her evening meal Mollie replaced half her usual portion of pot roast with a baked potato and nonfat yogurt topping instead of sour cream. (She especially liked the Mock Sour Cream potato topping on page 167.) Other foods rich in complex carbohydrates are whole grain pastas and breads, grains, fruits, corn, and other vegetables—all of which I use in recipes throughout this book.

The remainder of your calorie intake (10 to 20 percent) should be in the form of protein. Most people don't have any trouble getting enough protein—even on a vegetarian diet.

Lose Weight Naturally

Need to lose a few pounds? Here's an added bonus. Because the no-cholesterol diet is naturally low in fat, that means it's naturally low in calories. And that can translate into gradual weight loss.

One of the biggest steps you can take to lower your blood cholesterol, say experts, is to lose excess weight. Mollie found that switching from high-fat foods to low-fat, no-cholesterol ones automatically eliminated many of the calories that had allowed pounds to gradually creep up on her. That's not surprising. Fat contains twice as many calories, gram for gram, as either protein or carbohydrates. And it's more easily stored as body fat than the other two. By following the low-fat menu plans that I designed for her, Mollie easily lost 12 pounds after two months on her new diet.

KIDS AND CHOLESTEROL

Did Andy, the four-year-old neighbor mentioned in chapter 1, really need a cholesterol test? Or to watch the fat in his diet? Could be. It's estimated that at least 10 percent of our nation's children have cholesterol counts greater than 175. (The American Health Foundation says ideal levels are around 140.) And one recent study of 6,500 children found that 20 percent had levels above 185.

Because of such findings, many doctors stress that it's never too early to start thinking about cholesterol control. Some recommend routine screenings for all children age two and older if there's a family history of heart disease. (But don't restrict fat consumption for children under age two; they need the fat for proper development.)

Since all kids need some fat and cholesterol to grow, the key to cholesterol management is moderation and balance. If you teach children to develop good eating habits early in life, they will carry them to adulthood. Here are some cholesterol-controlling tips for parents who want to keep their children both happy and healthy.

• Fill the freezer with frozen juice bars instead of ice cream.
• Serve Mexican dishes—burritos, tostadas—piled with beans instead of meat. You'll get more fiber and much less fat and cholesterol. But be wary of commercial refried beans—they're often made with lard.
• Steer clear of snacks (such as many crackers, packaged baked goods, and cookies) that contain saturated oils, such as coconut, palm, or cottonseed oil.
• Declare the candy counter at the local Bijou off-limits. Instead, send your child to the cinema with low-fat popcorn, graham crackers, and pretzels (I prefer low-salt).
• Serve angel food cake. Kids particularly like it in cupcake form. Use fruit topping instead of icing. Angel food contains no egg yolks, and most brands have no oil whatsoever. But there are exceptions, so double-check labels just to be sure.
• Finish meals European-style, with fresh fruit for dessert rather than pastries.
• Freeze red, white, and green grapes (preferably seedless) and slices of bananas. Frozen grapes are great out-of-hand snacks; frozen bananas can be pureed in a blender, then served in ice cream cones.
• For birthday parties, package easy-seal plastic bags with an assortment of low-salt popcorn, pretzels, chopped dried fruit, and unsalted nuts. Pass out the packets as party favors.
• Offer hot or cold cereal with fruit for breakfast instead of bacon and eggs.

If you need to lose some pounds and aren't quite sure what your daily calorie allotment should be, here's an easy formula: Multiply your ideal weight by 15 (if you're reasonably active). If you should weigh 120, for instance, multiply 120 by 15 to give a daily calorie allowance of 1,800. If you're quite inactive, use 13 as the multiplier; if you're a super jock, increase the number to 17. Then make sure that your calories come from lean foods.

Almost Home

According to the National Heart, Lung, and Blood Institute and other authorities, you should begin to see some drop in cholesterol levels within two to three weeks of following a diet that incorporates these principles. In Mollie's case, her cholesterol dropped 15 points after the first month on the menu plans, bringing her down to 250. After six months, she was down another 45 points, to 205.

The last bend in the road to no-cholesterol cookery is learning about the various ingredients and techniques that can transform a potentially tedious no-meat, no-dairy diet into a delicious culinary adventure. I cover these easy-to-master tips and techniques thoroughly in chapter 4. For now, merely recognize that to maintain a healthy diet, you will need certain skills and equipment to prepare a wide variety of flavorful, satisfying dishes quickly and easily.

Essentially that's what this book offers you: delicious no-cholesterol cuisine that you will be proud to serve to anyone—even your meat-eating friends and relatives. Think of it as a gourmet approach that will engender a special feeling of accomplishment—and good health.

CHAPTER 3

STOCKING THE *No-Cholesterol* KITCHEN

Giving up high-cholesterol foods sounds easy, until you realize the central role they play in making things taste good. Most foods that are high in cholesterol also contain lots of fat. Fat molecules help convey flavor to your taste buds. You might call these molecules taste-translators. When you remove fat from food, your taste buds have a difficult time adapting to the new "language." This alone made devising the cholesterol-free diet a big challenge.

To overcome the "language" problem, I worked to develop the natural flavors in foods, especially onions and garlic. I learned to sauté them in just a little oil or wine to bring out their best characteristics. I also learned how to adjust seasonings to compensate for using less fat in recipes.

Baking, especially desserts, was tough at first. Some recipes—the ones that depended heavily on egg yolks, butter, or milk—had to be discarded altogether. But I discovered that others, especially those that leaned on ripe fruits for flavor, were successful with only small substitutions. I learned, for example, how to bind batters with arrowroot instead of eggs and how to make low-fat cookies crispy by leaving them in the oven for a little longer with the heat turned off.

I found that the real secret to no-cholesterol cooking is in choosing the finest ingredients available. To get the most taste out of your dishes, review the following foods.

Beans Are Basic

Beans, peas, and other legumes are the staple of many Third World cultures. And they're one of the cheapest and most available sources of cholesterol-lowering soluble fiber. In one study, men who ate 1½ cups of cooked beans a day decreased their cholesterol by an impressive 20 percent in three weeks. Some nutritionists recommend replacing half your daily meat intake with cooked beans as an alternative, low-fat form of protein. Once you've done that, you can work on cutting meat further—even eliminating it altogether for no-cholesterol cooking. Here are some of the beans and bean products I use most often.

Aduki beans. Also called adzuki or azuki, these beans are imported from Japan, where they are known as the king of beans. Aduki beans are meaty textured and hold together well after cooking—a bonus for bean

NO-CHOLESTEROL STAND-INS

For your own favorite recipes, try replacing the high-cholesterol, high-fat, highly refined ingredients in the left column with the no-cholesterol, low-fat ingredients on the right.

Instead of:	Try:
Beef or chicken stock, 1 cup	1 cup Vegetable Stock (page 113) seasoned with 1 tsp. miso paste
Butter, 1 Tbsp.	1 tsp. safflower oil
Cornstarch, 1 tsp.	1 tsp. arrowroot
Chocolate, 1 square (1 oz.)	3 Tbsp. carob powder
Gelatin, 1 Tbsp.	1–2 Tbsp. agar-agar flakes ½ bar kanten
Milk, 1 cup	1 cup soy milk 1 cup Nut Milk (page 244)
Ricotta cheese, 1 cup	1 cup crumbled firm tofu
Salt, 1 tsp.	¼ tsp. low-sodium soy sauce or tamari 1 tsp. herbal salt substitute
Shortening (for greasing pans), 1 Tbsp.	2 tsp. safflower oil 2–3 spritzes no-stick spray
Sour cream, 1 cup	1 cup Mock Sour Cream (page 167)
Sugar, 1 cup	½–¾ cup honey
Sweetened condensed milk, 1 cup	1 cup amazake (a thick, sweet rice beverage; also called amasake)
Whipped cream, 2 Tbsp.	2 Tbsp. Tofu Whipped Cream (page 229)
White bread crumbs, 1 cup	1 cup whole wheat bread crumbs 1 cup pita crumbs
White flour, 1 cup	⅞ cup whole grain flour
White rice, 1 cup	1 cup brown rice 1 cup wild rice

curries, soups, and marinated bean salads. Small and red, they also provide visual appeal when mixed with green vegetables. Available in Asian markets and natural-food stores, they will keep for about a year in a cool, dark place. Try them in Mexican Corn Stew (page 142).

Black beans. Also called turtle beans, these are typically used in Latin American recipes, such as black bean soup. Readily available in supermarkets, they are becoming part of the North American culture as more cooks discover their sweet, rich flavor. One word of warning: They color anything cooked with them, so feature them as the star of the dish, as in Cuban Black Beans and Rice (page 153), rather than inserting them as extras in other recipes.

Chick-peas. Popularly known as garbanzo beans, chick-peas are very starchy and sweet and lend a delicious flavor to soups. I also use them pureed in spreads and sandwich fillings. One favorite chick-pea dish of mine is Sprouted Bean Burgers (page 144).

Lentils and split peas. I always add a cup of lentils or split peas to wintertime soups. They are so rich tasting that my guests believe there's butter in the dish! These legumes are quick to cook, making them an easy addition to weekday menus.

Lima beans. Dried limas give a wonderful, buttery taste to winter soups, stews, and other hearty dishes. I especially like them in Boston Bean Soup (page 133). I also like to puree them with garlic, chili powder, and cumin for a quick sandwich spread. Sometimes I cook the puree with minced onions and green peppers seasoned with a little ground red pepper for low-cal, no-cholesterol refried beans.

Lima beans freeze well, so I often cook up a large batch at my leisure and store them in meal-size batches. Even the cooking water has a rich, buttery taste, so I save it to use as a delicious base for homemade soups.

Pinto and kidney beans. Mexican food fans will recognize these two southwestern beans as standbys for chili and taco fillings. I usually make a double batch and freeze extras by the cupful for impromptu dinners. Advantages of these two beans include their meaty texture, rich flavor, and eye-pleasing dark red color.

Soybeans. Although I sometimes cook soybeans to use like other beans, the most common ways I use them are in the forms of tempeh and tofu.

Tempeh (pronounced *tem*-pay) is a cultured soy food that looks like a small loaf of textured cheese. It has a meaty texture and a mild mushroomlike taste. It absorbs flavors very fast and holds its shape when cooked. Try tempeh in Spicy Indonesian Cutlets with Peanut Sauce (page 182) or in your favorite chili, lasagna, and stuffed-pepper recipes.

Originally made from just soybeans, tempeh is now available in multigrain mixtures. Look for it in the freezer section of health-food stores and some supermarkets. You can thaw it and use it right from the package, but I find tempeh absorbs flavors better if it is slightly steamed first. (Cut it into cubes and steam them for about 20 minutes.)

Tofu, a sort of soft cheese made from soybeans, can't be beat as a high-protein, no-cholesterol substitute for meat and dairy products. It has very little flavor of its own, so it fits into a wide variety of dishes, including egg-free quiches and all sorts of stir-fries. I knew I had reached success with tofu when a group of five-year-olds devoured my carrot cake with a tofu "cream-cheese" icing. They also loved Carob Pudding (page 245), which is made with tofu.

Two kinds of tofu are generally available: soft and firm. Soft tofu is good for blending into smooth dressings and desserts. Firm tofu, which holds its shape better, is more appropriate for stir-frying and general cooking.

Condiments to the Rescue

No-fat, cholesterol-free condiments are an essential part of the healthy cook's repertoire. They allow you to flavor foods in a way that enhances their natural qualities. Here are two that I consider indispensable.

Mustards. Mustard seeds have two separate chemicals that are responsible for their pungent flavor. One is activated by cold water and the other by hot water. But the results are the opposite of what you might expect. To make hot, spicy mustard, you add cold water to ground mustard seeds; to make milder mustard, you add hot water.

For inexpensive gourmet blends, prepare one of my favorite mustards (see "Savory Homemade Mustards" on page 30). Whichever type you make, spoon your mustard into a small jar and store it in the refrigerator. To keep the mustard from turning brown, place a small square of cheesecloth over the top of the jar and lay a thin slice of lemon on the cheesecloth before capping. Periodically replace the lemon slice—especially if starts to turn moldy. Your mustard will keep well for months.

Vinegars. I stopped spending $6.50 on raspberry vinegar when I discovered I could make my own for 50 cents. When fruits are at their peak of ripeness, I fill my supply of clear glass jars with jewel-like vinegars made from freshly picked produce.

Using seasoned vinegars is a great way to cut down on salad oil. The sweeter, more pungent flavor of vinegar allows you to get away with fewer high-calorie ingredients in salad dressings. I also use seasoned vinegars to

SAVORY HOMEMADE MUSTARDS

It's so easy to prepare your own mustard blends. Here are two of my favorites —one is hot and the other mild. If you like the basic flavor of the hot variety but prefer it a little less spicy, add a bit more oil or honey.

MILD BALLPARK MUSTARD

¼ cup ground yellow mustard seeds
3 tablespoons boiling water
1 tablespoon olive oil
¼ teaspoon honey

In a small bowl, stir together the mustard seeds, water, oil, and honey until smooth and pastelike. Transfer to a small, tightly lidded jar. Store in the refrigerator.

Makes about ⅓ cup.

HOT AND SWEET
GERMAN-STYLE MUSTARD

¼ cup ground yellow or brown mustard
    seeds
3 tablespoons apple cider vinegar
1 tablespoon olive oil
¼ teaspoon honey
    dried tarragon (to taste)

In a small bowl, stir together the mustard seeds, vinegar, oil, honey, and tarragon until smooth and pastelike. Transfer to a small, tightly lidded jar. Store in the refrigerator.

Makes about ⅓ cup.

BOTTLE YOUR OWN FLAVORED VINEGARS

You can easily make your own flavored vinegars. The recipe below is for raspberry vinegar, but you can make other flavors. You may substitute an equal amount of blueberries, for example, or you may use four large sprigs of your favorite herbs. Herbs I particularly like include tarragon, thyme, rosemary, and sage. If using berries, you might want to strain them out at the end of the standing period, but I like to keep the herbs in the jars for both decoration and identification. These vinegars keep for about a year on a pantry shelf.

RASPBERRY VINEGAR

2 cups apple cider vinegar
1 teaspoon honey
1 cup fresh raspberries

In a 2-quart saucepan over medium-high heat, bring the vinegar to a boil. Remove from the heat and stir in the honey.

Divide the raspberries between 2 half-pint jars. Add the hot vinegar. Cap the jars and let stand at room temperature for 48 hours. If desired, strain out the berries.

Makes 2½ cups.

marinate vegetables—eggplant or zucchini slices, fresh button mushrooms, bell peppers—before grilling them.

For a real culinary treat, try balsamic vinegar. This rich, rust-colored Italian vinegar is aged in special kegs and has a salty flavor that is great for no-cholesterol recipes. Sprinkle it over salad greens or lightly marinate kabobs in it before grilling. Basque Bean Salad (page 90) uses a balsamic-vinegar dressing.

Oils: The Cook's Choice

I've found no hardship in substituting oils for lard, shortening, and butter for everything from greasing baking pans to making cakes. Because I use such small quantities of oil, I try to buy small containers, and I store them in the refrigerator to make sure they don't turn rancid. Here are the oils I prefer most.

Olive oil. This type of oil is very high in heart-healthy monounsaturates. Olive oils differ in aroma, flavor, and even color, depending upon where the olives were grown and how pure the oil is. Virgin olive oil is 100 percent pure and not mixed with other refined oils. Within the virgin class are three major subclasses: *Extra virgin* is a light-golden oil with a delicate buttery flavor; it comes from the first pressing of the olive. *Fine virgin* and *semifine virgin* have darker colors and more pronounced flavors. Experiment to find the type you like best.

Safflower oil. High-quality safflower oil (the type I buy is very pale yellow in color) is virtually tasteless and works well in all kinds of dishes. Because safflower oil has a higher heat tolerance than olive oil, it does not smoke as quickly when used to grease baking sheets.

Sesame oil. Sesame oil comes in two versions: golden and deep bronze. The golden-colored version comes from raw sesame seeds and has a delicate flavor. The deep bronze oil is made from toasted seeds and has a heartier flavor. I prefer the darker oil, since it contributes so much flavor with just a tiny amount.

You can mix dark sesame oil with olive or safflower oil in salad dressings, Asian dishes, or even marinades. Keep sesame oil refrigerated, because it turns rancid quickly after pressing.

Secret Seasonings

These are among the seasonings that I use most often to bring out the best flavors of no-cholesterol foods.

Dried mushrooms. For a deep, rich flavor akin to beef broth, try soaking Asian dried mushrooms in hot water, then press them into a strainer to extract the liquid. Dried mushrooms are a staple in Szechuan and other Chinese recipes and have become a favorite seasoning for my no-cholesterol collection.

When buying them, look for small cellophane or boxed packages of about an ounce or two—remember they plump up considerably when soaked. They are not cheap, but a few can go a long way. Soak them for 10 minutes in very hot water, then slice off and discard the woody stems. The mushroom caps are ready to use in stir-fries, sautés, and soups. You can also puree them to make gravy. For a flavor treat, try Szechuan Hot-and-Sour Soup (page 121).

Garlic. Garlic has achieved a reputation as a cholesterol fighter. In some studies, it lowered elevated cholesterol levels. It also acted as a blood thinner, which may help protect against clogged arteries.

There are three ways to enjoy garlic: raw, roasted, and sautéed. Raw garlic is pungent and pervasive and best used in small quantities to enhance other ingredients (as in Mustard Dressing with Garlic, page 81).

Roasted garlic develops an astoundingly sweet taste and can be used straight from the oven or grill. As for sautéed garlic, the mellow, distinctive flavor falls somewhere between raw and roasted.

Dried and powdered garlic can be bitter, so I don't use them very much. To avoid chopping garlic cloves every day, I use this trick: Spend a few minutes chopping one entire bulb, then place it in a small wide-mouth jar. Cover with a generous layer of dry sherry or olive oil, tightly cap the jar and refrigerate it. (Be sure to store this mixture in the refrigerator; botulinus toxin may develop in unrefrigerated, nonacidic garlic blends.) To use, simply strain it out by the tablespoonful.

Herbs and spices. Most of us know an expert cook who can season dishes almost by feel with a pinch of this or a touch of that, but it takes time to learn salt-free seasoning. I give a detailed description of herbs and spices—both fresh and dried—in chapter 7, so you may find that a good place to begin.

Some words of advice about seasonings: The shelf life of most dried herbs is about six months. It's even less if they are exposed to intense light or heat, which is why you should store your herbs in a cool, dry, dark place. For best flavor, a general rule is to add herbs near the end of the cooking time. On the other hand, add spices near the beginning of the cooking time so their bitter oils can cook off.

Miso. Miso is a light brown paste that Asian cooks use the same way we use salt. It comes in many different varieties, flavors, and colors. Once made solely from soybeans, miso is now available in rice, barley, chick-pea, and other combinations. Most manufacturers recommend that you store it in the refrigerator where it will keep for months.

Miso is best added at the end of a cooked recipe. I know from experience it turns slightly bitter if heated too long. To try miso, see Miso Marinade for Vegetables (page 87).

Nutritional yeast. I used to eat a lot of brewer's yeast (for its B vitamins mostly), and I was glad to give it up when I discovered nutritional yeast, which has the same health benefits but tastes much better.

Brewer's yeast is grown on beer and has a strong flavor that is hard to disguise. Nutritional yeast is made from molasses and has a delicious taste. This yellow powder makes a nutritious addition to soups and salad dressings. And it's a fine replacement for table salt. You'll find it in many recipes in this book.

Salt substitutes. About 25 varieties of herbal salt substitutes (salt-free seasonings) line the shelf of my favorite co-op; about half that number are available in my local supermarket. You can purchase these herb-and-spice combinations in all sorts of flavors, including popcorn, Mexican, and garlic. Simply substitute them for salt—pinch for pinch—in most recipes. (I occasionally add a little more than the original salt amount, since the herbs and spices give a subtler flavor.)

Tamari. Tamari is a naturally brewed soy sauce. Unlike many types of soy sauce, tamari contains no wheat, which might interest those with wheat allergies. It has a stronger, darker flavor than commercial soy sauce since it is not diluted with water or fortified with extra table salt. You can use less tamari and still get plenty of flavor.

Wines and sherry. Once upon a time, I was challenged to create a fat-free spaghetti sauce. I couldn't imagine a decent blend of tomatoes, garlic, and spices without the fruity flavor of olive oil. But I remembered reading that you could "sauté" in wine, so I pulled out a bottle of Beaujolais and began mincing my garlic.

To everyone's surprise the sauce was heavenly. The wine added as deep a flavor as oil, and as it cooked down from a liquid, it became slightly caramelized. This gave the sauce an unusual barbecued flavor, almost as if I had added roasted red peppers. My next experiment was with dry sherry in place of butter to sauté vegetables for a vegetarian soup. It added a sweetness that was different from Beaujolais but quite delicious. By the way, I don't use the type of cooking sherry sold in supermarkets, because it contains added salt and is usually made from an inferior grade of sherry.

For those worried about the alcohol in wine, rest assured that dealcoholized wines work just as well. If you have trouble finding them or if you just prefer regular wine, you'll be interested in recent studies on alcohol by the U.S. Department of Agriculture. They showed that after 15 minutes of baking or simmering, 60 percent of the alcohol in wine and other spirits had cooked away—and so had a large portion of the calories.

The secret to sautéing with wine is to be sure the wine is hot before adding the vegetables. If you dump vegetables into cold wine, they absorb an unpleasantly alcoholic taste. Ideally, the hot wine will coat the vegetables, sealing in flavor and color. To substitute wine for oil, use this conversion ratio: for every tablespoon of oil eliminated, substitute ¼ cup wine or sherry—up to a maximum of ¾ cup per recipe.

Thicken without Fat

Many sauces are thickened with a roux made from flour and butter or some other fat. That makes them high in calories, fat, and possibly cholesterol. Other sauces are thickened with regular gelatin, which is an animal product that I prefer not to use. I've found that the following two thickeners work very well for low-fat, no-cholesterol cooking.

Agar-agar. A vegetable gum made from dried seaweed, agar-agar gels faster than regular gelatin so it's timesaving. Agar-agar comes in powdered form or in bars (called *kanten*) that you can crumble into flakes. Both are readily available in health-food stores. In general, use 1 tablespoon of the powder or flakes for each cup of liquid. Dissolve the agar-agar in cold water, then slowly simmer it. To try agar-agar, see recipes like Berry and Banana Kanten (page 242).

Arrowroot powder. Of all the major thickening agents (including flour, cornstarch, and others) I consider arrowroot the best for sauces. It produces a beautiful glaze and leaves no residual taste like the others sometimes do. Arrowroot is readily available in supermarkets (check the spice section).

For lump-free sauces, dissolve the arrowroot in a little cold liquid before adding it to hot mixtures. Cook until the mixture thickens. Recipes in this book that use arrowroot include Blueberry Sauce with Nutmeg (page 250) and Sweet Cherry Sauce (page 251).

Essential Whole Grains and Flours

Whole grains are the backbone of no-cholesterol cookery. They provide essential protein, a great deal of fiber, and a bonus of vitamins and minerals. When ground into flour, they enrich breads and other baked goods with their fiber and give a hearty texture that you don't get from white flour. Here are some of the whole grain products I use most.

Barley. An excellent source of soluble fiber, barley can contribute to lowering cholesterol levels. Barley is hulled after harvesting to remove the outside bran and reveal a pearly white interior. In this pearled form, barley is similar to white rice in nutrient composition.

Barley is primarily used in soups as a thickener, but it's excellent in pilafs and salads (see Southwestern Corn and Barley Salad, page 92). Modern cooks are finding that barley flour (ground raw pearl barley) has surprising advantages for bread and cake recipes. It contributes sweetness and a cakelike consistency normally achieved by adding milk products. That makes barley flour a good ingredient for no-cholesterol recipes.

Brown rice. Brown rice—the hulled but otherwise unrefined cousin of white rice—is a notable source of B vitamins, protein, and fiber. And with recent studies being done on the cholesterol-lowering benefits of rice bran, brown rice is showing up in everything from breakfast cereal to frozen dinners.

Four distinct varieties of brown rice are generally available in supermarkets and health-food stores, bringing the cook a wealth of possibilities in texture and flavor. The two most common types are long grain (which cooks

COOKING BROWN RICE: THE RIGHT TOUCH

I've found that cooking brown rice requires a slightly different technique than cooking white rice. Because brown rice is a whole grain, it takes longer to cook and soften. But cooking it too long can turn it into a gluey mess. So I developed the following cooking method that gives me tender, easily separated grains. It's slightly unorthodox in that it uses less water than usual, but it works with all types of brown rice.

BASIC BROWN RICE

4 cups brown rice
4 cups cold water (or as needed)

In a heavy-bottomed 3-quart saucepan over low heat, toast the rice for about 5 minutes, stirring frequently.

Add the water and raise the heat to medium. Bring the water to a boil and let the rice cook, uncovered, for 20 minutes. This will burst the grains of rice and allow some of the starch to cook off, preventing excess stickiness later.

Reduce the heat to low and check the water level—the water should just barely cover the rice. If needed, add more water. Cover the pan and cook the rice for 25 minutes, or until all the water has been absorbed. Don't stir the rice during this time.

Makes 6 cups.

into fluffy, separate grains) and short grain (which is quite a bit stickier). Brown basmati rice, a fairly new product, is perfect for Indian curries and stir-fries because of its delicate nutty flavor and chewy texture. The fourth type is sweet, or glutinous, brown rice. Asian cooks use this sticky rice for desserts, sushi, and mochi (a Japanese snack) as well as for grinding into rice flour.

Corn. This is the only cereal grain native to North America. Dried corn is used to make hominy for grits, *masa* for tortillas, corn flour for baked goods, and cornmeal for breads, muffins, and griddle cakes.

Supermarkets usually sell both white and yellow cornmeal. Some even carry the blue variety that is popular for southwestern dishes. I tend to prefer the yellow because it's highest in vitamin A. Water-ground (or stone-ground) cornmeal contains some of the corn's nutritious germ and therefore is more perishable than regular cornmeal. Store it in the refrigerator and try to use it within three months.

A newly popular dish made of ground cornmeal is polenta, a regional staple of northern Italy. To try it, see Creamy Polenta with Roasted Vegetables (page 147).

Couscous. This grain product is made from semolina flour and looks like tiny pellets. It's a staple in Morocco, Tunisia, and Algeria, where it's often steamed over broth or other savory liquids. The couscous available in most supermarkets and health-food stores is precooked and takes only 5 minutes to prepare.

Millet. You may be familiar with millet as a component of birdseed. For a nutty taste treat, try adding it to your own diet. You can add cooked millet to stuffings, puddings, casseroles, vegetable dishes, and breakfast cereals. I enjoy it in my morning oatmeal, my lunchtime vegetable soup, and my dinnertime chili. You can mix raw millet into bread dough for a crunchy texture, and you can even grind it into flour to add to cake and muffin recipes.

I always use this easy method of cooking millet: Slowly toast 1 cup of millet in a saucepan for about 3 minutes, or until it smells nutty. Add 1½ cups of water and bring to a boil. Cover the pan, reduce the heat to low, and simmer the millet for 30 to 40 minutes. Because millet freezes well, I sometimes cook up a large batch and store it in 1-cup containers for fast use on busy days.

Oats. Oats are an excellent source of protein and fiber because the bran is not removed from the oat during grinding. Because oats contain large amounts of soluble fiber, they have become popular in low-cholesterol recipes.

Three types of oats are readily available: steel-cut (Scotch), rolled, and quick-cooking. Steel-cut oats are the least processed, having been simply cut into two or three pieces. Rolled oats are taken a step further by being steamed and flattened with large rollers. Steaming inactivates certain enzymes that could cause rancidity when exposed to air. Quick-cooking oats are made from the smallest and thinnest flakes of the oat groat; they're partially cooked to allow them to absorb water quickly when fully cooked later.

Rye. Nutritionally, rye flour is similar to wheat flour. But you need to handle it a little differently when making bread because the rye has much less gluten and does not rise as quickly. It's generally used in combination with wheat or other flours. In addition, rye doughs are often a little stickier than usual and demand more kneading than all-wheat doughs. Dark rye flour has all of the original bran intact; light rye flour has been partially processed. To try a rye loaf, see Dark Rye Sourdough Bread (page 215).

Whole wheat. Wheat contains more gluten than other grains and is a good source of B vitamins and many minerals. Wheat is a fragile grain, however, and the fats in whole wheat begin to turn rancid very soon after the wheat berry is ground. I recommend refrigerating or freezing whole wheat flour in airtight bags.

I use two main types of whole wheat flour: bread flour (made from hard winter wheat) and pastry flour (from soft summer wheat). As its name implies, the bread flour is ideal for yeasted breads. It contains plenty of gluten, which helps breads to rise. You'll notice that most of the yeasted and sourdough breads in chapter 10 call for whole wheat bread flour. It is generally a darker, coarser flour than the pastry flour.

Whole wheat pastry flour contains much less gluten. It is a lighter, fluffier flour, with plenty of starch—making it the baker's choice for pastries, cookies, and pasta dough. Its texture and color will remind you more of white flour than whole wheat flour, but remember it has more fiber than white.

CHAPTER 4

TECHNIQUES AND *Tips*

Old habits die hard. Jody, who assists me in cooking classes that I teach, found it very difficult to switch from old-fashioned methods to low-fat cooking techniques. To her, sautéing, for instance, meant using mounds of butter; it never occurred to her that liquids such as vegetable stock work just as well.

Before one class, I asked Jody to put together a sauce for a later demonstration. The snag came when she started sautéing. She could not quite get the idea that she had to stir the stock and onions almost constantly for 15 minutes so they wouldn't stick. When Jody's cup of perfectly minced onions welded themselves to the bottom of the saucepan, she realized something was wrong.

To rescue the stuck onions, Jody plopped a stick of butter into the pan. The onions became unstuck, browned nicely and made a perfect sauce. But not a perfect low-fat, no-cholesterol sauce!

Well, we've all faced similar situations—and used a pile of fat to fix up recipes. Just about anyone can cook *with* fat; the trick is learning to cook *without* it. If you master the following no-fat cooking methods, you'll master the art of no-cholesterol cooking.

Braising. This method allows tightly covered food to cook gently in a small amount of liquid, much like a stew. Braised vegetables—such as carrots, potatoes, sweet potatoes, beets, peppers, onions, and garlic—absorb the flavor of the cooking liquid and retain their bright color and texture.

For best no-cholesterol results, start with vegetable stock, water, or wine. A typical amount would be ¼ cup of the liquid for every 2 cups of vegetables. Heat the liquid to simmering in a deep, heavy-bottomed pan, such as enameled cast iron or heavy stainless steel. Add the food, cover the pan, and cook over medium heat until the food is tender or until it reaches the point specified by the recipe. For an example of a braised recipe, see Mexican Corn Stew (page 142).

Broiling. Broiled correctly, vegetables like sweet potatoes, white potatoes, and squash turn out crisp and golden brown on the outside but tender and juicy on the inside. For best flavor, I often marinate vegetables first in lemon juice, low-sodium soy sauce, or Miso Marinade for Vegetables (page 87). Simply cut raw vegetables into attractive chunks, place in a shallow pan, and toss with enough marinade to coat evenly. Let them stand at least 3 hours (turning once or twice) for the flavors to penetrate.

If you use a marinade, you don't have to coat the vegetables with oil before broiling them. You don't even have to baste them with the marinade during broiling—though I often do to keep them tender and moist. If you broil without marinating first, drizzle some fresh lemon juice over the vegetables so they don't dry out as they cook.

Grilling. Before grilling potatoes, carrots, beets, turnips, jicama, or other dense vegetables, prebake them to speed the process. Simply slice them into pieces that won't fall through the grilling rack, then bake in a covered dish at 350° for 15 to 20 minutes. Transfer the vegetables to a hot grill and cook until tender. Baste them with lemon or lime juice, vegetable stock, low-sodium soy sauce or tamari, wine, or sherry as they cook.

Less solid vegetables may fall apart on the grill, but you may still want to experiment with them. Try halving a large beefsteak tomato and grilling it for just under 2 minutes—enough to warm the surface and brown it a little. Try skewering mushrooms, green beans, or snow peas before grilling; the skewers will prevent the vegetables from slipping through the rack and will allow you to turn them easily.

No matter what vegetables you're cooking, always make sure the coals are hot—burned down to a dark red glow. Among my favorite grilling recipes in this book is Grilled-Eggplant Salad with Teriyaki Marinade (page 85).

COOKING METHODS TO AVOID

When it comes to no-cholesterol cooking, *how* you cook is as important as *what* you cook. Many low-fat, cholesterol-free foods, such as pasta and potatoes, can lose their health benefits when fried in butter or otherwise cooked in fat. And vegetables or fruits can lose vitamins when cooked the wrong way. These are cooking methods I avoid like the plague.

Boiling. This method is fine for making tea and pasta, but that's about it. Most vegetables turn into mush when boiled.

Browning. You need plenty of fat—usually butter—in order to brown foods.

Deep-fat frying. This requires even more fat than simple browning. Besides sending your serum cholesterol to the moon, deep-frying often renders food difficult to digest.

Pan-roasting. Pan-roasting vegetables adds extra fat. And pan-roasting them with meat subjects them to the cholesterol-rich fatty juices that coagulate in the bottom of the pan (and usually become gravy).

Poaching. During the poaching process, food sits directly in a liquid, such as stock, juice, or wine, and absorbs some of the liquid's flavor. Poaching tends to use more liquid than braising and takes less time. Savory liquids, such as stock or dry sherry, are best for vegetables. Juice, dessert wines, and other sweet liquids work well with fruits, such as Ruby Apples (page 248) or Sweet Golden Pears (page 249).

You can use any kind of heavy pot that will allow food to cook slowly. Bring the liquid to the simmering point over medium-high heat before adding the food, then lower the heat to medium or medium-low and cook fruit or vegetables until they're easily pierced with a sharp knife.

Sautéing. You can sauté foods over medium to medium-high heat in cooking liquids instead of butter or oil. The trick is to stir the food frequently to prevent it from scorching or sticking.

Heat the cooking liquid until it steams slightly, then add the food. Stir everything quickly to coat the pieces with the cooking liquid. Sautéing at moderate temperatures develops wonderfully sweet flavors that are often lost in high-heat frying.

If the liquid evaporates before the food is tender (this can happen, especially with sherry), add ¼ cup more at a time. The excess liquid will cook off, so you don't have to worry about your sauté becoming too soggy.

Steaming. Steamed foods actually cook more quickly than those that are boiled. That's because steam is hotter than boiling water. Using a lid makes sure that food cooks very quickly and retains nutrients.

Asian cooks favor bamboo steamer baskets over the more common metal steamers. Bamboo baskets have no center post to get in the way of long, straight vegetables, such as asparagus spears. They can also be stacked on top of each other so you can cook many things at a time. Place longer-cooking foods on the bottom layer and more delicate ones on top. I have steamed carrots at the same time as mushrooms—on different layers—and both vegetables have turned out perfectly.

Stir-frying. A favorite of Asian cooks, stir-frying is generally done in a wok or large skillet set over high heat. Because of the high heat, the food must be continually moved around the pan with cooking chopsticks or a wooden spoon or spatula. (Wooden utensils don't break tender vegetables as easily as metal ones do.) A small amount of cooking liquid is used to prevent foods from scorching or sticking.

A wok is ideal for stir-frying because its rounded bottom and heavy metal construction allows heat to move evenly over the surface of the pan. For trouble-free wokking, be sure to season the pan before using (follow the manufacturer's instructions). And cut up all the vegetables and other foods completely *before* turning on the heat. Once the stir-fry is going, the heat will be on, so to speak, and you will have little time for anything else. For an easy stir-fry recipe, try Chinese Supper Stir-Fry (page 173).

Making Your Life Easier

People often worry that they'll be spending more time and money on no-cholesterol cookery than they were on their old, unhealthy diet. Happily, that needn't be so. Your grocery bills should actually be lower than when buying typical high-fat foods like meat and cheese. And you can save time by following simple tips concerning shopping, food storage, and choice of kitchen equipment. Here are some of my recommendations.

Shopping. Don't underestimate the value of a good shopping list. It will keep you from absentmindedly picking up high-fat or high-cholesterol items. You'll also save time if you make yourself a map of your usual market so you can group foods on your list according to how they're found in the store. (No more doubling back. And you can skip whole aisles of foods that aren't on your diet plan.) Most large supermarkets are laid out in a consistent pattern based on the plumbing and electrical circuits. The fresh main staples and refrigerated or frozen foods are usually located along the perimeter of the store. The packaged foods, impulse buys, and generally unhealthy items are in the center aisles.

The no-cholesterol diet demands that you become a careful label reader. Look for unsuspected fats (especially hydrogenated ones and tropical oils) and high-cholesterol ingredients. Many ordinary foods—among them soups, baked goods, sauces, and frozen dinners—contain alarming amounts of undesirable ingredients.

Storage. Spend a little time organizing your kitchen so all your no-cholesterol foods are stored in their proper places. Over the years, through trial and error, I've learned that some foods need refrigeration while others do well on a dark pantry shelf. Here's how I stock my no-cholesterol kitchen to minimize spoilage and maximize nutrients.

Refrigerator

All oils
Baking yeast
Miso
Nuts and seeds (can also be frozen)
Tofu
Whole grain cereals

Freezer

Cooked beans and grains
Tempeh
Whole grain flours (double bag to prevent frost buildup)

Pantry (away from light and heat)

Arrowroot powder
Baking powder and baking soda (replace every six months)
Carob powder
Dried fruit
Dried herbs and spices
Dried grains and beans
Honey, molasses, and other sweeteners
Low-sodium soy sauce or tamari
Nutritional yeast
Pasta
Vinegar

Cookware. Make sure you have the right utensils for no-cholesterol cookery. Choose *pans* for the way they heat well and evenly. You'll need heavy, durable pans for sautéing without fat. I've had my set of heavy, enameled cast-iron pots for more than 15 years, and they're my favorites for day-to-day cooking. Lighter metals often have hot spots that repeatedly burn food.

Other good combinations include aluminum or copper on the outside and stainless steel on the inside.

Because a no-cholesterol diet contains lots of fruits and vegetables that need chopping, you should have quality *knives.* I suggest buying at least a 6″ cook's knife, a 9″ chef's knife, and a short paring knife. Two serrated knives, one for bread and one for tomatoes, are also a good idea. When you purchase knives, look for a metal called molybdenum—a combination of carbon and stainless steel. It's soft enough to sharpen well and hold an edge like carbon steel, but it doesn't rust or spot. While you're at it, purchase a sharpening steel to keep a fine edge on your knives. Paradoxically, a dull knife is much more dangerous than a sharp one because it can slip off food much more easily.

I believe in *electrical appliances,* especially the food processor. My prep time is cut in half when I use it. I keep it on my counter, ready to use. A blender is also important for no-cholesterol cooking. I have gotten by with these two items for most recipes. While a hand mixer is also nice, I don't use mine much since I learned to whip egg whites in a blender or food processor. (Leave off the blender top or remove the processor feed-tube insert so you can incorporate enough air into the whites.) An electric citrus juicer is helpful. I usually juice fruit in quantity, then freeze the juice in small containers or ice cube trays for later use.

CHAPTER 5

LIGHT

Delights

APPETIZERS,
HORS D'OEUVRES,
AND SNACKS

t's a cold winter afternoon. The house is quiet but for the sound of the wind whistling against an upstairs windowpane. Suddenly, all hell breaks loose. Someone or something is attacking your kitchen. You rush in and find you are too late. Whatever-it-is has gotten into the refrigerator and the cupboards. Boxes and wrappers lie mangled and twisted on the kitchen floor. Last night's dinner leftovers are scattered over the counters like battle carnage.

Your premonition is confirmed. Your teenager is home from school.

Sighing, you begin to clean up the mess. But, you say to yourself, things could be worse. He could be at the local fast-food drive-in, scarfing up cardboard hamburgers with his friends. The fact that he isn't shows that you are winning at least a few skirmishes in the Healthy-Snack Wars.

How do you introduce nonmeat, nondairy snacks into your family's menu without inciting a full-scale revolt? How do you create a dinner party using strictly no-cholesterol appetizers without incurring the carnivorous wrath of your guests? How do you navigate the dangerous minefields of your own snacking habits?

This chapter, focusing on the "little dishes" in your life, will attempt to answer all of these questions. You'll find that with the right ingredients and techniques you can make delicious, healthy snacks that appeal to you and your family. What's more, with a bit of garnishing and a few insider's catering tips (see "Planning the No-Cholesterol Gourmet Dinner Party" on page 52), your snacks can be transformed into gourmet appetizers and hors d'oeuvres for entertaining.

Planning Ahead
for Between-Meal Pangs

One of the first things I noticed when I moved to Europe was that hardly anyone ate snacks. Eating was reserved for specific times, and people rarely deviated from the schedule. My French teachers bought pastries on the way to school, for example, but I never saw them nibble; they would judiciously wait until the appropriate coffee break. No one ate small, frequent meals the way my friends at home did.

Why is snacking so American? Maybe it's because miniature meals give us a feeling of independence and flexibility. We're in control of when and what we eat. We love to browse among different foods, selecting what looks good, in much the same way that we window-shop.

But just as an innocent window-shopping tour can turn into a costly shopping spree, offhanded snacking can degenerate into an ugly eating binge if you don't seize control over your snack foods.

When prepared with healthy ingredients, snacks are ideally suited to the no-cholesterol diet. They allow you to eat smaller amounts of food more often, and they keep your blood sugar even so you don't crave sweets or high-fat foods. Tasty snacks in the fridge encourage kids to come straight home from school without a detour to the local fast-food hangout. Taking snacks to work helps keep you alert and pleasant-tempered over those long afternoons at the office.

Light, easy-to-digest munchies for after-dinner hunger pangs enhance weight control and sleeping patterns: Metabolism slows down while you sleep, so it's difficult for your body to digest large amounts of food at night. *Small* snacks are the only healthy night snacks.

Snacking is also gaining support among the scientific community. According to a study in the *New England Journal of Medicine,* men who increased their number of meals lowered their blood cholesterol levels. The researchers explain that the effect was probably linked to insulin: When people eat large meals, their bodies produce more insulin, which stimulates cholesterol production.

The urge to snack usually hits when blood sugar—and energy—levels are lowest. But precisely for this reason few cooks feel up to preparing snacks on the spur of the moment. So they tend to grab onto whatever flotsam or jetsam happens to be floating by. The healthy snacker knows that the first step to resisting junk food is preparing and stocking a wide selection of healthy snack foods.

Each week I choose five or more quick and uncomplicated recipes, using ingredients already on hand, and assemble snacks for the week. I cut vegetables into strips and refrigerate them in plastic bags (celery, carrots, radishes, and bell peppers keep five days after cutting). I cook beans for a spread (see Simple Bean Spread on Rye Croutons, page 65) and toast bread rounds for croutons. For the price of a few minutes' prep time each morning, I can pack a healthy, no-cholesterol snack.

Parents know that sweets are a fact of life, so the smart parent substitutes sweet *healthy* snacks, made with natural sugars and minimal fat. These treats can be as simple as banana chunks rolled in coconut and frozen on a baking sheet or Ants on a Log (page 68). Stocking some crunchy TV snacks for drop-in guests, especially during football season, never hurts. Fall favorites include Savory Garlicky Popcorn and Chili Tortilla Strips (page 67).

Making the Most of Leftovers

To some cooks, the "well-planned leftover" may seem a paradox, like "fleet-footed tortoise," but it needn't be so. In fact, when you prepare recipes in quantity and freeze or refrigerate the excess, you'll be well stocked for on-the-go eating. Enter the well-planned leftover! And know that he is a multifaceted character actor who can play many roles.

I often cook family meals with snacking in mind. For example, for Sunday dinner I might make a batch of Southwestern Red-Bean Chili (page 61) and Red Pepper Cornbread (page 63). If I know I'll have little time for lunch one day in the week ahead because of a tight deadline, I'll make a double batch and refrigerate the leftovers. On the day in question, I can spoon leftover chili into a prewarmed Thermos and top it with chopped fresh cilantro. I'll wrap a wedge of leftover cornbread in a cotton napkin to carry along. When things settle down, I'll have a better lunch at my desk than I could have at most restaurants—and it's cholesterol-free! Leftover chili makes a great burrito, too, as in Southwestern Bread Wraps (page 70).

Marinated salads are great packers and keepers. When choosing salad ingredients, I avoid the delicate vegetables—tomato, avocado, and lettuce—which become too soggy when immersed in dressing to make light meals the next day. Cabbage, carrots, celery, raw seeds and nuts, tofu, and red or green bell peppers all marinate beautifully. Try Harvest Salad (page 68) or Warm Cauliflower Salad (page 62)—two tasty offerings that will keep for several days in the refrigerator and are delicious as late-afternoon snacks or light suppers after a hectic day.

If you love pasta for dinner, make an extra batch of the noodles and tomato sauce. Refrigerate leftovers separately to use in recipes like Next-Day Pizzas with Hot Peppers (page 63) or Noodles with Miso Sauce (page 62).

Turning Snacks into Special Occasions

To make your afternoon snack more of an event and therefore a more integral part of your regular meal patterns, you must spend some time creating the setting. Even on bleary, half-asleep mornings, I take the time to include a cloth napkin and real silverware in my lunchbox. (One friend, believe it or not, loves eating from takeout containers, so she buys them in quantity at restaurant-supply houses and packs her homemade, healthy snacks in them.)

You can use a plastic bottle for salad dressing and a large-mouth thermos for soup or chili to transport your snacks hard-hat style, but some people need something a bit more patrician—a small picnic basket, for example, or maybe a stacking set of Japanese lacquer boxes.

Everyday snacks can be magically transformed into elegant party hors d'oeuvres or gourmet dinner appetizers with some simple sleight of hand. Caterers and gourmet restaurant chefs know that meal presentation—the way food is garnished and arranged on the plate—is the key to its success. So spend an extra minute making your snacks look good.

To create cholesterol-free party platters, use lots of fresh vegetables and fruits around a centerpiece of hollowed-out bell peppers filled with cholesterol-free dips, such as Caper and Garlic Dip (page 56) or the Assorted Dips (page 57). Or try a fruit fondue: a selection of exotic fruits—mango, papaya, starfruit, kiwifruit, and fresh pineapple—cut into wedges, drizzled with lime juice and served with a dipping sauce of pureed strawberries, mint, and cinnamon.

The cardinal rule of successful entertaining is to use recipes that can be prepared ahead—and then refrigerated or frozen until needed. It's okay to include a few recipes that require some last-minute work, such as baking or broiling. But the bulk of your appetizer menu should be items that you can make ahead.

And it's simple to prepare healthy appetizers in advance. If your main appetizer is a tray of fresh vegetables of different shapes and sizes—snow peas, whole green beans, cherry tomatoes, miniature squash, and broccoli florets—simply clean and cut the vegetables several hours before your party and store them in plastic bags in the refrigerator.

PLANNING THE NO-CHOLESTEROL
GOURMET DINNER PARTY

Entertaining is much like choreographing a complex dance. All the creative work is done beforehand, behind the scenes. By the time the dancers come onto the stage, every movement and prop has to be in place, ready for the audience. Meanwhile, you, the choreographer, must stand in the wings, teeth chattering with anticipation.

Entertaining was probably enough of a challenge with your old butter-and-cream recipes. But how in the world can you please friends and business associates with a menu completely devoid of meat and dairy products? How does the no-cholesterol cook overcome the natural meatless-diet prejudice of mass numbers of carnivores?

I've catered parties attended by 700 guests, and I'm always fascinated by the effect of *presentation* on people's acceptance of food. A simple platter of fresh vegetables, cut into interesting shapes and arranged on a bed of banana leaves from the florist, became the most popular centerpiece at a black-tie business function. And a woven basket tray of miniature fruit kabobs (chunks of papaya, pineapple, and mango stuck on toothpicks) served with a fruit puree for dipping entranced a large group of fashion designers—especially when I arranged exotic flowers alongside the fruit.

The point is, both choices were simple no-cholesterol choices; both were winners among a group of traditional eaters who were old pros on the party circuit.

The secret of my success was not to hide the vegetarian nature of the fare but to *flaunt* it. Like a choreographer, I created a mood that was tailored to the personalities of the guests.

Mapping the Menu

How *do* caterers make everything run so smoothly and effortlessly? For starters, they carefully map out the menu, creating a mood with the colors, tastes, and textures of the food and the decor of the setting. They also schedule the cooking and preparation well in advance. If you do the same, you will have plenty of time to relax and enjoy the party.

Planning a successful no-cholesterol menu takes self-discipline. The goal is to impress your guests, but you do not want to "go where no man has gone before." Don't experiment with too many new recipes for the big event—or put too many items on your party menu. To assemble a successful menu, you must focus on three things: the mood you wish to create, the people you are entertaining, and the available seasonal foods you can choose from to showcase in your menu.

My most successful parties followed one simple formula: The more people on the guest list, the simpler the menu and the more make-ahead recipes on it.

Start by choosing a cuisine (such as Greek, Italian, or Chinese) and developing a menu around it. Choose four *dependable* recipes—appetizer, entrée, salad, and dessert—and one new dish. Lean on your old standbys (that's why they're *called* old standbys). If you also decide to add a new one and the recipe flops, your guests will scarcely notice amid the four tried-and-true.

Choose simple ingredients. Some caterers build menus around one or two easily available, seasonal foods at their peak flavor and texture. One memorable party featured wild mushrooms (served in a soup, a sauce, and a marinated green salad) and fresh papaya (added to the salad and sliced with lime for dessert).

A common concern among party givers is having too little food, yet more menus are ruined—and more cooks frazzled—by last-minute additions than by judicious subtractions. This is why careful planning well before your party is the first key to success.

Creating the Perfect Party Mood

The mood you create—from the colors of the food to the candles on the serving table—molds a strong impression and influences whether people are relaxed and enjoying your party.

Several subtle factors contribute to mood. Foods that are creamy, smooth, and heavy (sauces, rich red wines, mousses, and purees, for example) have a formal air about them. Dishes with crunch and a crisp texture are lively, light, and more informal. A mixture of the two creates interest for the eyes as well as the taste-buds.

Tableware and place settings also influence mood. Fine silver, gold-rimmed white china, and a heavy damask table-cloth lend a formal elegance that will put your guests on red alert, manners-wise. If you'd rather they relax and mingle, try a buffet with colorful plates, textured napkins, and pottery serving bowls.

Food temperature and color have a subtle effect. Bright, hot colors—fuchsia, yellow, orange—create sensual, exotic settings. Smooth-textured foods with warm colors, such as earth tones, red, brown, and dark green, are typically featured in cozy, family meals.

Making a Shopping and Cooking Schedule

About a week before a dinner party, I sit down with my party ideas and make a checklist:

Dinner-Party Checklist

Number of guests ____
   Couples ____
   Singles ____
Color theme for table _____
Serving time ____ P.M.
Style _____
(buffet or formal sit-down)
Recipes:

_____

_____

_____

_____

Cooking-ahead requirements
1. _____
2. _____
3. _____

(continued)

PLANNING THE NO-CHOLESTEROL
GOURMET DINNER PARTY—*Continued*

Then I make my shopping list. It includes a separate section for specialty-store ingredients. The "cooking-ahead requirements" note in my checklist informs me of any ingredients that need to be purchased in advance or cooked up ahead of time. I need to remind myself, for instance, if I must order any unusual ingredients or if I need to cook some foods—like beans—ahead of time before I can proceed with my recipes.

I schedule the cooking for the week before the party. I might bake a cake the weekend before, freeze it in layers, defrost it the night ahead, and decorate it the day of the party. I bake homemade bread and wrap and freeze it. I make and refrigerate sauces. I buy avocados and tomatoes for the salad at the beginning of the week and set them aside to ripen.

When the day of the party arrives, much of the meal is already prepared and I'm ready to enjoy myself.

Enjoying Your Own Party

Many hosts are so nervous that they can't enjoy their own party. However, whether the party's function is to unite old friends or to allow for corporate networking, the host should be able to participate in the festivities. If you can't enjoy your own dinner party, what's the point?

Relaxation is essential for true enjoyment. In my planning, I schedule a 30-minute break just before the guests arrive. It is sheer bliss to lie down, close my eyes, and drift off to Perle Mestaland. Somehow, the refreshment I gain from this brief respite always seems to transfer to my guests.

First-Course Appetizers
and Party Hors d'Oeuvres

The recipes in this section can serve double-duty in your entertaining repertoire. You can divide them into one-portion servings and present them as appetizer preludes to the main course. Or you can serve them as hors d'oeuvres on trays or chafing dishes (heated serving dishes), buffet-style.

Mushroom Kabobs

24 small mushrooms
2 teaspoons olive oil
½ teaspoon minced garlic
¼ teaspoon dried thyme
⅛ teaspoon ground red pepper (or to taste)
24 pineapple chunks

In a large bowl, combine the mushrooms, oil, garlic, thyme, and pepper. Let marinate for 1 hour at room temperature.

Preheat the broiler.

Drain the mushrooms and reserve the liquid. On each of 6 bamboo or metal skewers, alternate 4 mushrooms with 4 pineapple chunks. Broil 3″ to 4″ from the heat until the mushrooms are lightly browned, about 3 minutes. Turn and broil 3 minutes more.

Serve hot with the reserved sauce.

California Pizza Toasts

4 ounces soy mozzarella cheese, shredded
2 ounces soft tofu, drained
1 teaspoon minced garlic
¼ teaspoon dried oregano
¼ teaspoon dried basil
¼ cup tomato paste
1 large baguette whole wheat French bread

Preheat the broiler.

In a food processor or blender, puree the cheese, tofu, and garlic until smooth. Transfer to a bowl and stir in the oregano and basil.

Cut the bread diagonally into 20 (1″) slices. Spread each slice with a small amount of tomato paste and top with a dollop of the cheese mixture. Place on a baking sheet.

Broil 3″ to 4″ from the heat for 1 minute, or until lightly browned. Serve hot.

These colorful Russian kabobs are first marinated in aromatic herbs and cholesterol-lowering olive oil, then grilled until golden.

Serves 6.

Especially striking appetizers, these miniature pizzas are made on diagonal slices of French bread. If you can't find French bread, be sure to use bread made without dairy products. You may assemble the pizzas up to 5 hours ahead, cover with plastic wrap, and refrigerate. Broil right before serving.

Makes 20.

A Japanese friend of mine keeps a jar of this marinade in the refrigerator for up to six weeks and simply adds vegetables to it as she has them available. An overnight soak in the marinade produces crisp, pickled vegetables that are great on a buffet with richer hors d'oeuvres.

Makes 3 cups.

Tofu contains soybean protein, which has been shown to have a dramatic cholesterol-lowering effect. This creamy dip is a great partner for a platter of fresh vegetables. Be sure to choose a pepper with a flat bottom so it can stand upright to serve as a container for the dip.

Serves 16.

REFRIGERATOR PICKLED VEGETABLES

¼ cup rice wine vinegar
¼ cup apple cider vinegar
1 umeboshi plum, mashed, or 1 teaspoon salt
1 tablespoon low-sodium soy sauce or tamari
1 teaspoon honey or maple syrup
1 large seedless cucumber, halved lengthwise and sliced
     into thin half-moons
1 cup radish halves
1 cup carrot sticks

In a jar with a tight-fitting lid, combine the rice wine vinegar, apple cider vinegar, plum or salt, soy sauce or tamari, and honey or maple syrup. Add the cucumbers, radishes, and carrots.

Cap the jar and shake. Place in the refrigerator and let marinate at least overnight. Remove the vegetables from the marinade and serve.

CAPER AND GARLIC DIP WITH FRESH VEGETABLES

1 large sweet red or green pepper
1 cup cherry tomatoes
1 cup broccoli florets
1 cup whole snow peas
2 small zucchini or yellow summer squash, sliced diagonally
1 cup whole green beans
8 ounces mushrooms, halved
8 ounces soft tofu, drained
1 tablespoon capers, drained
1 tablespoon stone-ground mustard
2 teaspoons minced fresh tarragon or 1 teaspoon dried
2 teaspoons minced chives or scallions
2 teaspoons minced garlic

Cut the top off the pepper and discard the seeds and inner membrane. Place the pepper in the center of a large platter. Arrange the tomatoes, broccoli, snow peas, zucchini or squash, beans, and mushrooms around it.

In a food processor or blender, puree the tofu until smooth. Transfer to a small bowl and stir in the capers, mustard, tarragon, chives or scallions, and garlic. Spoon the dip into the pepper. Serve at room temperature.

Baked New Potatoes with Assorted Dips

20 unpeeled bite-size red potatoes
⅔ cup soft tofu, pureed until creamy
⅓ cup soy imitation bacon bits
1 tablespoon lemon juice
¼ cup minced chives or scallions
¼ cup Dijon mustard
1 cup chunky peanut butter
1 teaspoon ground red pepper
1 teaspoon low-sodium soy sauce or tamari

Preheat the oven to 350°.

Wash the potatoes, prick each once with a fork, and place on a large ungreased baking sheet. Bake for 30 minutes, or until soft.

Meanwhile, in a small bowl, combine the tofu, bacon bits, and lemon juice.

In another small bowl, combine the chives or scallions and mustard.

In a third bowl, combine the peanut butter, pepper, and soy sauce or tamari.

Place the warm potatoes on a platter and surround them with the dipping sauces.

I first tasted this appetizer at an upscale party in Marin County, California. After baking the red potatoes, the hostess piled them into a wicker basket lined with a cloth napkin. She placed the dips around the basket in colorful bowls.

Makes 20.

Pesto comes in various flavors. It can be made with different herbs and vegetables as well as the ubiquitous basil. The colorful pesto in this recipe is made from sun-dried tomatoes and is served in spears of pale green endive for a striking presentation. The recipe abounds with garlic, long known for its ability to ward off colds and flu and presently being examined for its cholesterol-lowering properties.

Serves 12.

Sun-dried-tomato pesto in endive spears

8 ounces oil-packed sun-dried tomatoes, drained well
½ cup fine cracker crumbs
4 cloves garlic, coarsely chopped
½ cup pine nuts
2 bunches Belgian endive, separated into spears
  fresh basil or cilantro (garnish)

In a food processor or blender, puree the tomatoes, crumbs, and garlic until smooth.

In a small frying pan over low heat, toast the pine nuts for 2 minutes, stirring continually. Add to the tomato mixture. Process until smooth.

Spread the pesto on endive spears. Garnish with basil or cilantro.

This cholesterol-free pâté tastes like chicken salad; it gets rave reviews whenever I serve it. In this recipe, it is spooned into cherry tomatoes and miniature cups made from fat slices of zucchini.

Makes 28.

Miniature stuffed vegetables

12 large cherry tomatoes
 2 large zucchini
 8 ounces tempeh, cut into large chunks
 1 teaspoon olive oil
 2 tablespoons low-sodium soy sauce or tamari
¼ cup minced celery
 3 tablespoons cholesterol-free mayonnaise
 2 tablespoons minced fresh parsley
 1 tablespoon minced scallions
   pinch of ground red pepper
   pinch of dried dill
   dill sprigs (garnish)

Slice the tops off the cherry tomatoes and remove the insides using the small end of a melon scoop. Slice each zucchini crosswise into 8 pieces. With the melon scoop, make a shallow well in the center of each slice.

In a large frying pan over medium-high heat, sauté the tempeh in the oil until lightly browned, about 10 minutes. Add the soy sauce or tamari and mash the tempeh into a thick paste.

Transfer the mixture to a medium bowl and add the celery, mayonnaise, parsley, scallions, pepper, and dried dill.

Spoon the mixture into the tomatoes and zucchini cups. Garnish with dill sprigs.

ASIAN NUT BALLS

2 cups finely ground, unsalted nuts, such as almonds, walnuts, or cashews
1½ cups cooked short-grain brown rice
½ cup grated onions
3 tablespoons nutritional yeast
1 tablespoon low-sodium soy sauce or tamari
1 tablespoon dried basil
1 teaspoon ground caraway seeds
1 teaspoon dried sage
½ cup prepared hot Chinese mustard

Preheat the oven to 350°.

In a large bowl, combine the nuts, rice, onions, yeast, soy sauce or tamari, basil, caraway, and sage. Form into 1" balls, adding a little water if needed for the mixture to hold together.

Place on an ungreased baking sheet and bake for 20 minutes. Serve hot with the mustard as a dip.

A savory, rich flavor weaves through these unusual hors d'oeuvres, which are made from an assortment of ground nuts seasoned with low-sodium soy sauce or tamari and nutritional yeast.

Makes 42.

Bypassing fatty cheeses and nuts, this pesto is a refreshing cholesterol-free alternative to traditional recipes. For variety, you can serve the pesto over hot pasta or as a spread on croutons or crackers.

Makes 16.

STUFFED MUSHROOMS WITH PARSLEY PESTO

16 large mushrooms
 3 tablespoons minced onions
 2 teaspoons minced garlic
 2 teaspoons olive oil
 2 tablespoons fine rye bread crumbs
 1/3 cup minced fresh basil
 2 tablespoons minced fresh parsley
 1/2 teaspoon minced fresh oregano
   herbal salt substitute (to taste)
   ground black pepper (to taste)
   shredded soy mozzarella cheese (optional)

Preheat the broiler.

Remove the stems from the mushrooms by wiggling them until they loosen. Mince the stems and set aside. Place the caps, round side up, on an ungreased baking sheet and broil 3″ to 4″ from the heat for 3 to 5 minutes, or until the mushrooms exude moisture. Set aside.

In a large frying pan over medium-high heat, sauté the onions and garlic in the oil for 5 minutes, stirring frequently to keep from browning. Add the minced mushroom stems and bread crumbs. Cook for 3 minutes.

Remove the pan from the heat and add the basil, parsley, oregano, salt substitute, and pepper.

Lightly coat a shallow baking dish or jelly-roll pan with no-stick spray. Arrange the mushrooms in the dish, hollow sides up. Spoon the basil mixture into the caps. Sprinkle with a little cheese (if using).

Broil until the filling is hot and bubbling, about 3 to 5 minutes. Serve hot.

On-the-Run Meals and Packable Lunches

The recipes in this section are all designed to provide quick cholesterol-free lunches. Some, such as the Southwestern Red-Bean Chili, taste better after an overnight mellowing in the refrigerator.

Southwestern Red-Bean Chili

2 pounds mushrooms, sliced
3 cups cooked and drained small red beans
3 onions, coarsely chopped
1 cup chopped celery
1 cup chopped carrots
2 tablespoons olive oil
1 teaspoon ground cumin
1 teaspoon dried basil
1 teaspoon chili powder (or to taste)
8 ripe Italian tomatoes, chopped
1 small can (about 2 ounces) green chilies, chopped
½ cup low-sodium soy sauce or tamari
½ cup red wine
3 tablespoons tomato paste
4 cloves garlic, minced
2 teaspoons ground red pepper (or to taste)

In a 6- to 8-quart heavy pot, combine the mushrooms, beans, onions, celery, carrots, oil, cumin, basil, and chili powder. Stir well to coat all ingredients with the oil. Cover and cook over medium heat for 10 minutes, or until the onions are soft.

Add the tomatoes, chilies, soy sauce or tamari, wine, tomato paste, garlic, and pepper. Increase the heat to high and bring to a boil. Lower the heat and simmer for at least 45 minutes (the flavors will improve the longer the chili simmers).

Some studies have shown that dried beans can help lower blood cholesterol levels. This spicy chili with a rich red color has plenty of beans—and is easy to make ahead in quantity and freeze for emergencies.

Serves 6 to 8.

Warm Cauliflower Salad

1 large head cauliflower, broken into small pieces
⅓ cup chopped celery
3 tablespoons light sesame oil
1 tablespoon chopped sweet red peppers
1 tablespoon lemon juice
1 teaspoon Dijon mustard
½ teaspoon curry powder
¼ teaspoon ground cinnamon
¼ teaspoon herbal salt substitute

In a large steamer, steam the cauliflower until tender but still crisp, about 8 to 10 minutes.

In a large bowl, combine the celery, oil, peppers, lemon juice, mustard, curry powder, cinnamon, and salt substitute. Add the warm cauliflower and toss to combine. Let stand for at least 5 minutes before serving.

This creamy noodle dish tastes as if it's loaded with rich dairy cheese, but the flavor comes from tahini, a paste made from sesame seeds. The sauce keeps for a week in the refrigerator and is equally delicious hot or cold. It's great over noodles, as in this recipe, or spooned over steamed vegetables or rice.

Serves 4.

Noodles with Miso Sauce

¼ cup water
½ cup thinly sliced mushrooms
¼–½ cup tahini
2 tablespoons minced scallions
1 tablespoon minced fresh parsley
2 tablespoons light miso
2 tablespoons hot water
2 cups cooked eggless noodles

In a large frying pan, heat the water until it's simmering. Add the mushrooms. Lower the heat, cover the pan, and let the mushrooms cook for 5 minutes.

Stir in the tahini, heating until it becomes creamy. Remove the pan from the heat. Add the scallions and parsley.

In a small cup, combine the miso and hot water. Stir into the sauce. Add the noodles and toss well.

NEXT-DAY PIZZAS WITH HOT PEPPERS

    2 whole wheat pitas
 ½ cup low-salt tomato sauce
 ½ green pepper, sliced into thin rounds
    2 tablespoons chopped marinated jalapeño peppers
 ½ cup shredded soy mozzarella cheese

Preheat the broiler. Lightly toast the pitas if desired.

Place the pitas (uncut) on an ungreased baking sheet. Spread each with tomato sauce, then top with the green peppers, jalapeños, and cheese. Broil until bubbly.

RED PEPPER CORNBREAD

       3 cups coarse cornmeal
       2 cups boiling water
 ¼–½ cup minced sweet red peppers
       3 tablespoons olive oil
    1–3 teaspoons herbal salt substitute
       1 cup soy milk
       1 tablespoon baking powder

In a large bowl, mix together the cornmeal, water, peppers, oil, and salt substitute. Let stand for 40 minutes. Stir in the milk and baking powder.

Preheat the oven to 400°.

Coat an 8″ × 8″ baking dish with no-stick spray. Place the empty dish in the oven for 1 minute, then remove (with hot pads) and pour in batter. (Preheating the dish creates a crisp outer crust.)

Bake the cornbread for 30 to 40 minutes, or until a toothpick inserted in the center comes out clean. Let cool, then cut into squares.

These spicy miniature pizzas are made from toasted pita bread topped with tomato sauce, sliced vegetables, and jalapeño peppers. I call them next-day pizzas because I often make them with leftover homemade tomato sauce the day after a pasta dinner.

Serves 2.

An ideal accompaniment to Southwestern Red-Bean Chili, this corn-bread tastes especially good warmed. Made with soy milk instead of dairy milk, this recipe is a no-cholesterol variation of a traditional favorite.

Serves 9.

An apple a day keeps the doc away—and maybe arterial plaque as well. According to some studies, apples wash away cholesterol-laden bile acids in the intestinal · tract. I like to use Red Delicious apples for this shake.

Serves 4.

Tempeh, an Indonesian soy food, is a great cholesterol-free substitute for beef. For these delicious sandwiches, it is cooked in a spicy marinade, then sandwiched between slices of rye bread. The soy mixture itself is also great for marinating vegetables for shish kebabs. Let them soak overnight.

Serves 2.

Morning-Glory Fruit Shake

2 cups sliced bananas
2 cups sliced strawberries
2 cups chopped pineapple or papayas
1 cup chopped peeled apples
½ cup ice cubes
1 teaspoon honey

In a blender container, combine the bananas, strawberries, pineapples or papayas, apples, ice cubes, and honey. Puree on high speed until smooth. Serve immediately.

Spiced Tempeh Sandwiches

1 pound tempeh
½ cup water
2 tablespoons low-sodium soy sauce or tamari
2 tablespoons dry sherry
1 tablespoon honey
1 teaspoon minced garlic
1 teaspoon ground coriander
½ teaspoon grated fresh ginger
   pinch of ground red pepper
4 slices rye bread
4 lettuce leaves or ½ cup radish sprouts
2 tomato or avocado slices

Cut the tempeh into 4 large pieces.

In a medium bowl, combine the water, soy sauce or tamari, sherry, honey, garlic, coriander, ginger, and pepper.

In a large no-stick frying pan over medium heat, lightly brown the tempeh on both sides. Add the marinade mixture and cook until the liquid evaporates. Remove from heat. Slice each piece of tempeh in half horizontally to make it thinner.

Place on half of the bread slices. Add lettuce or sprouts and tomatoes or avocados. Top with the remaining bread.

SIMPLE BEAN SPREAD ON RYE CROUTONS

2 cups cooked and drained chick-peas or pinto beans
3 cloves garlic
2 teaspoons herbal salt substitute
1 teaspoon lemon juice
1 teaspoon ground cumin (or to taste)
1-2 teaspoons water (optional)
1 tablespoon minced fresh parsley
20 slices round party-size rye bread

In a blender or food processor, puree the beans, garlic, salt substitute, lemon juice, and cumin until smooth. (If needed to facilitate blending, add the water.) Transfer to a medium bowl. Stir in the parsley. Refrigerate overnight to let the flavors blend.

Preheat the oven to 250°.

Place the bread in a single layer on a large ungreased baking sheet. Bake for 20 minutes per side, or until crisp. Let cool a few minutes. Spread with the bean mixture.

One of the easiest recipes in your lunchbox repertoire, this fiber-rich bean spread is equally delicious spread on croutons or wrapped into a burrito. The next time you cook up a pot of beans for a Mexican dinner, make extra for this simple but tasty spread. It freezes well and will keep in the refrigerator for a week.

Serves 10.

Wholesome Movie and TV Snacks

You should have a few trusty TV snacks on hand for those evenings when you feel like a couch potato. They can help you avoid the danger zone of salty nuts and chips. The following recipes make after-dinner snacking a healthy activity.

These tomato toddies are perfect for chilly evenings by the fire. They taste like warm, spicy Bloody Marys. But since they're nonalcoholic, they're much healthier. You can even make them ahead and serve them hot from a prewarmed thermos.

Serves 6.

Hot Tomato Toddies

6 cups low-sodium vegetable cocktail juice
  juice of 1 lemon (about ¼ cup)
  juice of 1 lime (about 2 tablespoons)
¼ teaspoon celery seeds
  dash of hot pepper sauce or ¼ teaspoon ground red
      pepper
3 stalks celery, halved

In a 2-quart saucepan, combine the vegetable juice, lemon juice, lime juice, celery seeds, and hot pepper sauce or red pepper. Bring to a boil over medium heat.

To serve, pour into mugs and add celery stalks for stirring.

No more greasy potato chips! In this recipe, paper-thin slices of red potatoes are baked until the moisture evaporates and the potatoes turn into crisp chips. The slicing is easiest if you use a food processor, but you can do it by hand, too.

Serves 10.

Oil-Free Potato Chips

1 pound red potatoes, well scrubbed
  herbal salt substitute (to taste)
  ground black pepper (to taste)

Preheat the oven to 300°.

Lightly coat a large baking sheet with no-stick spray. Using a sharp knife or a food processor fitted with a thin slicing blade, cut the potatoes into paper-thin slices. Spread the potatoes on the baking sheet in a single layer. Sprinkle lightly with the salt substitute and pepper.

Bake until lightly browned and crisp, about 10 to 15 minutes.

Savory Garlicky Popcorn

2 tablespoons honey
2 tablespoons tomato paste
1 teaspoon garlic powder
¼ teaspoon chili powder
¼ teaspoon paprika
6 cups air-popped popcorn

Preheat the oven to 200°.

In a 1-quart saucepan, combine the honey, tomato paste, garlic powder, chili powder, and paprika. Cook over medium heat, stirring frequently, until fragrant, about 3 minutes.

Place the popcorn in a large bowl. Drizzle with the honey mixture and toss to coat lightly.

Spread the popcorn on a large ungreased no-stick baking sheet. Bake for 15 minutes, stirring occasionally. Turn the oven off and let the mixture stand with the door closed for 1 hour, which helps the coating stick.

Chili Tortilla Strips

6 large corn tortillas
2 tablespoons olive oil
2 tablespoons chili powder
1 teaspoon ground cumin

Preheat the oven to 400°.

Lightly brush both sides of each tortilla with the oil. Using scissors, cut the tortillas into 1″-wide strips. Place in a single layer on a large ungreased baking sheet.

In a cup, mix the chili powder and cumin. Sprinkle over the strips. Bake for 15 to 20 minutes, or until crisp.

Make up plenty of this crunchy cholesterol-free snack. With the delicious garlic flavor, nobody will miss the butter. The popcorn will keep for five days in a tightly covered container.

Makes 6 cups.

These chips will become favorites of the Mexican-food lovers in your family. Crunchy and satisfying, they make good take-along afternoon snacks for kids and office workers.

Serves 6.

Ants on a Log

3 stalks celery, halved
½ cup peanut butter
¼ cup raisins

Stuff the cavity of each celery stick with peanut butter, then top with raisins.

A snack that's a winner with kids, this recipe is simple enough for them to make themselves. And it keeps for several days if tightly covered and refrigerated.

Makes 6.

Light Meals

These recipes are for those times when you don't have a huge appetite. They're sure to become family favorites for brunches, summer picnics, and late-night suppers.

Harvest Salad

1 cup corn
1 cup chopped green cabbage
1 carrot, thinly sliced
1 stalk celery, diced
⅓ cup chopped sweet red peppers
¼ cup pumpkin seeds
¼ cup olive oil
¼ cup water
3 tablespoons minced shallots
2 tablespoons lemon juice
1 tablespoon minced fresh dill
1 teaspoon Dijon mustard

A bright, colorful salad to celebrate harvest time, this recipe combines raw vegetables and seeds, giving you a chance to add plenty of fiber to your no-cholesterol diet.

Serves 4.

In a large bowl, combine the corn, cabbage, carrots, celery, peppers, and seeds.

In a small bowl, whisk together the oil, water, shallots, lemon juice, dill, and mustard. Pour over the vegetables. Let marinate for at least 1 hour before serving.

Rice-Paper Vegetarian Spring Rolls

2 large carrots
2 tablespoons chopped scallion tops
1 tablespoon olive oil
1 tablespoon minced fresh tarragon or 1 teaspoon dried
¼ teaspoon ground black pepper
16 rice-paper rounds, 6″ in diameter
2 cups cooked bean-thread noodles, snipped into 2″ pieces

Using a vegetable peeler, shave off long, thin slices of carrot. Place the carrots, scallions, oil, tarragon, and pepper in a large bowl. Toss well and let stand for 1 hour.

Fill a large bowl with warm water. Dip each rice-paper round into the water until softened and translucent, about 10 seconds. Remove and let drain on a clean dish towel.

Place about 2 tablespoons of the noodles and about 2 tablespoons of the vegetable mixture along the lower edge of each piece of rice paper, about 1″ from the edge. Fold the bottom of the paper over the filling; fold in both sides over the filling. Roll the bundle into a cylinder.

Place the rolls on a plate and cover with plastic wrap. Chill for 30 minutes. Serve cold.

Eh, what's up, Doc? Carrots, of course, which are on the list of healthy foods that can help lower cholesterol. These hors d'oeuvres are chock-full of carrots wrapped in rice paper—traditionally used in Vietnamese and Thai cuisines as an alternative to deep-fried egg-roll wrappings.

Makes 16.

A great light meal, southwestern style, these
burritos can be rolled
the night before and
packed for a picnic or an
on-the-road dinner when
traveling. They use left-
over Southwestern Red-
Bean Chili. If desired,
serve topped with
sprouts, shredded lettuce,
grated carrots, chopped
tomatoes, and sliced
avocados.

Serves 2.

Use aluminum foil or
parchment paper (avail-
able in cookware stores)
to wrap this savory vege-
table mixture before
cooking. The technique
keeps fat and calories
low and allows flavors to
mingle in the moist
packet. Lightly cooked
onions, the next best
thing to raw onions, may
help boost your level of
heart-protective HDL
cholesterol.

Serves 4.

Southwestern Bread Wraps

½ cup Southwestern Red-Bean Chili (page 61)
2 tablespoons Mexican salsa
1 teaspoon minced red onions
1 teaspoon minced fresh cilantro
½ clove garlic, minced
2 tortillas or chapatis

In a medium bowl, combine the chili, salsa, onions, cilantro, and garlic. Mash with a potato masher or fork.

Spread on tortillas or chapatis and roll to enclose the filling. If desired, warm in a toaster oven or microwave before eating.

Grilled Vegetables en Papillote

2 cups broccoli florets
1 red onion, thinly sliced
1 cup thinly sliced carrots
2 cloves garlic, minced
1 tablespoon olive oil
2 teaspoons chopped fresh tarragon
 juice of ½ lime

In a large bowl, combine the broccoli, onions, carrots, garlic, oil, tarragon, and lime juice. Let stand for 1 hour, stirring occasionally.

While the vegetables marinate, prepare a grill for cooking.

Cut aluminum foil or parchment paper into 4 circles about 10″ in diameter. Divide the vegetable mixture evenly among the circles. Fold into half-moon shapes, crimping the edges to seal.

Grill about 5″ to 6″ from medium-hot coals for about 10 minutes.

Mushroom Ragout on Rye Toast Triangles

1   ounce dried shiitake mushrooms
1   cup boiling water
½   cup dry sherry
1   teaspoon olive oil
3   medium leeks, thinly sliced
2   cups mushrooms, thinly sliced
1   teaspoon minced garlic
1   cup white wine
2   tablespoons arrowroot powder
    herbal salt substitute (to taste)
    ground white pepper (to taste)
4   slices rye bread

This recipe is so simple: dried and fresh mushrooms sautéed in sherry and olive oil, then the juices thickened into a rich sauce. Spooned over crisp rye toast triangles, it's a delicious light meal.

Serves 4.

Place the dried mushrooms in a small bowl and cover with the boiling water. Let soak for 15 minutes, then drain. Cut off and discard the stems. Slice the caps into thin strips. Set aside.

In a large frying pan over medium-high heat, heat the sherry and oil. Reduce the heat to medium and add the leeks. Sauté for 15 minutes, stirring frequently.

Add the soaked mushrooms, sliced mushrooms, and garlic. Cook for 10 minutes, stirring frequently. Strain, reserving the cooking liquid (if any). Set the mushrooms aside. Return the liquid to the pan.

In a small bowl, combine the wine and arrowroot until dissolved. Pour the wine mixture into the pan. Bring to a boil and cook, stirring with a whisk, until the sauce thickens. Season with salt substitute and pepper. Add the mushroom mixture to the sauce and heat through.

Meanwhile, toast the bread, then cut diagonally into quarters to form triangles. Place on a platter. Spoon the sauce over the toast.

CHAPTER 6

SALAD

Symphonies

Whenever I hear stories about children who hate vegetables, especially salad greens, it baffles me. Maybe the fact that I helped grow my own vegetables as a child and picked them myself gave me a feeling of kinship with the greenery on my dinner plate.

My father's garden overflowed with salad vegetables. Sitting along one side of the garden were two long, facing rows of lettuce heads, reminding me (in my giddy preteen years) of a beauty salon. There were the impeccably stoic Mrs. Icebergs, the exotic Miss Romaines, and the somewhat loose and floozy Red Leafs. It was almost a shame to pick the leaves and ruffle such imperturbable personalities. I would walk on tiptoe between the rows, afraid to disturb the "ladies," should they be sleeping under their hair dryers.

On summer evenings, my sister and I were given the special honor of harvesting. Ten minutes before dinner, we would grab our tiny baskets, pluck a few tender leaves of lettuce and only the ripest tomatoes and bring them inside to my mother, who did little to spoil the straight-from-the-garden taste. A small amount of salad dressing composed of simple ingredients— olive oil, lemon juice, vinegar, garlic, salt, and pepper—was stirred together or shaken in a glass cruet right before dinner, and that was about it. I still use a simple approach today, both for health reasons and because once you learn to appreciate the taste of fresh salad vegetables, you don't want to smother them under extraneous fluids.

Take Salads to Heart

With their bounty of vitamins, minerals, and fiber, salads contribute to your health in many ways. Studies suggest that some salad vegetables may lower blood cholesterol. In one experiment, subjects who ate about 2½ medium carrots every day lowered cholesterol levels an average of 11 percent.

Fresh-fruit salads may also help: Medical research teams in Italy, Ireland, and France have shown that apples can raise protective HDL-cholesterol levels; other studies have found that certain potent compounds in grapefruit lower total blood cholesterol and may even clean out plaque buildup.

Other salad ingredients, such as cooked dried beans, are backed by even more cholesterol-related research. These legumes provide plenty of soluble fiber, which has been discovered to sweep harmful LDL cholesterol out of the bloodstream. And salad dressings made with heart-healthy olive oil and garlic (which thins the blood to prevent clotting) can also provide some hearty benefits.

The Day-Round, Year-Round Salad Gourmet

In many parts of the country, cooks foolishly abandon salad making in the winter because fresh ingredients are not at their seasonal peak. This is absurd. Salads can be built around winter vegetables—spinach, lettuces, sweet red and green peppers; parsley, and cucumbers—and supplemented with cooked vegetables, beans and grains, or winter fruit to achieve year-round salad enjoyment.

Salads can be much more than a pause between soup and entrée. Some salads, such as vegetables tossed with cooked grains, beans, and fresh fruits, can be meals in themselves. Others, such as marinated selections, are a busy cook's boon, giving you on-the-run salads for hectic schedules.

Great salad making employs three important steps: selecting the best ingredients, presenting them aesthetically, and topping them with winning salad dressings.

Selecting Salad Ingredients

Unlike soup stocks, which hide the sins of less-than-perfect vegetables, salads magnify all the good and bad points of fresh fruits and vegetables. Once you know the flavors and textures of different fruits and vegetables, you can select your salad ingredients like an artist choosing paints for his latest masterpiece, using complementary colors, shapes, and tastes to compose a "canvas."

But before you can paint with your selections, you must first bring them home. Here are some important criteria for selecting the best vegetables at your neighborhood supermarket or fresh-vegetable outlet.

A GLOSSARY OF FRESH GREENS

Salad greens fill a bowl with colors ranging from bronze to the palest yellow. Greens like arugula and chicory, once considered exotic, are now the norm on gourmet tables. The following greens can cure you of the boring and not very nutritious iceberg-itis.

Arugula. Another name for arugula is rocket. It has small flat leaves and a piquant taste. You can find it in Italian groceries or gourmet markets. Its mustardy flavor combines well with the bite of radicchio lettuce or Belgian endive.

Belgian endive. Belgian endive breaks into spear-shaped leaves from its tight roll, lending a crisp texture and pale green color to your salad bowl. Because the leaves are firm and boatlike, they can also be filled with spreads or used as dipping appetizers.

Buttercrunch, red leaf, and green leaf lettuces. These popular varieties of loose-leaf lettuce are crinkled and crisp; the red leaf variety has a distinctive maroon trim on the outer leaves.

Cabbage. Red, green, savoy, and napa (Chinese) cabbage all add crunch and color to salads. Slice them into thin strips or dice into squares. Partially cut cabbage keeps best when wrapped tightly in plastic before refrigerating.

Chervil. A French version of parsley, fresh chervil has more of a bite than parsley. Chop it and sprinkle on greens or use it to top soups with a bit of color.

Chicory. Sometimes called curly endive, chicory has loose leaves that need careful washing to remove particles of sand. It has a bitter taste that works well with creamy dressings and milder greens.

Chives. Oniony and bright green, snippets of chives give you a lot of flavor and color for the money. They keep best

Bulbs (onions, garlic, leeks). Firm, well-shaped bulbs with no sprouts are best.

Fruit vegetables (tomatoes, peppers, eggplant, squash, cucumbers). Seek firm, bright, and shiny fruits that are heavy for their size.

Immature flowers (broccoli, cauliflower, artichokes). Good signs are compact, tight heads, firm green leaves, and no yellowing.

Leaf vegetables (spinach, lettuce). Make sure there is no wilting or brown or yellow spotting.

Mushrooms. The best mushrooms have tightly fitting caps that completely cover the gills (undersides).

Roots and tubers (potatoes, beets, carrots, turnips). Look for smooth shine, firmness, and bright color all the way to the leaves.

wrapped in aluminum foil in the refrigerator.

Cilantro. Also known as Chinese parsley, this leaf of the coriander plant has a citrus taste that some people find almost soapy. Cilantro is the distinctive flavor in many Vietnamese, Thai, and Mexican dishes; use it in combination with peanuts and soy dressings.

Fennel. With a mild licorice flavor, diced fresh fennel livens up any salad. Combine it with bitter greens like chicory and a lemony dressing.

Oak leaf lettuce. A tender lettuce, often a favorite of backyard gardeners, these leaves resemble those of their namesake tree. They wilt easily, so avoid pairing them with marinades.

Parsley. Always a welcome addition to salads (but rarely used except as a garnish), parsley adds deep color and sweet flavor. Keep parsley in sealed plastic bags in the refrigerator for up to two weeks.

Radicchio. An Italian native, this dark purple or red lettuce comes in a tight bunch about the size of a large fist. Only a few leaves, sliced into thin strips, are needed to set off a salad.

Romaine lettuce. A popular lettuce for marinated salads, especially Caesar salad, romaine is a sturdy leaf lettuce that has dark green outer leaves and pale inner ones. Sliced into strips, romaine combines well with red leaf or oak leaf lettuce.

Spinach. An excellent addition to any salad because of its dark leaves and crisp texture, spinach is also rich in fiber. Wash leaves carefully to remove sand and trim off any tough stems before adding spinach leaves to your salad bowl.

Watercress. A peppery plant that is the herald of early spring, watercress has long stems and penny-shaped leaves. It plays the garnish well, but it can also be mixed with lighter-colored greens for an attractive salad. Avoid yellow leaves.

Seeds and seed pods (beans, peas, snow peas). Pick only the wrinkle-free, moist, firm, and small-size ones.

Stalks (celery, bok choy). Look for young stalks that are firm and break crisply. Discard those that are pithy or have yellow leaves.

Presenting Your Salad

"The eye eats before the taste buds" goes the old saying. Or, as a friend of mine puts it, "the palette before the palate." And this is especially true for salads, which usually gain a great deal from fastidious presentation.

Presenting a salad may be compared with organizing the scenery for a stage play. You have a background and a foreground. Your salad bowls and plates act as the background and so should serve to enhance the interaction of the "actors" in the foreground. The use of contrasting colors, such as a cobalt blue plate to frame a selection of wild lettuce and yellow peppers, is one way to accomplish this.

One common mistake is to crowd a salad onto a minuscule plate—or to serve huge portions to compensate for a supposed lack of substance. Both strategies are fallacious. A salad is not an epic with a cast of thousands but more of a one-act play, with a small cast and a simple yet sweet plot line. Choose pleasing shapes, contrasting round cherry tomatoes, for example, with the spiky leaves of curly endive or the long ovals of whole snow peas. Choose colors that enhance each other, especially green and red, green and orange, or green and yellow.

Creating Winning Salad Dressings

Ask any good cook: The secret to great salads is not just super fresh ingredients but also a tasty salad dressing. Dressings are the magic potion that brings life and inspiration to vegetables and fruit. Heart-conscious eaters often think they have to sacrifice a salad dressing because of the fatty ingredients. But now that monounsaturated (olive) and polyunsaturated (safflower) oils are making headlines as cholesterol-lowering foods (see chapter 2), salad dressings are no longer something to skip. Although dressings loaded with large amounts of oil are not recommended, a careful recipe containing small amounts of cholesterol-lowering oils can be very beneficial.

Many people begin to expand their dressing repertoire by modifying their favorite vinaigrette recipe, replacing generic salad oil with a lesser amount of olive oil in hopes of cutting down the fat. But they soon discover a problem: When they alter the proportions of ingredients, the blend of flavors changes drastically. Salad dressings are delicate creations; they work only if their flavors are carefully balanced. Too much of any one flavor—be it sharp, tangy, or smooth—can upset the balance.

The old rule of thumb for oil and vinegar dressings is two parts oil to one part vinegar. But omitting a small portion of the oil tilts the pinball machine (the vinegar rings like a burglar alarm) because the oil acts as a flavor buffer, creating a harmonious blend that romances the taste buds.

But all is not hopeless. You can keep very close to the dressing's original flavor—and still lower the fat content—by *replacing* some oil with water, vegetable puree, vegetable juice, blended soft tofu, or even balsamic vinegar.

When I alter a traditional salad-dressing recipe, I automatically halve the amount of oil and substitute water. For example, a recipe that calls for ½ cup olive oil and ⅓ cup safflower oil (a total of approximately 13 tablespoons) would become ¼ cup olive oil, 2½ tablespoons safflower oil and 6½ tablespoons water. (Unsalted tomato or vegetable cocktail juice is acceptable in place of the water.) Automatically, I've cut the calories and fat by about half.

Bear in mind, however, that the resulting dressing will be less able to adhere to the salad vegetables. The raison d'être of dressings, after all, is to do just that—dress. A salad dressing that pools in the bottom of the bowl, leaving the lettuce naked (yikes!), is not fulfilling its mission in life. So to create a creamier, congealing outfit, I often add a small amount of pureed soft tofu. The tiny bit of fat in the tofu—much less than the original amount in the oil—helps the dressing congeal.

Note: To keep the balance of flavors when substituting for or reducing the oil, be cautious about adding stronger-tasting ingredients, such as grated onion, garlic, and ground red pepper. You may actually need to reduce them slightly because they'll have more impact than in the original recipe.

Another interesting base in some of my oil-free salad dressings is roasted and peeled sweet red peppers. Pureed roasted peppers lend a delicious barbecued flavor, a light rose color, and a smooth, silky texture. Green peppers have a similar effect, although they are not as sweet as red.

In winter, marinated salads can help awaken dull, sleepy palates. Marinades typically originate in hard economic times when leftovers are used as a staple and families search for creative recipes to relieve the boredom. Marinades are magical flavor enhancers. Less than perfectly fresh foods, such as leftover vegetables and cooked beans or grains, achieve new heights of flavor after 30 minutes in a marinade. For busy people, marinades are also an easy way to prepare menus in advance. Marinated vegetables, beans, and grains can keep for a week in refrigerated containers. January lunches in my house often revolve around a hearty soup and a green salad topped with marinated vegetables.

Marinades are usually composed of one salty and one sour ingredient. The French rely on fresh lemon juice and salt. Japanese cooks use miso and vinegar. For example, Miso Marinade for Vegetables (page 87) is perfect for cherry tomatoes or thick slices of cucumbers, bell peppers, daikon radishes,

TEN OIL-FREE SALAD DRESSINGS

It's easy to dress up salads with a collection of recipes such as these at your disposal.

SHIITAKE-MUSHROOM DRESSING

Japanese shiitake mushrooms offer a meaty flavor to this dressing. You can also use it as a versatile marinade that's great for tofu, steamed vegetables, or grains.

  1 cup water
  ½ ounce dried shiitake mushrooms
  ½ cup white wine vinegar
  ½ cup dry white wine
  2 teaspoons dried oregano
  1 teaspoon ground black pepper
  2 cloves garlic, minced
  ¼ teaspoon ground cloves

In a 1-quart saucepan, bring the water to a boil. Add the mushrooms and simmer for 20 minutes. Drain. Remove and discard the stems. Finely chop the mushroom caps.

Place the chopped mushrooms in a blender container. Add the vinegar, wine, oregano, pepper, garlic, and cloves. Blend for 30 seconds.

Makes about 2 cups.

RED RANCH SALAD DRESSING

Even if you're not a beet fan, you'll be amazed at the rich flavor of this silky dressing.

  1½ cups chopped, steamed beets
  1½ cups chopped, steamed carrots
  ½ cup water
  ¼ cup lemon juice
  2 tablespoons dried dill
  1 teaspoon herbal salt substitute

In a blender container, combine the beets, carrots, water, lemon juice, dill, and salt substitute. Blend at high speed until smooth, about 2 minutes.

Makes about 3½ cups.

LEMON-ROSEMARY DRESSING

Rosemary is an often-ignored herb. That's too bad. This dressing is one of my favorites for lettuce salads.

  8 ounces soft tofu, drained and
      crumbled
  1 cup tomato juice
  ½ cup lemon juice
  ½ teaspoon ground rosemary
  ¼ teaspoon dried oregano

In a blender container, combine the tofu, tomato juice, lemon juice, rosemary, and oregano. Blend at high speed until smooth, about 2 minutes.

Makes about 2½ cups.

or celery. Simply marinate the raw vegetables in the miso mixture for at least an hour and drain before serving.

Marinades keep for two weeks in the refrigerator in a tightly lidded jar or container. You can reuse them with each new batch of leftovers.

TOFU-MAYONNAISE DRESSING

Serve this creamy dressing as an all-purpose party dip or sandwich spread.

8 ounces soft tofu, drained and crumbled
3 tablespoons grated onions
2 tablespoons lemon juice
2 tablespoons rice wine vinegar
2 tablespoons water
1 tablespoon Dijon mustard
2 teaspoons apple juice concentrate
1 heaping teaspoon minced garlic
1 teaspoon ground white pepper

In a blender container, combine the tofu, onions, lemon juice, vinegar, water, mustard, concentrate, garlic, and pepper. Blend at high speed until smooth, about 2 minutes.

Makes about 1⅓ cups.

CUCUMBER-DILL DRESSING

Great over lettuce salads or sliced garden-ripe tomatoes.

1½ cups diced, peeled cucumbers
1 tablespoon herbal salt substitute
2 teaspoons minced fresh dill
2 teaspoons lemon juice
2 teaspoons minced red onions

In a blender container, combine the cucumbers, salt substitute, dill, lemon juice, and onions. Blend at high speed until smooth, about 1½ minutes.

Makes about 1¾ cups.

MUSTARD DRESSING WITH GARLIC

Perfect as a marinade on beefsteak tomatoes for a summer lunch.

¼ cup balsamic vinegar or Raspberry Vinegar (page 30)
¼ cup water
2 teaspoons Dijon or stone-ground mustard
2 teaspoons lemon juice
2 tablespoons minced garlic
1 tablespoon minced red onions
1 teaspoon minced fresh parsley

In a small bowl, whisk together the vinegar, water, mustard, and lemon juice. Stir in the garlic, onions, and parsley.

Makes about ¾ cup.

TOMATO-TARRAGON DRESSING

The rich flavor of the traditional French herb tarragon permeates this dressing.

1¼ cups low-sodium vegetable cocktail juice
½ cup grated onions
¼ cup white wine vinegar
1 teaspoon Dijon mustard
1 teaspoon dried tarragon
1 clove garlic, chopped
2 teaspoons minced fresh parsley

In a blender container, combine the juice, onions, vinegar, mustard, tarragon, and garlic. Blend at high speed until smooth, about 1 minute. Stir in the parsley.

Makes about 2 cups.

(continued)

TEN OIL-FREE SALAD DRESSINGS—*Continued*

SWEET DILL DRESSING

This dressing is good for delicate vegetables, such as cherry tomatoes, cucumbers,
and summer squash. And it makes an
excellent marinade for the same type of
vegetables.

- ¼ cup rice wine vinegar
- 2 tablespoons apple juice concentrate
- 2 tablespoons water
- 1 tablespoon lemon juice
- ½ teaspoon Dijon mustard
- ¼ cup minced red onions
- 2 tablespoons minced fresh dill
- 2 tablespoons minced fresh parsley

In a small bowl, whisk together the
vinegar, concentrate, water, lemon juice,
and mustard. Add the onions, dill, and
parsley.

Makes about 1¼ cups.

TOFU-DILL DRESSING

Creamy and reminiscent of buttermilk-
based ranch dressings.

- 4 ounces soft tofu, drained and
      crumbled
- ½ cup water
- ¼ cup minced fresh dill or 2
      tablespoons dried
- ¼ cup minced fresh watercress
      (optional)
- 2 tablespoons lemon juice
- 1 tablespoon rice wine vinegar
- 1 teaspoon Dijon mustard
- 1 teaspoon ground white pepper

In a blender container, combine the
tofu, water, dill, watercress (if using), lemon
juice, vinegar, mustard, and pepper. Blend
at high speed until smooth, about 2
minutes.

Makes about 1¼ cups.

VINEGAR-HERB DRESSING

Here's a basic vinaigrette—only it's much
lower in fat than usual.

- 2 ounces soft tofu, drained and
      crumbled
- ½ cup water
- ¼ cup red wine vinegar
- 2 teaspoons lemon juice
- 1½ teaspoons dried oregano
- 1½ teaspoons herbal salt substitute
- 1 teaspoon dried tarragon
- 1 teaspoon dried basil
- ¼ teaspoon Dijon mustard
- ¼ teaspoon ground black pepper
- ¼ teaspoon garlic powder
- ⅛ teaspoon vanilla

In a blender container, combine the
tofu, water, vinegar, lemon juice, oregano,
salt substitute, tarragon, basil, mustard,
pepper, garlic powder, and vanilla. Blend
at high speed until smooth, about 1 minute.

Makes about 1 cup.

Quick Salads for Busy Cooks

Is there such a thing as a quick gourmet salad? You bet—prepare vegetables in advance and refrigerate them in plastic bags. Keep marinades on hand and combine them with leftover grains and beans.

CHINESE VEGETABLE SALAD WITH KIWIFRUIT

1 cucumber
½ head green cabbage, thinly sliced
2 cups chow mein noodles (optional)
½ cup peeled and sliced fresh kiwifruit
½ cup raw peanuts or unsalted macadamia nuts
¼ cup chopped fresh cilantro
½ cup rice wine vinegar
⅓ cup honey
2 tablespoons sesame seeds
1 tablespoon grated onions
1 tablespoon low-sodium soy sauce or tamari
1 tablespoon grated fresh ginger
1 tablespoon dark sesame oil
1 teaspoon herbal salt substitute

Peel the cucumber. Halve it lengthwise, remove the seeds and slice the flesh into thin half-moons. Place in a large bowl.

Add the cabbage, noodles (if using), kiwis, peanuts or macadamia nuts, and cilantro. Mix well.

In a small bowl, whisk together the vinegar, honey, sesame seeds, onions, soy sauce or tamari, ginger, oil, and salt substitute. Pour over the salad and mix well. Let marinate for 1 hour before serving.

Flavorful dark sesame oil can be used in very small quantity to give a big taste. This salad may discolor if it stands too long, so I suggest eating it the same day you make it.

Serves 4 to 6.

Herbed Red-Potato Salad

Just a drizzle of cholesterol-free mayonnaise covers the steamed red potatoes in this recipe, making it as creamy as the deli version, yet cholesterol-free.

Serves 4.

    3 cups small unpeeled red potatoes
    2 tablespoons cholesterol-free mayonnaise
    1 tablespoon olive oil
    1 tablespoon chopped pimentos
2-3 teaspoons Dijon mustard
  ½ teaspoon lemon juice
  ½ teaspoon herbal salt substitute
  ⅓ cup chopped celery
  ⅓ cup diced green apples, such as Granny Smith
    1 tablespoon minced fresh chives
  ¼ teaspoon ground black pepper

Quarter the potatoes and steam over boiling water until tender, about 20 minutes.

In a large bowl, whisk together the mayonnaise, oil, pimentos, mustard, lemon juice, and salt substitute. Add the warm potatoes and toss well to coat. Let marinate for at least 1 hour.

Before serving, add the celery, apples, chives, and pepper. Taste for seasoning and add more lemon juice, salt substitute, or pepper, if needed.

Marinated Mushrooms

A traditional Ukrainian recipe, these marinated mushrooms may be prepared up to three weeks in advance and refrigerated. Sprinkle on quick salads for an added boost of flavor.

Serves 6.

  ½ cup water
  ½ cup lemon juice
    2 tablespoons olive oil
    1 bay leaf, crushed
    2 cloves garlic, minced
    6 whole black peppercorns
  ½ teaspoon herbal salt substitute
    2 cups small mushrooms, stems trimmed

In a 1-quart saucepan, combine the water, lemon juice, oil, bay leaf, garlic, peppercorns, and salt substitute. Bring to a boil over medium-high heat.

Place the mushrooms in a large bowl. Pour the hot marinade over them. Cover and refrigerate for 2 days. Drain and remove bay leaf before serving.

GRILLED-EGGPLANT SALAD WITH TERIYAKI MARINADE

½ cup low-sodium soy sauce or tamari
2 tablespoons safflower oil
2 tablespoons light molasses
2 tablespoons grated fresh ginger
6 cloves garlic, minced
1 medium eggplant, cut into 1″ × ½″ strips
1 sweet red pepper, thinly sliced
1 cup thinly sliced cucumbers
  red leaf lettuce, separated into leaves

In a large bowl, combine the soy sauce or tamari, oil, molasses, ginger, and garlic. Add the eggplant and toss well to combine. Cover and let marinate at room temperature for at least 2 hours, or overnight.

Preheat a broiler or stove-top grill.

Remove the eggplant slices from the marinade and place on a broiler pan or directly on the grill. (Reserve the marinade.) Broil or grill, turning once, until lightly browned on both sides.

Transfer to a large bowl. Add the peppers and cucumbers. Drizzle with 2 tablespoons of reserved marinade. Toss well. Spoon onto a platter lined with the lettuce leaves and serve warm.

This recipe was originally created to marinate chicken, but it pairs equally well with eggplant for a delicious grilled salad.

Serves 4.

SPROUTING GOOD HEALTH

Grow your own sprouts as a crunchy addition to salads, breads, sandwiches, stir-fries, and other dishes. They not only raise your fiber quotient, but also add vitamins, minerals, protein, and enzymes to a wide variety of meals.

To make your own sprouts, place ⅓ cup dried chick-peas (washed to remove stones) and ⅓ cup uncooked wheat berries in a clean 1-quart jar. Lay a double thickness of cheesecloth over the mouth of the jar and secure it to the rim with a rubber band. Fill the jar with water (through the cheesecloth lid) and let the chick-peas and wheat berries soak overnight.

In the morning, pour out the water, rinse the chick-peas and wheat berries twice under running water (you can do all this through the cheesecloth), and lay the jar on its side, slightly tilted, to let sprouts drain thoroughly. Place the jar in a dark spot; the sprouts will grow faster if kept in the dark.

Repeat the rinsing process twice a day—the idea is to keep sprouts moist but not waterlogged. In 2 to 4 days, you should have about 1 cup of ½″ to 1″ sprouts. Rinse well and use in your favorite recipes.

Gingered Cucumber and Squash Salad

A light sweet-and-sour dressing anoints this refreshing warm-weather salad. The vegetable combination can be marinated from early morning to dinnertime—just add the lettuce right before serving.

Serves 4 to 6.

1 teaspoon honey
4 teaspoons rice wine vinegar
½ teaspoon low-sodium soy sauce or tamari
1 tablespoon dark sesame oil
2½ cups thinly sliced seedless cucumbers
⅓ cup julienned sweet red peppers
1 cup thinly sliced zucchini or yellow squash
4 cups torn leaf lettuce

In a large salad bowl, whisk together the honey, vinegar, soy sauce or tamari, and oil. Add cucumbers, peppers, and squash. Toss well and let marinate for at least 30 minutes. Add lettuce, toss again, and serve.

CHINESE PICNIC COLESLAW

4 cups shredded napa (Chinese) cabbage
1 cup drained canned mandarin oranges
½ cup sliced water chestnuts
½ cup sliced seedless cucumbers
¼ cup drained canned litchi nuts
2 tablespoons minced fresh parsley
2 tablespoons cholesterol-free mayonnaise
1 tablespoon lime juice
1 tablespoon Dijon mustard
1 teaspoon dark sesame oil
1 teaspoon safflower oil
1 teaspoon grated fresh ginger

In a large salad bowl, combine the cabbage, oranges, water chestnuts, cucumbers, litchi nuts, and parsley.

In a small bowl, whisk together the mayonnaise, lime juice, mustard, sesame oil, safflower oil, and ginger. Pour over the vegetables and toss well.

MISO MARINADE FOR VEGETABLES

⅓ cup light-colored miso paste
3 tablespoons rice wine vinegar
3 tablespoons water
2 tablespoons dark sesame oil
2 scallions, minced
¼ teaspoon ground red pepper
4 cups chopped vegetables

In a large bowl, whisk together the miso, vinegar, water, oil, scallions, and pepper. Add the vegetables and toss well to combine. Cover and let stand at room temperature for least 1 hour, or overnight.

Bright with mandarin orange slices, this salad is an excellent side dish for picnics and parties.

Serves 6.

Any firm leftover vegetables—green or red peppers, cucumbers, cherry tomatoes, cabbage—taste delicious when steeped overnight in this marinade.

Serves 4.

THREE-SPROUT SALAD WITH LEMON DRESSING

I like to keep a steady supply of sprouts on hand for salads like this, as well as for adding to all sorts of other dishes. In this particular salad, I use home-sprouted chick-peas and wheat berries, plus store-bought radish sprouts. Feel free to experiment with other combinations. For basic sprouting directions, see "Sprouting Good Health" on page 86.

Serves 4 to 6.

1 cup chick-pea sprouts
1 cup wheat-berry sprouts
½ cup radish sprouts
1 large tomato, diced
¼ cup chopped scallions
¼ cup chopped fresh parsley
1 clove garlic, minced
⅓ cup olive oil
2 tablespoons lemon juice
2 cups torn red leaf lettuce
   herbal salt substitute (to taste)
   ground black pepper (to taste)

In a large salad bowl, combine the chick-pea sprouts, wheat-berry sprouts, radish sprouts, tomatoes, scallions, parsley, and garlic.

In a cup, combine the oil and lemon juice. Pour over the salad. Toss well and let marinate for 20 minutes.

Add the lettuce and toss again. Season with salt substitute and pepper.

Main-Dish Salads

These fresh and light main-dish salads draw on a variety of simple techniques for combining grains and beans with vegetables and fruits. In smaller portions, these salads can double as side dishes.

PASTA AND CORN SALAD WITH RED SAUCE

    2   cups cooked pasta
    1   cup cooked corn
    1   cup chopped tomatoes
¼–½   cup olive oil
    ¼   cup diced green peppers
    2   tablespoons red wine vinegar
    1   tablespoon lemon juice
    1   teaspoon dried basil
        herbal salt substitute (to taste)
        ground black pepper (to taste)

In a large bowl, combine the pasta, corn, tomatoes, oil, green peppers, vinegar, lemon juice, and basil. Let marinate for 10 minutes. Season with salt substitute and black pepper.

ORANGE SALAD WITH WALNUTS

    4   large navel oranges, peeled, sectioned, and cut into
            bite-size pieces
    3   tablespoons lemon juice
    2   tablespoons orange juice
    1   tablespoon honey
    1   tablespoon olive oil
    1   teaspoon ground cinnamon
    2   cups torn romaine lettuce
    ½   cup thinly sliced red onions
    ¼   cup chopped toasted walnuts
    2   teaspoons chopped fresh mint

In a large bowl, combine the oranges, lemon juice, orange juice, honey, oil, and cinnamon. Let marinate for 40 minutes at room temperature, stirring occasionally.

Add the lettuce, onions, walnuts, and mint. Combine well.

A red-wine vinegar dressing makes this a memorable salad to carry along on your next Fourth of July picnic. It's also a great way to use up leftover cooked pasta.

Serves 4.

This fruity salad combines the visual appeal of bright oranges and the contrasting texture of walnuts and crisp onions.

Serves 6 to 8.

In the Basque Pyrenees, meals are hearty and satisfying, like this full-meal salad, which combines savory beans and vegetables with a balsamic dressing. Balsamic vinegar's sweet and musky taste allows you to use less oil in recipes that include this ingredient.

Serves 6.

Basque Bean Salad

2 cups dried Great Northern beans, rinsed well and
    soaked overnight
5 cups Vegetable Stock (page 113)
1 cup dry white wine
1 medium onion, diced
½ cup minced fresh parsley
½ cup diced sweet red peppers
½ cup diced celery
½ cup balsamic vinegar
½ cup olive oil
2 tablespoons Dijon mustard
2 teaspoons minced garlic
1 teaspoon herbal salt substitute

Drain the soaked beans. Place in a 3-quart saucepan. Add the stock, wine, and onions. Bring to a boil over high heat. Cover the pot, reduce the heat to medium, and simmer for 2 hours, or until the beans are tender.

Drain the beans and onions and place in a large bowl. (Reserve any leftover liquid for another use.)

Add the parsley, peppers, celery, vinegar, oil, mustard, garlic, and salt substitute. Toss well. Serve warm.

Mango Salad
with Curry Dressing

6 ounces soft tofu, drained and crumbled
1 tablespoon honey
1 tablespoon lime juice
1 teaspoon lemon juice
1 teaspoon curry powder
1 teaspoon olive oil
⅛ teaspoon ground white pepper
5 cups torn romaine lettuce
1 cup cubed, peeled mango
2 tablespoons minced red onions

When it's mango season outside, tango inside with this tropical salad of bright orange and yellow. It can be presented as a simple one-course luncheon in summer or an elegant first course anytime.

Serves 6.

In a blender container, combine the tofu, honey, lime juice, lemon juice, curry powder, oil, and pepper. Blend at high speed for 1 minute.

In a large bowl, combine the lettuce, mango, and onions. Add the dressing and toss well.

MEXICAN RICE SALAD WITH ROASTED PEPPERS

    3 large sweet red peppers, seeded and halved
    1 jalapeño pepper, seeded and halved
    1 cup cooked short-grain brown rice
    1 cup cooked basmati rice
    1 cup cooked wild rice
    ½ cup minced fresh parsley
    ⅓ cup olive oil
¼–¾ cup diced yellow squash
    3 tablespoons lemon or lime juice
    1 tablespoon safflower oil
    ½ teaspoon ground cumin
    ½ teaspoon minced garlic
    ¼ teaspoon ground red pepper (or to taste)
    ¼ teaspoon ground black pepper
    ¼ teaspoon dried oregano

This salad combines a cheery mix of bright vegetables, the delicious barbecue flavor of roasted peppers, and high-fiber nutrition from three different kinds of rice.

Serves 4.

Preheat the broiler.

Cover a baking sheet with aluminum foil; place the red peppers and jalapeños on the foil, cut side down. Broil about 3″ from the heat for about 15 minutes, or until the skins blacken. Transfer to a brown paper bag. Close the bag and let the peppers steam (in their own heat) for 20 minutes so the skins will slip off easily. Remove the skins, pat the peppers dry on paper towels, then slice into thin strips.

Place the peppers in a large bowl. Add the brown rice, basmati rice, wild rice, parsley, olive oil, squash, lemon or lime juice, safflower oil, cumin, garlic, ground red pepper, black pepper, and oregano. Toss well to combine.

Southwestern Corn and Barley Salad

A satisfying combination of chewy cooked barley and corn kernels, this salad can be made in advance to carry along in lunchboxes or to take to a barbecue.

Serves 6.

3 cups cooked barley
2 cups cooked corn
³/₄ cup diced sweet red peppers
³/₄ cup chopped scallions
¹/₂ cup diced green peppers
¹/₄ cup minced red onions
¹/₄ cup lemon juice
¹/₄ cup olive oil
1 tablespoon minced fresh cilantro
2 teaspoons herbal salt substitute

In a large bowl, combine the barley, corn, red peppers, scallions, green peppers, onions, lemon juice, oil, cilantro, and salt substitute. Let marinate for 1 hour before serving. Adjust the seasonings as needed.

Warm Chopped-Vegetable Salad

On a chilly evening, paired with crusty bread and hot soup, this salad is a comforting meal in itself.

Serves 4.

1 carrot, thinly sliced
1 cup diced sweet red peppers
1 cup chopped broccoli
¹/₂ cup diced celery
1 cup dry white wine
1 tablespoon dry sherry
¹/₄ cup olive oil
2 tablespoons rice wine vinegar
1 tablespoon Dijon mustard
1 teaspoon lemon juice
   herbal salt substitute (to taste)
   ground black pepper (to taste)

In a 2-quart saucepan, combine the carrots, peppers, broccoli, and celery. Add the wine and sherry. Bring to a boil over medium-high heat. Cover the pan, reduce the heat to medium, and simmer for 5 minutes. Strain the vegetables and place in large bowl. Discard the liquid.

In a small bowl, whisk together the oil, vinegar, mustard, and lemon juice. Pour over the vegetables. Season with salt substitute and pepper. Serve warm.

CASHEW AND BEAN SALAD

    1 cup ice water
    ¼ cup thinly sliced red onions
    1½ cups broccoli florets
    1½ cups cauliflower florets
    1 cup cooked small red beans, such as aduki
    ⅓ cup olive oil
      juice of 1 large lemon
    1 tablespoon apple cider vinegar
    1 tablespoon low-sodium soy sauce or tamari
    1 teaspoon dry mustard
    1 teaspoon dried basil
    1 teaspoon herbal salt substitute
    ¼ cup chopped raw cashews

Cashews add crunch and protein to this winter salad; fiber-rich beans contribute cholesterol-lowering capacity. Use small red beans for a pleasing color contrast with the green broccoli.

Serves 4.

In a small bowl, combine the ice water and onions. Let stand for 15 minutes (this will take the bite out of the onions).

Steam the broccoli and cauliflower for 5 minutes, then drain and place in large bowl. Add the beans.

In a small bowl, whisk together the oil, lemon juice, vinegar, soy sauce or tamari, mustard, basil, and salt substitute. Pour over the vegetables and mix well.

Drain the onions. Add the onions and cashews to the salad right before serving.

Bulgur Wheat Salad with Apricots

Apricots make this a surprisingly sweet salad, colorful and rich tasting. And it's full of insoluble fiber—the kind that helps prevent colon cancer and digestive problems.

Serves 4.

1 cup bulgur
⅔ cup boiling water
1 small tomato, chopped
¼ cup chopped sweet red peppers
¼ cup chopped dried apricots
¼ cup chopped fresh mint
½ red onion, minced
2 tablespoons olive oil
5 sprigs parsley, chopped
   juice of ½ lemon

In a small bowl, combine the bulgur and water. Cover with a plate and let stand for 25 minutes, or until the water is absorbed. Fluff with a fork.

Meanwhile, in a large bowl, combine the tomatoes, peppers, apricots, mint, onions, oil, parsley, and lemon juice. Toss well to combine.

Add the warm bulgur and combine well.

Salads for Entertaining

Fresh salads lend themselves to easy entertaining. Most of the recipes in this section can be prepared in advance, requiring only last-minute garnishing.

Spicy Chinese Noodles

6 ounces whole wheat or buckwheat pasta
⅓ cup diced sweet red peppers
¼ cup chopped scallions
¼ cup low-sodium soy sauce or tamari
2 tablespoons dark sesame oil
1 tablespoon grated fresh ginger
1 tablespoon chopped macadamia nuts
1 tablespoon minced garlic
1 tablespoon minced fresh cilantro
1 teaspoon ground red pepper (or to taste)
½ teaspoon honey

In a large pot of boiling water over medium-high heat, cook the pasta for 8 minutes, or until tender. Drain well. Place in a large bowl.

Add the red peppers, scallions, soy sauce or tamari, oil, ginger, nuts, garlic, cilantro, ground red pepper, and honey. Toss well. Let salad marinate for 1 hour before serving.

Lemon-Rice Salad

½ cup Tofu-Mayonnaise Dressing (page 81)
1 tablespoon low-sodium soy sauce or tamari
2 tablespoons lemon juice
3 cups cooked long-grain brown rice
½ cup chopped scallions
½ cup diced green peppers
¼ cup minced fresh parsley
¼ cup diced celery
1 lemon, thinly sliced

In a large bowl, mix the dressing, soy sauce or tamari, and lemon juice. Add the rice, scallions, peppers, parsley, and celery. Let marinate for at least 30 minutes. Garnish with the lemon slices just before serving.

This salad uses fiber-rich whole wheat or buckwheat noodles. It gets its kick from ground red pepper; you can make it hotter or milder by adjusting the amount.

Serves 4.

A perfect picnic recipe, this salad can be made up to two days ahead of time.

Serves 4 to 6.

An elegant first course for a dinner party, this recipe was inspired by a salad I tasted at the famous Greens Restaurant in San Francisco.

Serves 8.

Winter Pear and Spinach Salad with Balsamic Vinegar

4 cups torn spinach
2 large Bosc pears, thinly sliced
2 tablespoons minced red onions
6 tablespoons balsamic vinegar
6 tablespoons water
2 tablespoons olive oil
1 teaspoon Dijon mustard
1 clove garlic, minced

Place the spinach leaves on a large platter or individual salad plates. Arrange the pears on the spinach in a fan pattern. Sprinkle with the onions.

In small bowl, whisk together the vinegar, water, oil, mustard, and garlic. Drizzle over the salad. Serve immediately.

The tart/sweet combination of citrus, spinach, pine nuts, and red onions blends well with the light olive-oil and honey dressing.

Serves 6.

Sweet Grapefruit, Orange, and Kiwifruit Salad

4 oranges, peeled and sectioned
2 large pink grapefruit, peeled and sectioned
2 kiwifruit, peeled and sliced
2 tablespoons honey or maple syrup
½ teaspoon ground nutmeg
½ teaspoon ground cinnamon
3 cups torn spinach
¼ red onion, thinly sliced
¼ cup toasted pine nuts
3 tablespoons olive oil
   herbal salt substitute (to taste)
   ground black pepper (to taste)

In a large bowl, combine the oranges, grapefruit, and kiwis. Add the honey or maple syrup, nutmeg, and cinnamon. Toss to combine. Let stand 15 minutes.

In a medium bowl, toss together the spinach, onions, nuts, and oil. Season with salt substitute and pepper.

To serve, arrange a small mound of the greens on a plate and top with the fruit mixture.

Ratatouille Salad in Lettuce Cups

1 large onion, chopped
2 large cloves garlic, minced
¼ cup dry sherry
4 cups chopped eggplant
2 cups chopped zucchini
1 teaspoon dried basil
1 teaspoon dried oregano
1 teaspoon herbal salt substitute
2 cups chopped sweet red peppers
3 large tomatoes, chopped
lettuce leaves

This ratatouille salad is a surprisingly delicious combination of cooked and crunchy vegetables.

Serves 6 to 8.

In a large heavy frying pan over medium-high heat, sauté the onions and garlic in the sherry for 5 minutes, or until the onions are soft but not browned.

Add the eggplant, zucchini, basil, oregano, and salt substitute. Cover the pan, reduce the heat to low, and simmer the mixture for 15 minutes.

Add the peppers and tomatoes. Cook for 2 minutes, stirring frequently. Remove from the heat and transfer to a heatproof bowl. Chill for 20 minutes.

To serve, line individual plates with the lettuce leaves. Spoon on the salad.

Green Rice and Avocado Salad

2½ cups cooked basmati rice
½ cup diced avocados
½ cup sliced mushrooms
⅓ cup minced fresh parsley
¼ teaspoon minced garlic
¼ cup Vinegar-Herb Dressing (page 82)
½ cup tomato wedges
¼ cup julienned sweet red peppers

In a large bowl, combine the rice, avocados, mushrooms, parsley, and garlic. Add the dressing and toss well. Let marinate for 1 hour. Before serving, garnish with the tomatoes and peppers.

Of Spanish origin, this unusual salad combines parsley and avocado with steamed basmati rice, creating a bright green-and-white dish that refreshes the eye. Garnish it with strips of red pepper and tomato.

Serves 4.

Green and White Bean Salad

3 cups sliced (1″) green beans
1 cup cooked white beans, such as Great Northern or navy
⅓ cup minced fresh parsley
¼ cup olive oil
3 tablespoons lemon juice
2 teaspoons Dijon mustard
2 shallots, minced
½ teaspoon herbal salt substitute
¼ teaspoon dried sage
   ground black pepper (to taste)

In a large bowl, combine the green beans, white beans, parsley, oil, lemon juice, mustard, shallots, salt substitute, sage, and pepper. Let marinate for at least 1 hour. Serve at room temperature.

One of my favorite green-bean salads, this concoction forms a colorful addition to any menu. If fresh green beans are hard to find, thaw a package of frozen green beans. Use them right from the package.

Serves 6 to 8.

Peanutty Pasta Salad

    4 cups cooked whole wheat linguine or rotelle (spirals)
    1 cup sliced green beans
    1 sweet red pepper, cut into strips
    1 large cucumber, sliced
    6 scallions, sliced
    ⅓ cup chopped unsalted roasted peanuts
    ½ cup olive oil
    ¼ cup chunky peanut butter
    ¼ cup water
    3 tablespoons low-sodium soy sauce or tamari
    2 tablespoons lemon juice
    ¼–1 teaspoon ground red pepper
    ¼ teaspoon ground cumin
    ⅛ teaspoon ground turmeric

In a large bowl, combine linguine or rotelle, beans, red peppers, cucumbers, scallions, and peanuts.

In another bowl, whisk together the oil, peanut butter, water, soy sauce or tamari, lemon juice, ground red pepper, cumin, and turmeric. Pour over the salad and mix well. Let marinate for 1 hour before serving.

This salad is quite spicy if you use the full amount of ground red pepper. If you prefer it milder, use just a little. It's high in fiber and goes well in a picnic lunch.

Serves 6.

CHAPTER 7

SOUP

Sorcery

Whenever my friend Lisa and I craved excitement, we would go to San Diego and eat dinner at a tiny restaurant called The Prophet. Managed by an eccentric religious group, it was one of the first vegetarian restaurants in southern California. Needless to say, The Prophet made very little profit.

It was the early 1970s, and Lisa and I were cooking together in a small café in Escondido, about 50 miles away. We were always on the lookout for new recipes, and The Prophet offered an abundance of these. The cooks may not have had much business sense, but one thing they did extremely well was make soup. I recall one visit when we tasted an incredible concoction called Beet-Orange Soup. Lisa and I decided immediately that we had to have the recipe. When we learned that the cooks never divulged the ingredients to anyone, we did the only thing we could do: We conducted culinary espionage. We sat in a booth for hours, sipping and writing notes on a paper napkin. If I remember correctly, we went through four bowls each.

It took a few more visits (and some heavy arguments between Lisa and me), but we were finally able to duplicate the recipe back at our own restaurant. Our first surprise—understandable in those days of high-fat vegetarian fare—was that this marvelous creation had no cream or butter. It turned out that Beet Soup with Orange Juice and Green Onions (our name for the replica on page 119) got its rich flavor from a gentle sauté of vegetables in sherry and a dash of cumin.

Each of the soups in this chapter is brimming with nutrients and flavor and uses new ways to obtain rich taste or creamy texture. For example, the Dairyless Cream of Spinach Soup (page 117) blends a mixture of cooked oats and vegetables to achieve its smooth, thick consistency. And the Chilled Leek and Potato Soup (page 128) uses a puree of new red potatoes to wield its creamy magic.

You'll find that soups are especially suited for no-cholesterol cooking and menu planning for a number of reasons. First, no-cholesterol soups can be a valuable low-fat source of vitamins, minerals, and fiber, so you can build an entire meal around the soup course without sacrificing essential nutrients.

Second, compared with some other courses, soups are relatively easy to cook—once you understand the guiding principles and get some practice with the basic techniques of vegetarian soup making.

Third, because soup stores so easily, one evening's work can stock you up for a week's worth of easy meals. The flavor of some soups, in fact, is *enhanced* by spending a few nights in the refrigerator.

Finally, even dyed-in-the-wool carnivores (no blasphemy intended) are often fond of vegetable soups—a reminiscence, perhaps, of childhood. For me the memory is of my grandmother's kitchen, which brimmed with the aroma and flavor of homemade soup stock, colorful vegetables, and hearty grains and beans. It's the memory of walking in the door at early evening, rosy-cheeked from the chilly weather, and being greeted by a large bowl of homemade soup and a hunk of crusty bread.

Hokey? Yes, but the best memories often are.

The Tricks of the Trade

Your adventure in no-cholesterol soup making can be equally nostalgic. Vegetables and soups are no strangers to each other; the trick, of course, is learning how to make a *wide variety* of delicious vegetarian soups quickly and efficiently. It is no easy art. Though some people think that soup making is as simple as boiling water, professional chefs know that concocting a truly tasty soup is more magician's alchemy than basic chemistry.

My own bag of tricks includes a number of techniques that will make you feel like a wizard brewing a magic potion.

Stocking up. A flavorful stock is the first key to your soup's success, so it's helpful to have a variety of homemade stocks stored in the freezer. I usually try to have on hand at least a container each of Garlic Broth (page 113), which is a good substitute for chicken broth, and Vegetable Stock (page 113), an all-purpose stock for cream soups, chilled soups, and full-meal soups.

The sweet sauté. Vegetables, especially strong-flavored ones like onions and garlic, need the direct heat of the sauté to cook off the bitter flavors and coax out the sweeter ones. Applying the same principle that Asian cooks employ in stir-frying, I use a low-fat combination of dry sherry and oil to coat the vegetables in my soups and seal in their moisture content. This extra step helps prevent the soup vegetables from overcooking or burning while retaining much of their bright color and nutritional value.

Soup-er seasonings. Certain herbs and spices are especially effective in enhancing the natural flavors of vegetables, grains, and beans. Knowing which seasonings to use with which ingredients (see the herb and spice chart on page 108) will not only increase the flavor of your soups but also allow you to bypass salt. Fresh herbs, snipped into the bowl directly from your garden or windowsill, will add an elegant touch to your meal presentations.

Creative cream substitutes. Using a blender or food processor, you can achieve the rich smoothness of gourmet cream soups with pureed vegetables, nut milk, or cooked oats.

Chilled soups. Made with vegetables and fruits at the peak of freshness, a cold soup can be either a graceful pause between courses at an evening dinner party or a meal by itself when served with crusty rye bread and a fresh green salad. Chilled soups, such as the ones presented in this chapter, are an easy way to vary your no-cholesterol diet and provide extra vitamins, minerals, and fiber in the bargain.

Tasteful presentation. Soup can look like the dullest course in a meal or one of the brightest, depending on your presentation. Sweetheart Strawberry Soup (page 130), for example, is best spooned into glass bowls frosted for 20 minutes in the freezer and then garnished with a perfect leaf of fresh mint. Serve hearty Mediterranean Pesto Soup (page 122) in stoneware crocks with a basket of no-cholesterol breadsticks.

Essentially, no-cholesterol soup making relies on four basic steps: (1) preparing a flavorful soup stock, (2) preparing a vegetable sauté that forms what I call a flavor base, (3) seasoning with the proper herbs and spices, and (4) combining the flavors of the vegetables and stock using slow-cooking techniques.

Step 1: Preparing a Flavorful Cholesterol-Free Stock

Because a flavorful stock is the foundation of many no-cholesterol soups, it should be sturdy enough to hold its own as a simple broth. Yet it should be flexible enough to blend with a wide variety of spices, seasonings, tastes, and aromas—cooked rice, diced vegetables, or a sprinkling of fresh herbs—to produce a gourmet soup. You can make several vegetable-based stocks that exude an aroma and flavor to match the best beef or chicken stock.

Always use vegetables with the richest flavors, such as tomatoes, carrots, garlic, mushrooms, onions, potatoes, and winter squash. Avoid waxed vegetables—such as peppers or cucumbers—and beet or carrot greens, which will give the stock a bitter, acidic flavor. To use the stock for a variety of soup recipes, don't add herbs, spices, or condiments, except for fresh parsley.

A creative chef I once worked with in Sedona, Arizona, conjured up another way to make great vegetarian stock. While I watched out of the corner of my eye, he would squirrel away the peels, tops, and other odds and ends of the vegetable ingredients he used for other dishes. Then, on Sundays, he would pull out these leftovers and simmer them for 2 hours on low heat. Presto! The fragrance of the simmering stock filled the kitchen as he produced a delicious vegetable stock.

Today, I follow the same thriftiness in my home: My freezer contains a bag for vegetable ends. Into it go carrot trimmings, garlic and onion peels, mushroom stems, tomato cores—all the leftovers from the week's vegetable chopping. When I collect about a cup of pieces, I have enough to start a pot of stock.

The key to savory stock is, as the Pointer Sisters say, a "slo-o-o-w hand." In cooking terms, this translates to *slow simmer:* The stock should bubble gently but not boil. If you cook green vegetables too fast, their bitter acids are released, giving the stock an unpleasant taste that will detract from all your soup recipes.

After letting the stock cool and straining it, you can store it for your next day's lunch or next week's dinner party with a simple trick: Simply pour the cooled stock into ice cube trays and freeze it. In a few hours, flick the cubes into heavyweight sealable plastic bags, filling each bag with four to eight cubes, depending on their size. Four cubes, when defrosted, make about ½ cup of stock. The reason for separating the cubes into bags is that it is easier to defrost a few cubes than a whole tray.

Step 2: Sautéing Vegetables

Sautéing the vegetables specified in each recipe is the all-important second step in successful no-cholesterol soup making. The sauté will determine how little fat (and salt) you can get away with. Cooks who try to skip or streamline this step at the front end of the recipe must often compensate for the lack of flavor at the back end, which means adding a lot of unnecessary salt just before serving or at the table.

Sautéing works so well because direct stove-top heat brings out the rich oils in vegetables—especially in the potent ones like onions and garlic—while allowing the harsher acids to evaporate. A gentle sauté exposes the vegetables to a more intense heat than they would ever encounter in simmering liquid. What's more, the sherry or oil you use as your sauté liquid will hold the flavors the vegetables release, much like alcohol seals and holds a perfume.

Once again, speed of cooking is the key: When vegetables are *slowly* sautéed—at *medium* heat, not high heat—they reach a peak of flavor and taste. Students in my cooking classes have tried this sautéing technique on their favorite soup recipes and consistently remark on greatly improved flavor—with much less salt!

I recommend as a sauté medium a very small amount of olive or safflower oil, dry sherry or white wine, or vegetable stock. With delicate vegetables like mushrooms and tomatoes, flavors are better enhanced with oil or alcohol; with stronger vegetables, like onions and garlic, you'll find that stock or even water works well.

The order in which you add the vegetables to the sauté is also crucial. Use the list below as a guide for adding certain vegetables before others, and allow each to cook for a minute or so before going on to the next type. Each vegetable will jettison its bitter oils and then turn bright in color, signaling the release of its sweeter flavor. This small amount of cooking gives each vegetable time to make an individual impression on the soup and assures a delicious batch of soup vegetables every time.

Never cook your vegetables to the browning point unless the recipe specifically instructs you to. Browning indicates a loss of sweetness, desirable in certain recipes like Sweet Onion Soup (page 126) but not in most vegetable soups.

In a sauté, herbs lose their impact more quickly than vegetables, so for the most flavor you should add them *after* the vegetables have softened.

Vegetable Sauté Order

1. Heat the sauté medium (oil, stock, juice, wine, or water) in a soup pot over high heat until it simmers (small bubbles appear). Reduce the heat to medium.
2. Start by sautéing the strong-tasting vegetables, such as onions, leeks, scallions, and shallots. Aromatics like onions have bitter oils that cook

off within the first few minutes. Let them cook to the soft, almost translucent stage to develop sweetness.

3. If your recipe calls for ground spices, such as caraway, cinnamon, cumin, curry, and coriander, add them now. They are sturdier than herbs and require more cooking time to release their flavor. Cook for 2 minutes.

4. Add root vegetables, such as carrots, turnips, and beets. Stir to coat and cook for 3 to 5 minutes.

5. Add stalk and cabbage-family vegetables, such as celery, green and red cabbage, broccoli, and cauliflower. Stir to coat and cook for 2 minutes.

6. Add vine vegetables, such as peas, beans, summer squash, and peppers. Stir to coat and cook for 2 minutes.

7. Add tomatoes, stir to coat and cook for 1 minute.

8. Add mushrooms, stir to coat and cook for 3 minutes.

9. Add garlic, stir to coat and cook for 2 minutes.

10. Add fresh or dried herbs, stir to coat and cook for 1 minute.

Step 3: Seasoning Soups without Salt

Once you've developed a hearty flavor base from your sauté, seasoning is next. Remember to season during the last 10 minutes of sautéing to retain the most herb flavor. Some herbs, such as dill and basil, lose much of their potency if cooked longer than 15 minutes.

Believe it or not, herbs and spices "communicate" with each other when they are added to soups. I learned all about this when I became a diet and menu consultant for a special study on patients with heart disease. I was asked to create a variety of low-fat, salt-free recipes that would delight typical "meat-and-potatoes" eaters—about as easy a task as feeding a herd of elephants with one bag of peanuts!

After much experimenting, I began to see a logical pattern forming: Combining certain herbs and spices produced predictable results, similar to the way that mixing various paints produces other colors.

I now divide herbs and spices into nine groups, as shown in my herb and spice chart on page 108. The name of each group indicates the results of using a seasoning in that group. For example, herbs from groups 1 through 4 sweeten foods in various subtle ways; spices from group 9 bring out the heat in foods. It is important to remember that the herb or spice itself may not taste sweet, hot, or pungent. Rather, it will bring out that flavor from the food that it seasons.

Using this chart, you can season salt-free with very little guesswork.

HOW SWEET—OR SAVORY—IT IS!

1. Savory-sweet herbs. These herbs add sweetness to main dishes, soups, salads, and sauces. They include celery seed, tarragon, mint, parsley, and chervil. They are mild tasting and combine well with most salad vegetables, oil-based dressings, and cream soups.

2. Licorice-sweet herbs and spices. Anise and fennel, the seasonings in this group, are used for desserts, breads, and salads.

3. Nutty-sweet spices. These spices are often combined with those in group 4 and are used primarily for sweetness in desserts, pastries, custards, pies, and breads. Included are caraway, cinnamon, cloves, mace, and nutmeg.

4. Spicy-sweet spices. This group adds a little kick to the sweetness, as in cardamom and allspice. Cardamom is often used in curries and spice breads. Allspice is famous as a pumpkin pie ingredient because it does such a good job of transforming pumpkin's bland taste.

5. Sour herbs and spices. Dill weed and dill seed are delicately sour and enhance the flavor of foods containing lemon juice. They're often used in vinegar-based dressings.

6. Onion herbs. Chives are the only member of this group—they add a light onion flavor.

7. Pungent herbs and spices. When used with caution, this group gives rich flavor to watery soups and enhances or tempers other spices or strong flavors. Included are cumin, coriander, oregano, rosemary, sage, thyme, and turmeric. These are seasonings that I am careful not to overuse since they increase in flavor as they cook.

8. Basic background seasoners. These old standbys are favorites for seasoning soups, main dishes, casseroles, and sauces. You probably use them often: basil, garlic, paprika, savory, cilantro, bay leaf, marjoram, and saffron.

9. Hot shots. This group spices things up and includes ground red pepper, peppercorns (white, green, or black), mustards (yellow, brown, or white), ginger, and horseradish.

Which Herbs and Spices Do You Use?

Herbs and spices not only work together in different ways, they also act and react differently with different vegetables. For example, rosemary and sage enhance the sometimes-dull taste of potatoes and winter squash, which is one reason Thanksgiving menus often include these spices.

The following list shows which soup vegetables respond best to which herbs and spices. It is especially handy when you are substituting one ingredient for another and want to know what it will require in terms of extra seasoning.

Here's how it works: If your soup relies heavily on tomatoes (such as Mediterranean Pesto Soup, page 122), good accompaniments would be herbs and spices in the "Tomato" category: basil, bay leaf, celery seed, oregano, and rosemary.

Asparagus: Lemon, mustard seed, tarragon
Beans, dried: Cayenne, cumin, parsley, sage, summer savory
Beans, fresh: Dill, lemon, summer savory
Beans, lima: Bay leaf, chili pepper, mustard seed
Beets: Allspice, bay leaf, caraway, dill, ginger
Broccoli: Caraway, dill, mustard seed
Brussels sprouts: Basil, caraway, nutmeg, tarragon
Cabbage: Caraway, dill
Carrots: Allspice, bay leaf, caraway, fennel, mint, thyme
Cauliflower: Basil, caraway, curry powder, dill, garlic, lemon, oregano, summer savory, tarragon
Eggplant: Marjoram, oregano
Lettuce: Basil, celery seed, chervil, dill, marjoram, parsley
Onions, green, white, or yellow: Caraway, chervil, dill, garlic, parsley
Peas: Basil, dill, rosemary, sage, summer savory
Potatoes: Chives, oregano, paprika, parsley, rosemary, sage, summer savory, tarragon
Spinach: Basil, celery seed, chervil, dill, marjoram, parsley
Squash, summer: Basil, garlic, marjoram
Squash, winter: Cinnamon, coriander, curry powder
Sweet potatoes: Cardamom, cinnamon, cloves, nutmeg
Tomatoes: Basil, bay leaf, celery seed, oregano, rosemary

HOW TO GROW YOUR OWN FRESH HERBS

It may be chilly outdoors, but spring can still be as close as your own windowsill, which is usually the best location for an indoor herb garden. Herbs need the intensity of a southern exposure: The warm sun extracts the protective oils that shield the plants against disease and insects.

If you don't have a sunny, south window, you may need to place the herbs under a grow light. Set up a table in the basement or a spare room, suspend the light over your seedlings, and let it shine 24 hours a day for best results. Herb seedlings planted indoors in March can soon be transplanted in your outdoor garden.

The advantage of growing your own fresh herbs is twofold: You get a bright green covering on your windowsill, and herbs impart vibrant color and taste to most foods—especially soups.

Here are some growing tips:

• When starting herb plants, choose sandy soil that allows good drainage; most potting soils are fine because their nutrients let the plants develop strong roots. (The soil should not be too rich, however; some gardeners believe that poorer soil produces better, stronger-tasting herbs.) If you make your own mixture, experts recommend one-third each (by weight) of soil, sand, and compost.

• Pack the soil into clay or plastic pots and give the herb seedlings plenty of light as they develop.

• Some herb favorites that are easy to start indoors from seed include basil, chervil, coriander, marjoram, parsley, savory, and chives. Dill seeds don't germinate as easily as some others. Thyme, rosemary, tarragon, mints, and sage grow best from cuttings; look for these herbs in pots at your local nursery.

• When your herb plants look healthy and show plenty of new growth, you can begin cutting sprigs to use for recipes. Fresh herbs are less concentrated than dried, so use twice as much when you're substituting fresh in recipes.

• Clip (and use) your fresh herbs often. Pinch back any flowers that try to bloom. Clipping the plant encourages it to produce faster, and pinching off the flowers keeps the plant's flavor in the leaves—where you want it for seasoning.

• If you reap an especially abundant crop, you can dry some of the herbs for storage. Gather the bunched herbs and tie the stems together with string. Hang them upside down in a paper sack. Put the sack into a back corner of a coat closet for three to four weeks, or until the herbs are dry enough to store. The sack catches loose leaves and stems that fall off during the drying process while still allowing plenty of air to circulate to prevent mold.

Step 4: Combining the Vegetables and the Stock

The final step in no-cholesterol soup making is the slow simmer of the stock, vegetable sauté, and seasonings. Some soups require less than 30 minutes cooking time and so are perfect for busy cooks. Others require an hour or more. One way to streamline this step is to simmer the soup for 10 minutes, then let it cool and refrigerate it overnight. The overnight steeping will accomplish much of the same flavor blending that my grandmother achieved with 3 hours of boil and bubble, toil and trouble at the stove.

To get the most flavor out of your sauté, cook the vegetables in the same pot in which you'll be simmering the soup. When you have sautéed all the vegetables, herbs, and spices in this pot, simply pour in the required amount of stock, increase the heat, and bring the soup to a boil, then lower the heat to medium and simmer the soup to allow the flavors to blend.

Better yet, make your soup the night before you plan to serve it. Let it cool, then refrigerate it in a tightly covered container. The seasonings will have a chance to blend and develop overnight, and the soup will taste richer the next day.

To make a thicker, heartier soup, try pureeing half the soup in a blender and then pouring it back into the pot. Another trick is to add lima beans, lentils, or split peas as the soup cooks; wave your magic wand and watch the soup thicken before your eyes.

Presenting Your Soup

Despite the fact that most people are fond of soup, it is simply not the favorite course of some humans, spelled k-i-d-s. It is the rare mother who has not heard the groan, "Yecch, soup," for no apparent reason at some point in her child's life.

You can make the soup course especially appealing to family and guests by setting the right mood. First, serve your soup in bowls that enhance its color and texture. Minestrone, for example, appears better in a plain, white bowl that doesn't compete with its multitude of colors and textures. Delicate cream soups look beautiful in glass or fine, pale-colored china. Hearty, full-meal soups stand out in sturdy stoneware, heavy crockery, or even wood.

When people do bypass the soup course, it is often because they think it is just too heavy. They want to save their appetite for other courses, such as dessert. So try to simplify the menus on which you serve soup. Let hearty soups star as the main attraction—don't undermine their appeal with a lot of other complex-tasting dishes. Usually a large salad, some crusty bread or breadsticks, and a lean dessert are enough to round out a hearty soup meal.

On the other side of the coin, serve first-course soups in small quantity: 1/2- to 3/4-cup servings are usually adequate. And choose light soups, such as Orange-Carrot Soup with Ginger (page 125), for this part of the meal. Avoid hearty soups that will compete with the main entrée.

To give a lighter feeling to the soup course, try breaking the rule that soups must always be served steaming hot. A room-temperature or chilled soup is often a more refreshing first course, especially on a warm spring or summer evening.

Storing Soup

Soups freeze better than almost any other kind of cooked food. Put your freezer to work during several stages of soup making. Here are some tips.

- If you're planning to freeze a soup, undercook it just a little so that the vegetables will still be crisp and bright in color when you reheat it.
- Before freezing let the cooked soup come to room temperature, preferably in a cool spot.
- Pour soup into food-grade plastic containers or doubled zipper-type bags. Fill only three-quarters full because the soup will expand as it freezes.
- Freeze the soup until solid. It's best to package soups in 2-cup portions, so you won't have to thaw too much at a time. (Though you'll find no meat or fish soups in this book, do not refreeze any because they can develop harmful bacteria during the process.)

Basic Soup Stocks

I consider these two stocks indispensable for no-cholesterol cookery.

VEGETABLE STOCK

4 cups water
1 cup chopped vegetables

In a 2-quart saucepan, combine the water and vegetables. Bring to a boil over medium-high heat. Reduce the heat to the lowest setting and simmer the stock, uncovered, for 2 hours. Strain before using.

Inject extra nutrition and taste into this stock by replacing the water with leftover liquid from steamed vegetables or cooked beans.

Makes about 2¼ cups.

GARLIC BROTH

4 garlic heads
6 cups water
2 cups chopped vegetables
3 sprigs parsley
2 bay leaves, crushed

Separate the garlic heads into individual cloves but don't peel them. Place in a 3-quart saucepan. Add the water, vegetables, parsley, and bay leaves. Bring to a boil over high heat, then reduce the heat and simmer for 2 hours on low. Strain.

What a delicious broth you get from simmering four heads of garlic for 2 hours!

Makes about 3¾ cups.

Mock Cream Soups

Cream soups usually taste rich because of the fat they contain, but you can have that rich taste even without fat. All you need is a blender or food processor and the right ingredients. The following recipes show you how.

HUNGARIAN CREAM OF POTATO SOUP

Cooked, pureed potatoes are one secret to creamy nondairy soups that taste as good as they look. A substantial dose of paprika —a mild red pepper—is the Hungarian influence in this potato soup.

Serves 4.

1 cup diced onions
½ cup dry white wine
2 cups diced red potatoes
½ cup diced carrots
1 tablespoon paprika
2 cloves garlic, minced
½ teaspoon dried thyme
3 cups Vegetable Stock (page 113)
  herbal salt substitute (to taste)
  ground white pepper (to taste)
1 tablespoon chopped chives (garnish)

In a 3-quart saucepan over medium-high heat, sauté the onions in the wine for 10 minutes, stirring frequently to prevent browning.

Add the potatoes, carrots, paprika, garlic, and thyme. Sauté for 5 minutes, stirring frequently. Add the stock, bring to a boil, then lower the heat to medium. Cover the pot and simmer the soup for 20 minutes, or until the potatoes are very tender.

Remove from the heat and let cool for 10 minutes. Working in batches, puree the soup in a blender or food processor. Return the soup to the pot, heat through, and season with salt substitute and pepper. Serve garnished with the chives.

Butternut Squash Soup
WITH FIVE SPICES

½ cup chopped onions
2 tablespoons minced garlic
1 tablespoon grated fresh ginger
⅓ cup dry sherry
1 tablespoon olive oil
4 cups cubed butternut squash
2 cups Vegetable Stock (page 113)
1 tablespoon lemon juice
½ teaspoon ground coriander
½ teaspoon ground nutmeg
¼ teaspoon ground cumin
¼ teaspoon ground cinnamon
1 tablespoon grated lemon rind (garnish)

In a 3-quart saucepan over medium-high heat, sauté the onions, garlic, and ginger in the sherry and oil for 10 minutes, stirring frequently to prevent browning. If the vegetables stick, add a small amount of stock.

Add the squash and stock. Bring to a boil. Reduce the heat to medium, cover the pot and simmer for 25 minutes.

Remove from the heat. Let cool for 10 minutes. Working in batches, puree the soup in a blender or food processor. Add the lemon juice, coriander, nutmeg, cumin, and cinnamon.

Cover tightly and refrigerate overnight to develop flavors. Heat through and serve garnished with the lemon rind.

Orange winter squash makes this visually stunning soup perfect for a chilly winter's day. Serve it topped with grated lemon rind to complement the five spices.

Serves 4 to 6.

Carrots always lend a rich, autumnal color to pureed soups. Here they are seasoned with a delicious mixture of sherry, orange, and ginger.

Serves 6.

CARROT BISQUE

½ cup minced onions
¼ cup dry sherry
1 tablespoon olive oil
8 large carrots, chopped
1 tablespoon grated fresh ginger
3 cups Garlic Broth (page 113)
1 cup minced scallions
1 tablespoon minced garlic
1 tablespoon orange juice concentrate
2 tablespoons minced fresh cilantro (garnish)

In a 3-quart saucepan over medium-high heat, sauté the onions in the sherry and oil for 10 minutes, stirring frequently to prevent browning. Add the carrots and ginger. Cook for 5 minutes, stirring occasionally.

Add the broth, scallions, and garlic. Bring to a boil, lower the heat to medium, and cover the pan. Simmer for 20 minutes, or until the carrots are tender.

Remove from the heat. Let cool for 10 minutes. Working in batches, puree the soup in a blender or food processor. Return the soup to the pot and add the juice concentrate. Heat through. Serve garnished with the cilantro.

TAHINI CREAMED VEGETABLE SOUP

1 onion, chopped
2 cloves garlic, minced
¼ cup dry white wine
2 cups chopped carrots
1 cup chopped celery
¼ cup chopped fresh parsley
4 cups Vegetable Stock (page 113)
2 teaspoons curry powder
½ cup tahini
  low-sodium soy sauce or tamari (to taste)

Tahini, a silky paste made from ground sesame seeds, is the secret to this soup's creamy texture. Be careful when reheating the soup because the tahini will separate if boiled.

Serves 4 to 6.

In a 3-quart saucepan over medium-high heat, sauté the onions and garlic in the wine for 10 minutes, stirring frequently to prevent browning.

Add the carrots, celery, parsley, and ½ cup of the stock. Cook for 10 minutes. Add the remaining stock and curry powder; bring to a boil. Lower the heat to medium and simmer, uncovered, for 20 minutes.

Remove from the heat. Let the soup cool for 10 minutes. Working in batches, puree the soup with the tahini in a blender or food processor. (If necessary to facilitate blending, add a little more stock.) Season with soy sauce or tamari.

Dairyless Cream of Spinach Soup

- 1 cup minced onions
- ¼ cup chopped scallions
- ¼ cup dry sherry
- 2 teaspoons olive oil
- 2 cups chopped spinach
- ¼ cup chopped fresh parsley
- ¼ cup chopped celery
- 4 cups Garlic Broth (page 113)
- ⅓ cup rolled oats
- 1 teaspoon herbal salt substitute
- ¼ teaspoon dried thyme
- ¼ teaspoon ground white pepper

Thickened with a mixture of cooked oats and vegetables, this soup will delight Popeye fans. Its fragrance and bright color make it an ideal launch for a spring menu.

Serves 6.

In a 3-quart saucepan over medium-high heat, sauté the onions and scallions in the sherry and oil for 5 minutes, stirring frequently. Add the spinach, parsley, and celery. Cook for 5 to 7 minutes, stirring occasionally.

Add the broth, oats, salt substitute, thyme, and pepper. Bring to a boil, then lower the heat to medium, cover, and simmer for 20 minutes.

Remove from the heat. Let the soup cool for 10 minutes. Working in batches, puree in a blender until thick and smooth. Return to the pot. Reheat.

Bright red peppers turn this recipe into a cheery first course for entertaining or special family occasions. It can also be a meal in itself, paired with crusty black bread and a tossed green salad.

Serves 6 to 8.

RED PEPPER CREAM SOUP WITH THYME

5   large sweet red peppers, seeded and halved
1   large onion, chopped
1   tablespoon olive oil
6   cups Vegetable Stock (page 113)
1   large russet potato, chopped
1   teaspoon minced garlic
½   teaspoon dried thyme
    herbal salt substitute (to taste)
    ground black pepper (to taste)

Preheat the broiler.

Cover a baking sheet with aluminum foil; place the red peppers on the foil, cut side down. Broil about 3″ from the heat for about 15 minutes, or until the skins blacken. Transfer to a brown paper bag. Close the bag and let the peppers steam (in their own heat) for 20 minutes so the skins will slip off easily. Remove the skins and pat dry with paper towels.

In a 3-quart saucepan over medium-high heat, sauté the onions in the oil for 5 minutes, stirring frequently to prevent browning. Add the stock, potatoes, garlic, and thyme. Bring to a boil, then lower the heat to medium and simmer, uncovered, for 20 minutes.

Add the peppers and remove the soup from the heat. Let cool for 10 minutes. Working in batches, puree the soup in a blender or food processor. Return to the pot, season with salt substitute and pepper, and heat through.

Hot Soups for Cold Winter Nights

When winter winds howl, serve the following recipes as the main course for a family supper or Sunday football game fare. They all freeze beautifully, so don't hesitate to make a double batch.

Beet Soup with Orange Juice and Green Onions

1 onion, chopped
2 cloves garlic, minced
1/3 cup dry sherry
1 tablespoon olive oil
4 cups Vegetable Stock (page 113)
2 1/2 cups chopped unpeeled beets
1/2 cup orange juice
1/4–1/2 teaspoon ground cumin
2 tablespoons minced scallions
2 tablespoons minced fresh parsley

The unusual flavor combination of fresh beets and oranges makes this an elegant cold-weather soup for entertaining. If possible, let the soup sit overnight in the refrigerator so the flavors can deepen.

Serves 4 to 6.

In a 3-quart saucepan over medium heat, sauté the onions and garlic in the sherry and oil for 10 minutes, stirring frequently to prevent browning. Add the stock and beets. Bring to a boil. Lower the heat and simmer, uncovered, for 30 minutes, or until the beets are tender.

Remove from the heat. Let cool for 10 minutes. Working in batches, puree the soup in a blender or food processor.

Return the soup to the pot. Add the orange juice and cumin. Heat through. Just before serving, stir in the scallions and parsley.

Orzo is a tiny Italian
pasta shaped like rice; it
lends a chewy texture to
this exuberant Mediter-
ranean soup. Bitter esca-
role is also traditionally
Italian.

Serves 4.

ESCAROLE SOUP WITH ORZO

    3 cups chopped onions
    2 tablespoons olive oil
    1 pound escarole, cut into bite-size strips
    1 tablespoon chopped garlic
 5-6 cups Vegetable Stock (page 113)
  ³/₄ cup orzo
       herbal salt substitute (to taste)
       ground black pepper (to taste)
  ³/₄ cup fine rye bread crumbs

In a 3-quart saucepan over medium-high heat, sauté the
onions in the oil, stirring frequently, until limp and transpar-
ent but not browned, about 5 to 7 minutes. Add the escarole
and garlic; cook until the escarole wilts.

Reduce the heat to medium-low. Add the stock. Simmer,
uncovered, for 20 minutes.

Add the orzo and cook for 10 minutes, or until the
pasta is tender. Season with salt substitute and pepper.

Before serving, toast the bread crumbs in a small dry
frying pan over medium heat until lightly browned. Spoon
over each serving of soup.

The oft-neglected sweet
potato comes center stage
for this stunning soup—a
good Thanksgiving alter-
native to candied yams.

Serves 4.

ANN'S SWEET POTATO SOUP

  ²/₃ cup minced onions
    1 tablespoon olive oil
    1 carrot, sliced thinly
    1 large sweet potato, diced
    1 russet potato, diced
  ¹/₃ cup chopped celery
    3 cups Garlic Broth (page 113)
    2 bay leaves, crushed and wrapped in a piece of
           cheesecloth
  ¹/₄ teaspoon ground nutmeg
    1 tablespoon minced fresh chives (garnish)

In a 3-quart saucepan over medium-high heat, sauté the onions in the oil for 5 minutes, stirring frequently to prevent browning. Add the carrots, sweet potatoes, russet potatoes, and celery. Cook for 5 minutes.

Add the broth, bay leaves, and nutmeg. Bring to a boil, then lower the heat to medium and simmer, uncovered, for 20 minutes. Discard the bay leaves.

Remove from the heat. Let the soup cool for 10 minutes. Working in batches, puree the soup in a blender or food processor. Return it to the pot, heat through, and serve garnished with the chives.

SZECHUAN HOT-AND-SOUR SOUP

6 cups Vegetable Stock (page 113)
2 ounces dried shiitake mushrooms
1 teaspoon dark sesame oil
½ cup chopped scallions
1 teaspoon grated fresh ginger
6 ounces firm tofu, cut into 1″ squares
2 tablespoons arrowroot powder
¼ cup dry sherry
    juice of 1 lemon
2 tablespoons low-sodium soy sauce or tamari
½ teaspoon ground red pepper
    ground black pepper (to taste)

In a 2-quart saucepan, bring the stock to a boil. Remove from the heat, add the mushrooms and let stand for 30 minutes. Strain, reserving the liquid. Remove and discard the mushroom stems. Slice the caps into thin strips.

In a 3-quart saucepan over medium-high heat, heat the oil. Add the scallions and ginger; sauté for 2 minutes. Add the tofu and cook for 1 minute. Add the stock and mushrooms.

In a small bowl, dissolve the arrowroot in the sherry, lemon juice, and soy sauce or tamari. Add to the soup and cook, stirring, until the soup thickens slightly. Add the red pepper and black pepper.

Traditional hot-and-sour soup gets its distinct aroma and flavor from dried shiitake mushrooms. Soak them ahead of time to create a rich broth, which can then be added to the simmering soup.

Serves 8.

Mediterranean Pesto Soup

Good pesto can be made from a variety of ingredients, basil being the most well known. This version of a traditional Mediterranean soup uses an unusual blend of fresh parsley and spinach; you'll rely on it in winter when fresh basil is hard to find.

Serves 6.

Soup

¼ cup dry sherry
1 teaspoon safflower or olive oil
6 scallions (including greens), thinly sliced
4 cups Vegetable Stock (page 113)
2 large carrots, diced
1 cup canned Italian tomatoes, with their liquid
1 cup diced russet potatoes
1 cup peeled and cubed winter squash
½ cup chopped celery leaves
½ cup pastina or other small pasta
⅓ cup chopped leeks
2 tablespoons tomato paste
⅛ teaspoon saffron threads
1 teaspoon ground black pepper
1 teaspoon herbal salt substitute

Pesto

½ cup chopped spinach
½ cup minced fresh parsley
¼ cup chopped walnuts or pine nuts
3 cloves garlic, minced
2 teaspoons olive oil
1 teaspoon dried basil
1 teaspoon miso
6 thick slices whole grain bread

To make the soup: In a 3- or 4-quart saucepan over medium heat, heat the sherry and oil. Add the scallions and sauté until bright in color, about 1 minute. Add the stock, carrots, tomatoes, potatoes, squash, celery, pastina, leeks, tomato paste, and saffron. Bring to a boil.

Reduce the heat and simmer for 30 minutes, or until the potatoes are soft. Add the pepper and salt substitute.

To make the pesto: In a blender or food processor, process the spinach, parsley, walnuts or pine nuts, garlic, oil, basil, and miso into a thick paste.

To serve, spread the pesto on the bread. Place 1 slice in the bottom of each soup bowl. Ladle the soup over it.

Fennel Soup Italian-Style

1 large onion, chopped
½ cup diced celery
2 cloves garlic, minced
2 tablespoons olive oil
2 tablespoons dry white wine
4 cups Vegetable Stock (page 113)
1 large head fennel, diced
1 cup diced small red potatoes
1 teaspoon herbal salt substitute
½ teaspoon ground black pepper
⅓ cup chopped sweet red peppers (garnish)

In a 3-quart saucepan over medium-high heat, sauté the onions, celery, and garlic in the oil and wine for 10 minutes, stirring occasionally to prevent browning.

Add the stock, fennel, and potatoes. Bring to a boil. Cover the pan, lower the heat to medium, and simmer for 40 minutes. Add the salt substitute and black pepper. Serve garnished with the red peppers.

Momma's Mock Chicken Soup

4 cups Garlic Broth (page 113)
1 large carrot, diced
1 potato, diced
1 cup cubed winter squash
1 parsnip, diced
½ cup diced daikon radishes
3 cups chopped greens, such as spinach, parsley, or mustard
light miso or low-sodium soy sauce or tamari (to taste)

In a 3-quart saucepan over medium-high heat, bring the broth to a boil. Add the carrots, potatoes, squash, parsnips, and radishes. Cover, reduce the heat, and simmer for 20 minutes, until the potatoes are soft.

Add the greens and season with the miso or soy sauce or tamari.

Raw fennel lends a sharp licorice taste to salads. Here it is simmered to bring out a milder flavor.

Serves 4.

Welcome to the world's first no-cholesterol "chicken soup." The rich flavor comes from the garlic broth.

Serves 4 to 6.

Spinach and Wild Rice Soup

Here's a hearty soup to enjoy after a day on the slopes or cross-country trails. It's especially good with Swedish rye bread.

Serves 6 to 8.

1 onion, chopped
1 large potato, diced
3 bunches spinach, destemmed and chopped
2 tablespoons olive oil
4 cups Vegetable Stock (page 113)
2 cups cooked wild rice
   herbal salt substitute (to taste)
   ground black pepper (to taste)

In a 3-quart saucepan over medium-high heat, sauté the onions, potatoes, and spinach in the oil for 10 minutes, stirring frequently to prevent browning. Add the stock and bring to a boil.

Cover the pan, reduce the heat to medium, and simmer for 20 minutes, or until the potatoes are tender.

Remove from the heat. Let cool 10 minutes, then puree half of the soup in a blender or food processor. Return to the pot. Add the wild rice, heat through, and season with salt substitute and pepper.

Tomato-Cilantro Soup

The South-of-the-Border influence is evident in this deliciously spicy concoction, lightly flavored with cilantro. For an unusual one-dish meal, serve it over hot pasta.

Serves 8.

2 onions, minced
2 cloves garlic, minced
¼ cup dry sherry
1 teaspoon olive oil
4 cups chopped fresh tomatoes
1 cup diced sweet red peppers
¼ cup diced celery
2 tablespoons chopped canned green chilies
2 cups Garlic Broth (page 113)
2 tablespoons chopped fresh cilantro
½ teaspoon ground red pepper
¼ teaspoon ground cumin
   herbal salt substitute (to taste)
   ground black pepper (to taste)
   fresh cilantro (garnish)

In a 3-quart saucepan over medium-high heat, sauté the onions and garlic in the sherry and oil for 10 minutes, stirring frequently to prevent browning. Add the tomatoes, red peppers, celery, and chilies. Cook for 5 minutes.

Add the broth, cilantro, ground red pepper, and cumin. Bring to a boil, then lower the heat and simmer for 45 minutes. Season with salt substitute and pepper. Serve garnished with the cilantro.

ORANGE-CARROT SOUP WITH GINGER

1 cup chopped onions
2 teaspoons safflower oil
4 cups Vegetable Stock or Garlic Broth (page 113)
2 cups chopped carrots
1 cup diced potatoes
3 cloves garlic, minced
1/3 cup ground cashews
2 teaspoons grated fresh ginger
2 tablespoons dry sherry
1 tablespoon orange juice concentrate

With a spicy, exotic character, this soup is a great first course to curried vegetables or pasta.

Serves 6.

In a 3-quart saucepan over medium heat, sauté the onions in the oil until soft but not browned, about 5 minutes. Add the stock or broth, carrots, potatoes, and garlic. Bring to a boil.

Cover, reduce the heat and simmer for 15 minutes, or until the carrots and potatoes are soft.

Remove from the heat and let cool for 10 minutes. Working in batches, puree the soup with the cashews in a blender or food processor until creamy.

Return the soup to the pot and reheat.

While the soup is reheating, in a small frying pan, sauté the ginger in the sherry for 3 minutes. Remove from the heat. Stir in the juice concentrate. Add to the soup and serve hot.

If your market carries sweet Vidalia onions, be sure to try this fragrant soup—delicious on a chilly day with crusty brown bread.

Serves 4.

Sweet Onion Soup

4 medium Vidalia onions, thinly sliced
⅓ cup dry white wine
2 tablespoons minced garlic
1 tablespoon whole wheat flour
4-5 cups Vegetable Stock (page 113)
1 tablespoon herbal salt substitute
1 teaspoon dried thyme
1 tablespoon low-sodium soy sauce or tamari
¼ cup minced scallions (garnish)

In a 3- or 4-quart saucepan over medium-low heat, sauté the onions in the wine, stirring frequently, for 25 minutes. The onions will begin to brown slightly and get very soft; be careful not to burn the onions. Add the garlic and flour. Cook, stirring, for 2 minutes. Add the stock, salt substitute, and thyme.

Raise the heat to medium-high and bring the soup to a boil. Reduce the heat to low and simmer, uncovered, for 30 minutes. (Add additional stock if the soup becomes too thick.) Add the soy sauce or tamari. Serve garnished with the scallions.

This delicate consommé is made with a mixture of wild and domestic mushrooms simmered in sherry.

Serves 4.

Mushroom-Essence Soup

2 cups chopped onions
1 tablespoon olive oil
6 cups water
1 cup chopped mushrooms
1 cup chopped wild mushrooms, such as chanterelle
1 ounce dried shiitake mushrooms
¼ cup dry sherry
2 sprigs parsley
  herbal salt substitute (to taste)
  ground black pepper (to taste)
2 tablespoons minced red onions (garnish)
2 tablespoons minced scallions or chives (garnish)
½ cup thinly sliced mushrooms (garnish)

In a 3-quart saucepan over medium heat, gently sauté the onions in the oil for 15 minutes, stirring frequently to prevent browning. Add the water, chopped mushrooms, wild mushrooms, shiitake mushrooms, sherry, and parsley. Raise the heat to medium-high and bring the soup to a boil. Reduce the heat to medium-low and simmer, uncovered, for 45 minutes.

Place a colander over a large pot or bowl and line it with a double thickness of cheesecloth. Pour the soup into the colander and press the vegetables against it with the back of a wooden spoon to extract as much juice as possible.

Return the liquid to the pot and season it with salt substitute and pepper. Serve the soup garnished with red onions, scallions or chives, and mushrooms.

Cold Soups for Hot Summer Days

Summertime and the livin' is easy—and so is your menu planning if you play your soups right. Colorful and refreshing chilled soups—some of them made days ahead—are just the ticket for hot summer nights.

Most cold soups taste better if refrigerated overnight, so try to prepare them ahead. Stored in tightly covered containers, they easily keep for two to three days. Remember to stir the soup well before serving.

Be sure to use only the freshest, most colorful fruits and vegetables because the ingredients are simple and not heavily seasoned. Farmers' markets and local farms are great places to pick up ripe tomatoes and plump, juicy berries if you don't have your own backyard garden.

Cold soups can turn an outdoor buffet or picnic into a gourmet gathering. Bring your soup to a picnic in a chilled thermos and serve it in tall glass mugs that have been stored in the beverage cooler. When serving cold soup on an outdoor buffet table, keep the soup tureen cold by placing it inside a larger bowl of crushed ice. At home, try serving cold soups in glass bowls frosted for 20 minutes in the freezer.

If available, new red potatoes or yellow Finnish potatoes are especially good in this delicate, creamy vichyssoise.

Serves 6.

CHILLED LEEK AND POTATO SOUP

1 yellow onion, finely chopped
1 teaspoon safflower oil
2 cups chopped potatoes
1 cup sliced leeks (white part only)
4 cups Vegetable Stock or Garlic Broth (page 113)
1 teaspoon herbal salt substitute
1/4 teaspoon ground white pepper
2 tablespoons chopped fresh chives (garnish)

In a 3-quart saucepan over medium-low heat, slowly sauté the onions in the oil until soft but not browned, about 5 to 7 minutes. Add the potatoes and leeks. Cook for 5 minutes; add a small amount of the stock or broth if the vegetables begin to brown.

Add the remaining stock and bring to a boil. Cover, reduce the heat, and simmer for 15 to 20 minutes, or until the potatoes are soft. Add the salt substitute and pepper.

Remove from the heat and let cool for 10 minutes. In a blender, puree half of the soup until smooth. Combine with the remaining soup and chill for 2 hours. Serve garnished with the chives.

There's no secret to this delicious soup—except perfectly ripe melons. Serve it in frosted glass bowls as the first course to a dinner party.

Serves 4.

TWO-MELON SOUP

2 cups diced cantaloupe
2 cups diced casaba melon
1/3 cup lime juice
1 tablespoon honey
3 tablespoons chopped fresh mint leaves

In a blender or food processor, puree the cantaloupe, casaba, lime juice, honey, and 2 tablespoons of the mint leaves. Pour into a large bowl and chill for 20 minutes. Serve garnished with the remaining mint.

CHILLED PAPAYA-PINEAPPLE SOUP

4 cups cubed pineapple
3 cups diced papaya
  juice of 2 oranges
  juice of 1 lime
1 tablespoon honey
½ teaspoon ground nutmeg

In a blender or food processor, combine the pineapple, papaya, orange juice, lime juice, honey, and nutmeg. Puree until smooth. Pour into a large bowl and chill for 30 minutes. Serve in tall glasses or frosted bowls.

CHICK-PEA AND TOMATO GAZPACHO

4 cups low-sodium vegetable cocktail juice
3 cups diced tomatoes
1 cup cooked chick-peas
½ cup diced green peppers
½ cup cooked corn
½ cup diced cucumbers
¼ cup minced red onions
¼ cup chopped fresh parsley
2 tablespoons lime juice
2 tablespoons rice wine vinegar
1 teaspoon honey
1 teaspoon herbal salt substitute
½ teaspoon ground black pepper
1 clove garlic, minced
¼ teaspoon ground red pepper
¼ teaspoon dried marjoram

In a large bowl, mix the vegetable juice, tomatoes, chick-peas, green peppers, corn, cucumbers, onions, parsley, lime juice, vinegar, honey, salt substitute, black pepper, garlic, red pepper, and marjoram. Chill overnight.

An island treat, this rich-tasting soup is also rich in enzymes—papain from the papaya and bromelain from the pineapple—that help digest protein. (By all means, use fresh pineapple.) In Hawaii, this soup is garnished with small white orchids.

Serves 4 to 6.

Gazpacho—the fresh salad-soup of Spain—comes in many varieties. Here's a delicious high-fiber version made with cooked chick-peas and fresh tomatoes.

Serves 8.

This fruit soup, an old favorite, can be made with practically any combination of fruits in season. Traditionally, its base is yogurt or whipped cream, but this recipe tastes just as good without dairy products.

Serves 6.

Sweetheart Strawberry Soup

2 cups sliced strawberries
2 cups chopped cantaloupe
½ cup chopped honeydew or casaba melon
1 cup pineapple juice
1 cup orange juice
1 cup apple juice
  juice of 1 lemon
2 tablespoons honey
1 teaspoon chopped fresh mint (garnish)
½ teaspoon ground nutmeg (garnish)

In a blender or food processor, combine the strawberries, cantaloupe, honeydew or casaba, pineapple juice, orange juice, apple juice, lemon juice, and honey until very smooth. Pour into a large bowl and chill thoroughly. Serve garnished with mint and nutmeg.

High-Protein Chowders and Full-Meal Soups

You know those days when the kids tease the dog and the dog chases the cat and the cat knocks over the milk and by late afternoon the last thing you want to do is cook? Well, for those days, have on hand one of these chowders or full-meal soups.

FRESH-CORN AND PEPPER CHOWDER

5 ears of corn
5 cups Garlic Broth (page 113)
1 cup chopped onions
1 teaspoon olive oil
1 cup diced sweet red peppers
1 cup diced red potatoes
2 carrots, diced
2 stalks celery, diced
1/4 cup whole wheat pastry flour
2 tablespoons chopped canned green chilies
1/2 teaspoon ground black pepper
1/4 teaspoon ground red pepper
1 tablespoon herbal salt substitute
2 tablespoons chopped fresh chives (garnish)

Remove the kernels from the corn cobs and set aside (you should have about 2½ cups). Place the cobs in a 3-quart saucepan. Add the broth and bring to a boil over medium-high heat. Reduce the heat and simmer for 1 hour. Discard the cobs and reserve the stock.

Wash and dry the pan. Add the onions and oil. Sauté over medium heat for 10 minutes, stirring frequently to prevent browning. Add the red peppers, potatoes, carrots, and celery. Cook, stirring occasionally, for 10 minutes.

Add the flour and cook for 2 minutes, stirring frequently. Add the reserved stock and bring to a boil.

Cover, reduce the heat to medium, and cook for 10 minutes. Add the reserved corn kernels. Cook for 10 minutes, or until the potatoes are very tender.

Remove from the heat and let the soup cool for 10 minutes. Working in batches, puree half of the soup in a blender or food processor. Return the soup to the pot. Add the chilies, black pepper, ground red pepper, and salt substitute. Heat through. Serve garnished with the chives.

In corn season, buy whole ears of corn, scrape off the kernels with a sharp knife, and try this savory soup. Cooking the cobs gives extra flavor to the soup.

Serves 6 to 8.

Greek Lentil Soup

The vinegar in this tomato-based soup lifts the everyday lentil to new heights.

Serves 6 to 8.

1 stalk celery, chopped
1 small carrot, chopped
1 small russet potato, chopped
½ onion, chopped
1 tablespoon olive oil
5 cups Vegetable Stock (page 113)
1 cup dried lentils, washed well
1 cup low-sodium tomato sauce
1 bay leaf, crushed and wrapped in cheesecloth
¼ cup red wine
2 teaspoons red wine vinegar
¼ teaspoon ground cinnamon
   herbal salt substitute (to taste)
   ground black pepper (to taste)

In a 3-quart saucepan over medium-high heat, sauté the celery, carrots, potatoes, and onions in the oil for 10 minutes, stirring frequently. Add the stock, lentils, tomato sauce, and bay leaf. Bring to a boil.

Lower the heat to medium and simmer the soup, uncovered, for 45 minutes, or until the lentils are soft. Add the wine, vinegar, and cinnamon. Season with the salt substitute and pepper. Discard the cheesecloth before serving.

Simple Split-Pea Soup

An easy split-pea soup that can be made in double or triple batches, then frozen for emergency meals.

Serves 6 to 8.

1 cup minced onions
1 tablespoon olive oil
3 cups dried split peas, washed well
2 large carrots, grated
2 tablespoons dry sherry
1 teaspoon herbal salt substitute
1 teaspoon dried marjoram
½ teaspoon ground rosemary
5 cups Vegetable Stock (page 113)

In a 3-quart saucepan over medium-high heat, sauté the onions in the oil for 5 minutes, stirring frequently to prevent

browning. Add the split peas, carrots, sherry, salt substitute, marjoram, and rosemary. Sauté, stirring frequently, for 3 minutes. Add the stock.

Bring to a boil, then reduce the heat to medium-low and simmer, uncovered, for 45 minutes.

Boston BEAN SOUP

- 2 cups dried lima or pinto beans, washed well
- 1 large onion, coarsely chopped
- ¼ cup dry white wine
- 2 tablespoons dark sesame oil
- ⅓ cup chopped celery
- 4 cloves garlic, minced
- 6 cups Vegetable Stock (page 113)
  juice of 1 lemon
- 1 tablespoon molasses
- 1 tablespoon tomato paste
- 1 teaspoon ground cumin
- 1 teaspoon ground coriander
  pinch of ground red pepper
- 1 teaspoon red wine vinegar
  herbal salt substitute (to taste)
  ground black pepper (to taste)

Bostonians are famous for baked beans; here's a tasty no-cholesterol alternative. Lima or pinto beans are favored here for their richness and high fiber content. Be sure to allow time to presoak the beans overnight.

Serves 6 to 8.

Place the beans in a large bowl and cover with cold water. Let stand overnight, then pour off the soaking water. Set the beans aside.

In a 3-quart saucepan over medium-high heat, sauté the onions in the wine and oil for 10 minutes, stirring frequently to prevent browning. Add the celery and garlic. Cook for 5 minutes.

Add the reserved beans, stock, lemon juice, molasses, tomato paste, cumin, coriander, and red pepper. Bring to a boil, then reduce the heat to medium. Simmer, uncovered, for 2 hours, or until the beans are soft.

Add the vinegar. Season with the salt substitute and black pepper.

CHAPTER 8

BEANS, GRAINS, AND *Pasta*

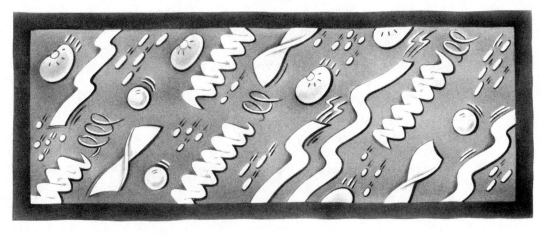

Years ago, when I first fell in love with beans and grains, my first act of wooing was to purchase two dozen large glass jars. Into these jars I stuffed all the colorful beans and grains I could carry home from the health-food store bins. Then I placed the jars on shelves along one entire wall of my kitchen, which then resembled a kind of frontier-town general store. It took all my restraint not to run out and buy a crinoline petticoat.

There was only one thing wrong with this picture. I did not have the foggiest notion how to cook beans and grains.

After several weeks elapsed and not one jar had been opened, I invited my cooking mentor, April, to fix dinner. My plan was that she would make a few dishes with these wonderful (albeit virgin) ingredients and initiate me into their world.

When April arrived, she rinsed a cupful of pinto beans, dumped them in a bowl and then covered them with boiling water. "Soak them first," she advised. "It cuts way down on the cooking time."

Out of a large shopping bag, she pulled a stainless-steel pressure cooker and placed the soaked pinto beans in it. Then she cooked some lentils, boiled a few handfuls of long spinach noodles, and started a vegetarian spaghetti sauce. While all this was going on, she told me the "life story" of beans and whole grains, which, she informed me, have the longest history of any foods on the planet. To one who always imagined our prehistoric ancestors chomping away on large animal bones or climbing banana trees, this came as a bit of a surprise.

Not that prehistoric cultures knew what to do with these foods any more than I did; what these people did, according to April, was collect wild grains and eat them without cooking them. Not until 7000 B.C. or so did ancient civilizations start cooking grains into porridge or roasting them over a fire before grinding. The first bread was made from thick cakes dried in the sun—some of these have actually been found intact in Stone Age settlements.

Romans developed the use of grains even further with rotary milling stones. Flour was ground for baked goods—coarse for the poor and sifted for the rich (big surprise). As our civilization evolved, we moved farther away from our ancestors' diet of whole grains and legumes.

By the time April had finished her story, dinner was ready. The pintos had turned into a delicious soup. The lentils had transformed into a pureed pâté seasoned with sage and thyme. The pasta emerged from the oven as a layered vegetable lasagna.

Legumes: Vegetarian Protein Plus

That evening opened my eyes to a new satisfying array of vegetarian protein. Legumes—members of the bean and pea family—are an excellent source of protein and, when combined with grains, make a complete set of amino acids that constitute protein. On the societal level, this advantage turns into a potential gold mine for a world increasingly concerned about its food supply—it requires many more acres of land to produce a pound of meat protein than a pound of vegetable protein from beans and grains.

Beans, grains, and pasta make sense to the personal pocketbook, as well. A 1-cup serving of pinto beans, for example, costs about one-tenth as much as the equivalent amount of red meat. So eating "low" on the food chain makes sense economically as well as ecologically.

The other nutritional benefits of beans, grains, and pasta are well known: Besides the serum cholesterol-lowering benefits (see chapter 3), these foods have very little fat, a good amount of protein, and some B vitamins, calcium, iron, and potassium. Further, they contain practically no sodium and plenty of soluble fiber.

So why don't more Americans add these foods to their diet? The main obstacle is the time factor. Unlike beef, which can be on the table in 15 minutes, some grains and most beans take several hours to cook. But this obstacle can be hurdled: Scientists at the U.S. Department of Agriculture have developed quick-cooking processes that many manufacturers are employing. So you can now find in stores many grains and beans that are already presoaked and dried, reducing cooking time to 10 to 30 minutes. (You can do something similar at home by presoaking or cooking beans and grains, then freezing them for quick future meals.)

The second obstacle is more of a stigma: Beans still cry poverty to many Americans who associate them with the Depression years when more expensive protein was scarce. Many people simply do not want to rekindle these memories, nor do they want others to think that they are having financial problems. However, this prejudice is slowly dissolving as health becomes a higher priority for many. In fact, things are turning upside down: Beans and grains are becoming rather chic items in the food world. Pasta, of course, has been the au courant food of the rich and famous for quite a few years now. And many top-name chefs are exploiting the publicity afforded oat bran and other substances to spruce up their repertoire with health-oriented recipes.

A third reason beans haven't exactly set the culinary world on fire is that they set many "colonary" systems on fire. Simply put, beans often cause gas and bloating. That's because they contain undigested sugars and dietary fiber which ferment in the colon. Several methods to deal with this unfortunate situation are outlined below.

Finally, there is the old myth that beans and grains simply will not taste good no matter what you do to them. You can destroy this myth with any one of the recipes in this chapter.

Basic Rules for Cooking Beans and Peas

Cooking times for dried beans and peas vary tremendously—from 30 minutes to 3 hours. See the bean table in "Cooking Beans and Grains" on page 140 for specifics. All beans must undergo three basic steps: rinsing, soaking, and simmering.

Step 1: Rinsing. Because beans and peas are gathered straight from the field, small pebbles and little balls of mud can slip into even the most carefully sorted batch. Fill a pot with cold water and pour the beans into it. Stir the water with your hands, sifting the beans and removing any pebbles or imperfect beans. Drain the beans through a colander and return them to the pot.

Step 2: Soaking. Fill the same pot with boiling water, covering the beans with about 2″ of water. Let the beans soak for 1 hour. They will absorb most of the water. Pour off any excess and rinse the beans one more time. Some say this helps make the beans more digestible.

Step 3: Simmering. Once again fill the pot with cold water. This time add a strip of kombu, or kelp, which is available in health-food stores. Cooking beans with kombu is a Japanese technique said to make beans easier to digest. It also adds plenty of flavor to the bean-cooking water. Bring the water and beans to a boil, cover the pot, reduce the heat to low, and simmer the beans for the time shown in the bean table on page 140. Every now and then, skim off any foam that rises to the top of the pot. This foam is very bitter and will flavor the beans if left in the pot. When the beans are tender enough to be easily mashed on the side of the pot with the back of a wooden spoon, they are done.

Let the beans cool and then divide them into 1- or 2-cup portions. Spoon into freezer-quality plastic bags and stack them in your freezer. I always make double or triple the quantity that I need, then freeze the extra to cut cooking time later.

Basic Rules for Cooking Whole Grains

Most whole grains need much less cooking time than beans, usually 1 hour at most. You can tell that grains are finished cooking if they've doubled in size and absorbed most of the liquid in the cooking pot. Cooked grains should be tender and chewy but not mushy.

You can cut down on the cooking time by presoaking the grains overnight in cold water. Grains cook best in a covered heavy pot. If your pot is thin-bottomed, add water occasionally to prevent the grain from scorching.

Toasting. To bring out the best flavor in grains, I often toast them beforehand in the same cooking pot. Don't add oil; instead, place the pot over low heat and stir the grain until a fragrant aroma emerges. Then add the liquid required for cooking.

Flavoring grains. Some cooks like to use liquids other than water to cook grains, such as tomato or vegetable cocktail juice, Vegetable Stock (page 113), or Garlic Broth (page 113). Others add minced onions, garlic, or herbs to the water to flavor the grain as it cooks. This is an especially effective technique if the grain is to be used unadorned as a side or main dish.

Grains can be frozen after cooking and cooling. They make great salads when marinated, but for the best flavor, marinate them while still warm. They absorb much more vinegar this way.

A Word about Pressure Cookers

Pressure cooking can cut total cooking time for grains and beans by one-third to one-half. Many cooks rely on this technique to help incorporate these foods into their diet. Stainless steel pressure cookers are the best because they don't corrode as aluminum ones do. They typically cost around $100. A good pressure cooker should last you a lifetime.

COOKING BEANS AND GRAINS

Here are the basic cooking times—both regular and pressure-cooking—for 1 cup of grain or presoaked beans. Please note that the water amounts given are approximate and may vary due to weather, the age of the beans or grain, and the cooking method chosen. Note, too, that certain items are not suitable for pressure-cooking. Buckwheat and bulgur, for example, get mushy when prepared by that method. Oats and quinoa cook too quickly to make pressure-cooking practical. And chick-peas, lentils, and split peas have skins that can come loose and clog the steam vent.

Bean (1 cup soaked)	Water (cups)	Regular Cooking Time	Pressure- Cooking Time	Yield (cups)
Aduki	3	2 hr.	75 min.	2
Black	3	2 hr.	75 min.	2
Black-eyed peas	2	1½ hr.	1 hr.	2
Chick-peas	4	3 hr.	—	2
Great Northern	3	1½ hr.	1 hr.	2
Kidney	3	2 hr.	75 min.	2
Lentils	2	1½ hr.	—	2
Limas	2	2 hr.	75 min.	2
Mung	3	2 hr.	75 min.	2
Navy	3	2 hr.	75 min.	2
Pinto	4	2 hr.	75 min.	2
Split peas	2	45 min.	—	2

When pressure-cooking beans and grains, follow these guidelines.

Beans. Rinse and soak beans as described on page 138. Drain, then use 3 cups of water for each 1 cup of soaked beans. Place the water and beans inside the pressure cooker, secure the lid, and attach the pressure valve. Cook on medium-high heat until the pressure comes up (the valve will begin to move and then stop moving as the steam equalizes). Reduce the heat to medium-low and cook for the required time as indicated in the bean table above.

When the beans are finished cooking, bring the pressure down before opening the lid of the pressure cooker: Do this by removing the pot from the stove and running cold water over the lid. Then carefully lift off the valve. Twist off the lid and check the beans for doneness. If tender, drain the beans and use.

Note: Never pressure-cook lentils, split peas, or chick-peas. They have

Grain (1 cup)	Water (cups)	Regular Cooking Time	Pressure-Cooking Time (minutes)	Yield (cups)
Barley	2–3	1 hr.	50	3
Buckwheat	3	30 min.	—	3
Bulgur	4	20 min.	—	4
Millet	2–3	45 min.	20	3
Oats	3	20 min.	—	3
Quinoa	2	15 min.	—	3
Rice (basmati)	1½	45 min.	20	1½
Rice (brown)	1½	45 min.	20	2
Rye (whole)	2	1 hr.	45	2
Wheat (whole)	2	1 hr.	45	2

skins that slip off during cooking; the skins can clog the valve and cause the lid to blow off.

Grains. Toast the grain as described on page 139 and then place in the pressure cooker along with water (1½ cups water for each 1 cup of grain). Secure the lid and attach the pressure valve. Cook on medium-high heat until the pressure comes up (the valve will begin to move and then stop moving as the steam equalizes). Reduce the heat to medium-low and cook for the required time as indicated in the grain table above.

When the grain is done cooking, bring the pressure down before opening the lid of the pressure cooker. Remove the pot from the stove, run cold water over the lid, and then carefully lift off the valve. Twist off the lid and check to see if all the water has been absorbed. If done, remove the grain from the pot and use.

Family Entrées

Here are some tasty ways to introduce beans to your family. They're filling enough to be meals in themselves—or they can be dressed up with the addition of a tossed salad, some hot bread, and a light dessert.

Mexican Corn Stew

This spicy stew is a favorite of Mexican-food fans—its fire comes from the minced fresh jalapeño peppers. Pass around a bowl of guacamole as a garnish.

Serves 6 to 8.

1 cup dried small red beans, rinsed
3 tablespoons olive oil
1 cup chopped onions
1 tablespoon minced garlic
2 sweet red peppers, diced
½ cup thinly sliced carrots
½ cup thinly sliced celery
¼ cup diced jalapeño peppers
6 cups water or Vegetable Stock (page 113)
3 cups corn
3 tablespoons minced fresh cilantro
2 teaspoons ground cumin
2 teaspoons ground coriander
½ teaspoon ground red pepper (optional)
2 cups crushed tortilla chips

Place the beans in a large bowl and cover with cold water. Let soak overnight, then drain off excess water. Place in a Crockpot.

In a large frying pan over medium-high heat, heat the oil. Add the onions and garlic. Sauté until the onions are soft, about 3 to 5 minutes. Add the red peppers, carrots, celery, and jalapeños. Cook for 3 minutes, stirring frequently.

Add to the Crockpot. Add the water or stock, corn, cilantro, cumin, and coriander. Cover the pot and turn to low. Cook for 6 to 8 hours, or until the beans are tender and the stew is thick. Add the ground pepper (if using) and serve in warmed bowls. Top each serving with tortilla chips.

VEGETARIAN RED PEPPER AND ARTICHOKE PAELLA

¼ cup boiling water
¼ teaspoon saffron threads
2 large onions, thinly sliced
¼ cup olive oil
3 cups basmati rice, washed and drained
1 large sweet red pepper, thinly sliced
4 cloves garlic, minced
5½ cups Vegetable Stock (page 113)
1 tablespoon low-sodium soy sauce or tamari
½ teaspoon ground red pepper (or to taste)
1 teaspoon herbal salt substitute
½ teaspoon ground black pepper
8 ounces marinated artichokes, drained
¼ cup slivered almonds

In a small bowl, combine the water and saffron. Let steep 20 minutes.

In a large frying pan over medium-low heat, sauté the onions in the oil for 10 minutes, stirring frequently to prevent browning.

Add the rice, red peppers, and garlic. Sauté, stirring, for 5 minutes. Add the stock. Bring to a boil and let simmer, uncovered, for 15 minutes. Add the saffron and water.

Cover the pan, turn the heat to the lowest setting and let steam 10 to 15 minutes, or until all the water is absorbed. Add the soy sauce or tamari and ground red pepper. Season with salt substitute and black pepper. Mix well.

Pour into a serving bowl. Serve topped with the artichokes and almonds.

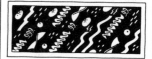

Paella means celebration, usually a feast saluting the catch of the day on the Spanish coast. Here's a vegetarian version with the same seasonings: saffron and garlic. It has an assortment of sautéed and marinated vegetables.

Serves 4 to 6.

The hamburger lover in your family is probably too astute to be tricked by these simulations. But after you top these burgers with mustard, lettuce, tomatoes, and sprouts, he or she just might not care. (For instructions for sprouting chick-peas and wheat berries, see "Sprouting Good Health" on page 86.)

Serves 6.

Sprouted Bean Burgers

- 1 cup sprouted chick-peas
- 1 cup sprouted wheat berries
- ½ cup grated carrots
- ½ cup mashed potatoes
- ¼ cup grated onions
- ½ teaspoon herbal salt substitute
- ¼ teaspoon dried basil
- ¼ teaspoon dried thyme
- ¼ teaspoon ground black pepper
- ⅛ teaspoon ground rosemary
    low-sodium soy sauce or tamari (to taste)
- 1-2 cups whole wheat bread crumbs
- 1 teaspoon canola oil

Place the chick-peas, wheat berries, carrots, potatoes, onions, salt substitute, basil, thyme, pepper, and rosemary in the bowl of a food processor. Puree. Add soy sauce or tamari to taste.

Transfer to a large bowl. Stir in enough bread crumbs to make a mixture that holds together. Form into 6 patties.

Fry in the oil on a nonstick griddle over medium heat.

Indian Rice Pilaf with Vegetables

Curried rice turns this pilaf into a spicy international dish. You can serve it as is or dress it up Indian-style with side dishes of chutney, peanuts, and dried fruit.

Serves 4.

- 1 cup chopped onions
- 4 cloves garlic, minced
- 1 tablespoon cumin seeds
- 1 tablespoon grated fresh ginger
- 2 teaspoons safflower oil
- 2 cups basmati rice, washed and drained
- 4 cups Vegetable Stock (page 113)
- ⅔ cup raisins
- 2-3 teaspoons curry powder
- ⅓ cup chopped scallions
- ⅓ cup raw peanuts or cashews

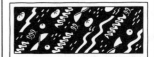

In a large frying pan over medium-low heat, sauté the onions, garlic, cumin, and ginger in the oil for 10 minutes, stirring frequently to prevent browning. Add the rice and sauté an additional 3 minutes, stirring constantly. Add the stock, raisins, and curry.

Bring to a boil and let the mixture cook uncovered for 15 minutes. Cover the pan, reduce the heat, and simmer for 10 to 15 minutes, or until all the liquid has been absorbed. Stir in the scallions and peanuts or cashews.

Basic BEAN SOUP

 1 cup dried beans, rinsed
 1 cup chopped onions
 2 teaspoons minced garlic
 1 tablespoon olive oil
 ½ cup diced celery stalks and leaves
 ½ cup diced sweet potatoes or carrots
 ½ cup diced tomatoes
 5″ piece kombu (kelp)
 6 cups Vegetable Stock (page 113)
 ¼ cup white miso
 1 tablespoon mirin (Japanese rice wine)
 1 tablespoon minced fresh parsley

Place the beans in a large bowl and cover with cold water. Let soak overnight, then drain off excess water. Set aside.

In a 3- to 4-quart pot over medium-high heat, sauté the onions and garlic in the oil for 10 minutes, stirring frequently to prevent browning. Add the celery, sweet potatoes or carrots, tomatoes, and kombu. Continue to sauté, stirring frequently, for 5 minutes. Add the stock and bring to a boil.

Reduce the heat to medium, add the beans, cover and simmer for 1⅓ hours, or until the beans are tender. Remove and discard the kombu.

Pour ½ cup of the soup into a small bowl, add the miso, and stir until the miso is blended. Pour back into the pot and add the mirin and parsley.

There's little as satisfying as a thick soup that brings a taste of fiber-rich beans and vegetables with every spoonful. This recipe will satisfy the busy cook as well, since it can be made ahead and easily incorporates any leftovers you have in the refrigerator. Use your choice of pinto, lima, or Great Northern beans.

Serves 6 to 8.

Spinach Fried Rice

1½ cups chopped spinach
  2 cloves garlic, minced
  1 teaspoon dark sesame oil
⅓ cup dry sherry
  1 cup diagonally sliced celery or bok choy
  1 cup thinly sliced mushrooms
  3 cups cooked long-grain brown rice
¼ cup sliced scallions
  2 tablespoons low-sodium soy sauce or tamari

In a wok or large frying pan over medium-high heat, sauté the spinach and garlic in the oil for 2 minutes, stirring constantly. Transfer to a platter.

In same pan, heat the sherry and sauté the celery or bok choy and mushrooms, stirring constantly, for 3 minutes. Add the rice, scallions, and spinach. Heat through. Season with soy sauce or tamari.

Vegetarian Sierra Stew

  3 cups dried kidney beans, rinsed
  2 tablespoons olive oil
  1 large onion, thinly sliced
  4 cloves garlic, minced
  1 green pepper, coarsely chopped
10 ounces canned tomatoes, with liquid
  1 cup coarsely chopped green cabbage
½ cup diced red potatoes
  1 tablespoon chili powder
½ teaspoon ground cumin
  4 cups water or Vegetable Stock (page 113)
½ cup brown rice
    herbal salt substitute (to taste)
    ground black pepper (to taste)

Place the beans in a large bowl and cover with cold water. Let soak overnight, then drain off excess water. Place in a Crockpot.

Whip up this simple recipe in 20 minutes and watch the delight on your family's faces. It's a delicious way to satisfy Chinese fried-rice cravings without the fat that usually accompanies those recipes.

Serves 4.

This tasty stew is hearty enough for a camping trip to the High Sierras, from where, by the way, its name originated.

Serves 6 to 8.

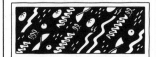

In a large frying pan over medium-high heat, heat the oil. Add the onions and garlic. Sauté until the onions are soft, about 3 to 5 minutes. Add the peppers, tomatoes, cabbage, potatoes, chili powder, and cumin. Continue cooking, stirring frequently, for 3 minutes, then transfer to the Crockpot.

Add the water or stock and rice. Cover the pot and turn to low. Let cook for 6 to 8 hours, or until the stew is thick, and beans and rice are tender. Season with salt substitute and pepper.

CREAMY POLENTA WITH ROASTED VEGETABLES

1 Japanese eggplant, halved lengthwise and sliced thickly
8 large mushrooms
8 scallions
1 cup cherry tomatoes
¼ cup olive oil
1 tablespoon low-sodium soy sauce or tamari
1 tablespoon dried thyme
1 cup coarse cornmeal
1 cup cold water
2 cups boiling Vegetable Stock (page 113)

Preheat a broiler or stove-top grill.

In a large bowl, combine the eggplant, mushrooms, scallions, and tomatoes. Drizzle with the oil and soy sauce or tamari and sprinkle with the thyme. Toss well and let marinate while you make the polenta.

In a heavy 2-quart saucepan, combine the cornmeal and water. Whisk in the hot stock. Bring to a boil over medium-high heat. Reduce the heat and cook, stirring with a whisk, until thick. Cover the pan and turn off the heat.

Remove the vegetables from their marinade (reserve the liquid). Broil or grill the vegetables until lightly browned, turning once halfway through the cooking time.

Divide the warm polenta among 3 or 4 plates and arrange the vegetables on top. Drizzle with leftover marinade.

Polenta, a soft-cooked cornmeal that's growing in popularity, is perfect for a chilly winter evening. You can also bake the cooked polenta and serve it in slices for a more elegant presentation.

Serves 3 to 4.

On the Lighter Side

For those evenings when you want a lighter cooking burden or just less to eat, here are some of my favorite light-meal bean, grain, and pasta dishes.

JALAPEÑO-PEPPER AND WILD-MUSHROOM RISOTTO

Risotto—rice cooked to a cereal consistency—is made from Italian Arborio rice, the only rice that cooks to a creamy texture without dissolving. I serve it with a sauté of peppers and wild chanterelle mushrooms, the delicate flavor of which enhances the rice.

Serves 4 to 6.

7 cups Garlic Broth (page 113)
½ cup minced onions
⅓ cup minced jalapeño peppers
2 cloves garlic, minced
½ cup dry white wine
2 tablespoons olive oil
2 cups sliced wild mushrooms, such as shiitake or chanterelle
1½ cups Arborio rice

In a 2-quart saucepan over medium-high heat, bring the broth to a boil. Reduce the heat and keep the broth warm, just barely simmering.

In a 3-quart saucepan over medium-high heat, cook the onions, jalapeños, and garlic in the wine and 1 tablespoon of the oil for 2 minutes. Reduce the heat to medium and continue cooking the vegetables for 8 minutes, stirring frequently to prevent browning. Add the mushrooms and cook, stirring occasionally, until the mushrooms begin to exude moisture. Add the rice and stir to coat with the cooking liquid.

Add 1 cup of the hot broth and cook, stirring, until the liquid is absorbed. Add broth ½ cup at a time, cooking after each addition until the liquid is absorbed. Continue until the rice is tender and all the broth has been absorbed, about 20 to 30 minutes. Serve hot, drizzled with the remaining olive oil.

REFRIED MEXICAN BEANS

½ cup minced onions
2 tablespoons minced garlic
2 tablespoons olive oil
3 cups cooked pinto beans
1 tablespoon minced jalapeño peppers
½ teaspoon ground cumin
½ teaspoon salt (optional)

In a large frying pan over medium-high heat, sauté the onions and garlic in the oil for 10 minutes, stirring frequently to prevent browning. Add the beans and mash with a spoon. Add the jalapeños, cumin, and salt (if using). Heat through, stirring constantly.

WILD RICE WITH MUSHROOMS AND PECANS

¼ cup diced onions
¼ cup diced celery
¼ cup diced carrots
¼ cup dry white wine
1 tablespoon safflower oil
2 cups sliced mushrooms
1 cup wild rice
2½ cups Vegetable Stock (page 113)
2 tablespoons minced fresh parsley
2 tablespoons chopped toasted pecans

In a 3-quart saucepan over medium heat, sauté the onions, celery, and carrots in the wine and oil for 5 minutes, stirring frequently to prevent browning.

Add the mushrooms and wild rice. Cook for 5 minutes, or until the mushrooms begin to exude moisture.

Add the stock and bring to a boil. Cover, reduce the heat to low, and cook for 25 minutes, or until all the water has been absorbed. Stir in the parsley and pecans.

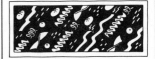

You can make great refried beans without lard! The secret of this recipe is a substantial dose of Mexican spices.

Serves 6.

Wild rice is a special treat in our house, often mixed with other rice in a medley. Here it goes solo, livened up with savory sautéed mushrooms and crunchy pecans.

Serves 4 to 6.

Black Beans with Cumin and Garlic

2 cups washed black beans
3 cups Vegetable Stock (page 113)
¼ cup minced onions
2 jalapeño peppers, minced
5 cloves garlic, minced
1 teaspoon ground cumin
2 tablespoons olive oil
¼ cup dry sherry
¼ cup minced fresh parsley

Place the beans in a large bowl and cover with cold water. Let soak overnight, then drain off excess water. Transfer to a 3-quart saucepan. Add the stock. Bring to a boil over medium-high heat. Reduce the heat to medium and cook for 45 to 60 minutes, or until the beans are almost tender. Drain.

In a large frying pan over medium-high heat, sauté the onions, jalapeños, garlic, and cumin in the oil for 5 minutes, stirring frequently to prevent browning. Add the sherry and cook for 1 minute.

Add the beans and cook, stirring frequently, for 10 minutes. Serve sprinkled with the parsley.

Asian-Style Quinoa

6 cups water
2 cups quinoa
1 tablespoon dark sesame oil
2 tablespoons low-sodium soy sauce or tamari
½ cup diagonally sliced scallions
½ cup diagonally sliced carrots
¼ cup dry sherry
8 ounces firm tofu, cut into chunks

Serve your cholesterol-lowering beans with some spice! This dish is ultra simple, but it'll warm you when the chilly winds blow. You can freeze leftovers to wrap in sandwich burritos later.

Serves 4 to 6.

Quinoa is a grain from the South American Andes that's rich in protein and other nutrients. In this recipe, it is combined with stir-fried vegetables in an Asian sauce.

Serves 6 to 8.

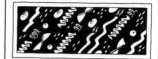

In a saucepan over medium-high heat, bring the water and quinoa to a boil. Cover the pan, reduce the heat to low and simmer for 20 minutes. Stir in the oil and 1 tablespoon of the soy sauce or tamari. Transfer to a large platter and keep warm.

In a wok or large frying pan over medium-high heat, sauté the scallions and carrots in the sherry for 5 minutes, stirring constantly. Add the tofu and remaining soy sauce or tamari. Cook for 1 minute, stirring occasionally. Pour over the quinoa.

BROWN-RICE SALAD WITH MINT IN LETTUCE CUPS

 3 cups cooked short-grain brown rice
 ½ cup chopped red onions
 ½ cup chopped fresh mint
 ½ cup chopped fresh parsley
 ¼ cup peas
 ¼ cup minced sweet red peppers
 ¼ cup olive oil
 ¼ cup lemon juice
 1 teaspoon minced garlic
 1 teaspoon herbal salt substitute
 ½ teaspoon ground white pepper
 1 head red leaf lettuce
12 strips sweet red peppers (garnish)

In a large bowl, combine the rice, onions, mint, parsley, peas, red peppers, oil, lemon juice, garlic, salt substitute, and ground pepper. Toss well and let marinate for 1 hour at room temperature.

Wash and separate the lettuce leaves; dry thoroughly. Place 2 or 3 leaves together, forming a cup. Repeat until you have 6 cups.

Divide the salad evenly among the cups. Garnish with the pepper strips.

The delicate flavors of mint and lemon mingle in this springtime salad, served in a curled lettuce leaf and garnished with sweet red pepper strips.

Serves 6.

Noodle and White-Bean Salad with Low-Oil Vinaigrette

If you make this pasta and bean salad in the morning, the flavors will have a chance to blend by dinnertime. Store, covered, in the refrigerator, then bring to room temperature before serving. You can find soba noodles—a delicate buckwheat pasta often used in Japanese recipes—in most health-food stores and Asian markets.

Serves 4.

1 cup cooked soba
1 cup cooked white beans
1 cup julienned carrots
1 cup broccoli florets
1/2 cup sliced scallions
1/4 cup minced fresh parsley
3 tablespoons apple cider vinegar
2 tablespoons olive oil
2 tablespoons low-sodium soy sauce or tamari
1 tablespoon dark sesame oil
1 tablespoon lemon juice
1/8 teaspoon ground red pepper

In a large bowl, combine the soba, beans, carrots, broccoli, scallions, parsley, vinegar, olive oil, soy sauce or tamari, sesame oil, lemon juice, and pepper. Let marinate for at least 1 hour, or overnight. Serve at room temperature.

Three-Color Rice

Can you guess what the three colors are? (Hint: They come from peas, corn, and carrots.)

Serves 4.

1/4 cup minced onions
2 teaspoons minced garlic
1 teaspoon olive oil
1/2 cup peas
1/2 cup corn
1/2 cup diced carrots
1/4 cup dry sherry
3 cups cooked short-grain brown rice
2 tablespoons minced fresh parsley

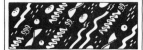

In a large frying pan over medium-high heat, sauté the onions and garlic in the oil for 5 minutes, stirring frequently to prevent browning. Add the peas, corn, carrots, and sherry. Let simmer for 5 minutes, then add the rice. Heat through, stirring frequently. Sprinkle with the parsley before serving.

CUBAN BLACK BEANS AND RICE

1 cup washed black beans
4 cups Vegetable Stock (page 113)
³/₄ cup chopped onions
4 cloves garlic, minced
1 tablespoon cumin seed
2 tablespoons olive oil
1½ cups long-grain brown rice
½ cup chopped green peppers
½ cup chopped sweet red peppers
2 cups Garlic Broth (page 113)
   low-sodium soy sauce or tamari, to taste

Place the beans in a large bowl and cover with cold water. Let soak overnight, then drain off excess water. Transfer to a 3-quart saucepan. Add the stock. Bring to a boil over medium-high heat. Reduce the heat to medium and cook for 25 to 35 minutes, or until the beans are almost tender. Drain.

In a large frying pan over medium heat, sauté the onions, garlic, and cumin in the oil for 10 minutes, stirring frequently to prevent browning. Add the rice, green peppers, and red peppers. Cook, stirring for 2 minutes. Add the beans and broth.

Bring to a boil, cover and cook for 40 minutes, or until the rice is tender. Season with soy sauce or tamari.

"I Love Lucy's" Ricky Ricardo loved his beans and rice, and so do most Cubans. Black beans are used in this recipe for their rich flavor that combines well with cumin and garlic. You can make this dish spicier with a sprinkle of ground red pepper or hot pepper sauce.

Serves 4 to 6.

International Pasta Recipes

If you think pasta is just spaghetti and tomato sauce, think again. A favorite of chefs around the world, pasta can transform a few basic ingredients —flour, water, oil, vegetables, garlic—into a recipe worthy of a magazine cover. And pasta is a perfect food for the no-cholesterol diet since you can make so many meatless sauces. So when you tire of the same old spaghetti and tomato sauce, try these easy variations on a theme.

This recipe has three components: a rich-tasting sauté of vegetables, a seasoned tofu mixture that takes the place of cheese, and a thick tomato sauce. Make any or all of the parts ahead of time and assemble just before serving. If you use whole grain noodles, you get plenty of cholesterol-lowering fiber.

Serves 6 to 8.

FIVE-VEGETABLE LASAGNA

  1 cup sliced onions
  2 teaspoons minced garlic
 ½ cup dry sherry
  3 cups thinly sliced zucchini
1½ cups chopped spinach
  1 cup sliced mushrooms
  1 cup chopped tomatoes
 ¼ cup minced fresh parsley
 12 eggless spinach lasagna noodles
 16 ounces firm tofu, well drained and crumbled
  1 tablespoon honey
  1 tablespoon herbal salt substitute
  2 teaspoons dried basil
1½ teaspoons dried oregano
 ½ teaspoon ground black pepper
  1 cup Salt-Free Tomato Sauce with Mushrooms
      (page 161)
 ⅓ cup toasted whole wheat bread crumbs

In a large frying pan over medium-high heat, sauté the onions and garlic in the sherry for 10 minutes, stirring frequently to prevent browning. Add the zucchini, spinach, mushrooms, tomatoes, and parsley. Lower the heat to medium

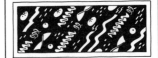

and cook for 15 minutes, stirring frequently. Remove from the heat and set aside.

In a large pot of boiling water over high heat, cook the noodles for 8 minutes. Drain and rinse with cold water. Set aside in a single layer.

In a small bowl, combine the tofu, honey, salt substitute, basil, oregano, and pepper.

Preheat the oven to 350°.

Lightly oil a 9″ × 13″ baking pan. Spread half of the vegetable mixture in the bottom of the pan. Top with half of the tofu mixture and half of the noodles (overlap as needed to fit). Repeat the layers with the remaining vegetables, tofu, and noodles.

Top with the tomato sauce. Sprinkle with the bread crumbs. Cover with foil and bake for 45 minutes. Uncover and bake for 15 minutes.

Saffron Orzo

1½ cups orzo
¼ cup dry sherry
⅛ teaspoon saffron threads
2 tablespoons minced onions
1 teaspoon minced garlic
1 teaspoon olive oil
2 tablespoons chopped chives

In a large pot of boiling water over high heat, cook the orzo until just tender, about 10 minutes. Drain and set aside.

In a small bowl, combine the sherry and saffron. Let steep for 10 minutes.

While the saffron is steeping, in a large frying pan over medium heat, sauté the onions and garlic in the oil for 5 minutes, stirring frequently to prevent browning. Add the saffron and orzo.

Continue cooking and stirring for 5 minutes, or until the orzo has taken on golden color. Sprinkle with the chives.

Orzo, a tiny rice-shaped pasta, turns harvest gold from the saffron in this recipe. Soaking saffron threads in sherry before combining them with the pasta makes the color spread more evenly.

Serves 4.

MAKE YOUR OWN NO-CHOLESTEROL PASTA

Pasta making requires the skills of a professional chef, right? Nope. With a food processor, a hand-cranked pasta machine, and a good recipe, you can make enough fettuccine in 7 minutes to serve two hungry pasta eaters.

Even with the bare essentials—a bowl, a floured board, and a sharp knife—you can learn to knead, roll, and cut good pasta with the best Italian mamas. In fact, I learned the process from a friend's Italian grandmama, who laid out the simple ingredients with such reverence that I knew I was in for a culinary treat.

Perfect pasta is a delicate balance of three elements: flour, water, and kneading. Too much of any one element and the dough's silky elasticity vanishes. Though many people think that good pasta must include eggs, in truth eggs are only options. Even oil isn't really necessary.

The following technique will guide you through the stages of making basic pasta dough. Once you practice and produce a passable pasta, try some of the variations listed on the opposite page.

BASIC PASTA DOUGH

1 cup whole wheat pastry or unbleached flour
¼ cup water (approximate)
1 teaspoon olive oil (optional)
  pinch of herbal salt substitute

To make the dough with a food processor: Place the flour, water, oil (if using), and salt substitute in the bowl of a food processor. (The oil will make the pasta dough smoother but can be omitted to lower the calorie content.) Process with on/off turns to lightly combine. Continue to process until the dough forms a ball and cleans the sides of the bowl. (You may need to add 1 to 3 teaspoons more water to get to this point.) Proceed to the kneading step.

To make the dough by hand: In a large bowl, mix the flour and salt substitute. Make a well in the center of the flour and add the oil (if using). Use a fork to lightly incorporate the oil into the flour. When a loose lump of dough forms, begin adding water by tablespoonfuls. If needed, incorporate more flour and water in small amounts until a stiff dough forms. Proceed to the kneading step.

To knead the dough: Throughout kneading, be careful to add flour very gradually. In the beginning stages, the dough is apt to absorb flour and can get tough very quickly. Your goal is to knead the stickiness out of the dough rather than to cover it with flour.

Lightly sprinkle flour on your hands and all sides of the dough. Knead the dough on a lightly floured board or between your hands. After about 5 minutes, the dough should be smooth and elastic.

You can test it by stretching a piece: It should stretch several inches without breaking. Flatten the dough into a pancake and flour it well. Now that it is fully kneaded, the flour will not be absorbed as much. Choose your rolling method.

To roll the dough by machine: Position the rollers at the widest setting. Roll the flattened dough through the machine. Fold the dough into thirds, turn it 90° and roll it through again. This should give you an even rectangle of dough to cut into even strips.

Lightly flour both sides of the dough. Roll the rectangle of dough one time each through successively narrower settings until it is about $1/16''$ thick. Cut the strip in half for easier handling. Flour the dough well on both sides and feed through the cutting blades. Separate any sticky strands and hang on a rack or lay on a floured board to dry for 30 minutes. Proceed to cooking step.

To roll the dough by hand: With a lightly floured rolling pin, roll the dough to $1/16''$ thick. Lightly flour both sides of the dough. Starting at an edge, roll up the dough to form a jelly roll. Cut the roll into strips about $1/4''$ thick. Unroll each strip, separate sticky strands and let dry on a rack or floured board for 30 minutes. Proceed to cooking step.

To cook the pasta: In a large pot, bring 2 quarts of water to a rapid boil. Add the pasta and cook for 1 to 2 minutes. A teaspoon of olive oil in the water will help keep the noodles separate, but is not essential. Drain and serve immediately.

Serves 2.

SPINACH NOODLES

Basic Pasta Dough (opposite page)
2 tablespoons thawed and finely chopped frozen spinach, squeezed dry

Follow the directions for the basic pasta. Add the spinach during the kneading stage.

Serves 2.

HERB NOODLES

Basic Pasta Dough (opposite page)
2 tablespoons minced fresh basil, oregano, or thyme

Follow the directions for the basic pasta. Add the herbs during the kneading stage.

Serves 2.

BEET NOODLES

Basic Pasta Dough (opposite page)
2 tablespoons pureed cooked beets

Follow the directions for the basic pasta. Add the beets during the kneading stage.

Serves 2.

A friend's Italian grand-
mother taught me to
make this dish; it was a
favorite from her native
Venice and a standard
side dish—summer or
winter—at Sunday supper.

Serves 4 to 6.

Chefs sometimes pass on
their favorite recipes. This
was a south-of-France
standby of a friend who
cooked in a small north-
ern California café. I love
the bright contrast of
beet and spinach pastas
topped with an unusual
pesto made from walnuts
and garlic. It's rich, so
serve it in small amounts.

Serves 6.

Nona's Pasta with Beans

1 cup chopped onions
1-1½ cups chopped tomatoes
3 cloves minced garlic
1 tablespoon olive oil
2 cups cooked eggless elbow macaroni
2 cups cooked navy beans
½ cup minced fresh parsley
1 teaspoon dried oregano
½ teaspoon dried basil
herbal salt substitute (to taste)
ground black pepper (to taste)

In a large frying pan over medium-high heat, sauté the onions, tomatoes, and garlic in the oil, stirring frequently to prevent browning. Add the pasta, beans, parsley, oregano, and basil. Heat through. Season with salt substitute and pepper.

Red and Green Pasta with Walnut Sauce

⅔ cup walnuts
⅓ cup hot water
3 tablespoons olive oil
½ teaspoon minced garlic
2 tablespoons chopped parsley
1 tablespoon herbal salt substitute
½ teaspoon ground black pepper
3 cups hot cooked Spinach Noodles (page 157)
3 cups hot cooked Beet Noodles (page 157)

In a blender or food processor, puree the walnuts, water, oil, and garlic until a smooth paste forms. Spoon into a large bowl and stir in the parsley, salt substitute, and pepper.

Add the pastas and toss well.

Baked Eggplant and Tomato Pasta Casserole

1 large eggplant, thinly sliced
2 cups thinly sliced onions
4 tablespoons minced garlic
2 tablespoons olive oil
4 tomatoes, chopped
1 cup diced green peppers
1 cup diced sweet red peppers
½ cup dry red wine or Vegetable Stock (page 113)
4 tablespoons tomato paste
2 tablespoons honey
1 tablespoon herbal salt substitute
3 cups cooked whole wheat rotelle
½ cup toasted whole wheat bread crumbs

Preheat the oven to 300°.

Place the eggplant slices directly on an oven rack and bake for 10 minutes. Turn the slices and bake for 10 minutes. Remove from the oven and set aside.

Increase the oven temperature to 350°. Lightly oil a 9″ × 13″ baking dish.

In a large frying pan over medium-low heat, sauté the onions and garlic in the oil for 10 minutes, stirring frequently to prevent browning. Add the tomatoes, green peppers, red peppers, wine or stock, tomato paste, honey, and salt substitute. Cover and cook for 10 minutes.

Place half of the eggplant in the baking dish and top with the rotelle. Spoon half of the sauce over the rotelle. Add another layer of eggplant and the remaining sauce. Sprinkle with the bread crumbs. Bake for 25 minutes.

A new version of eggplant parmigiana—without the Parmesan! Bread crumbs are a delicious substitute in this highly seasoned, rich-tasting casserole, redolent of fresh herbs and garlic. The special cooking of the eggplant in the beginning allows it to dry out so it absorbs more flavor from the sauce during baking.

Serves 6.

The elegant cuisine of Thailand brings us this salad of cellophane noodles flavored with peanuts, lemon juice, and sesame oil. Serve it with a glass of iced jasmine tea for an outdoor summer lunch.

Serves 4.

THAI NOODLE AND VEGETABLE SALAD

¼ cup water
3 tablespoons lemon juice
2 tablespoons dark sesame oil
2 tablespoons safflower oil
4 teaspoons low-sodium soy sauce or tamari
1 tablespoon peanut butter
1 tablespoon herbal salt substitute
1 teaspoon minced garlic
4 teaspoons rice wine vinegar
2 teaspoons honey
1 cucumber
3 cups shredded romaine lettuce
3 cups cooked cellophane noodles
1 cup snow peas
½ cup julienned sweet red peppers
¼ cup raw peanuts
¼ cup diagonally sliced scallions

In a small bowl, whisk together the water, lemon juice, sesame oil, safflower oil, soy sauce or tamari, peanut butter, salt substitute, garlic, vinegar, and honey. Let stand for 10 minutes while you prepare the salad.

Peel the cucumber. Halve it lengthwise, scoop out the seeds, and slice the flesh into half-moon shapes. Place in a large bowl. Add the lettuce, noodles, peas, peppers, peanuts, and scallions.

Pour the dressing over the salad and toss well. Serve immediately.

Easy Pasta Toppings

Everyone should have a repertoire of fast-cooking pasta toppings. I like to have one or two sauces in the freezer for unforeseen "emergencies," such as guests or relatives popping in unexpectedly. Serve your choice with home-made pasta.

SALT-FREE TOMATO SAUCE WITH MUSHROOMS

1 cup minced onions
2 tablespoons minced garlic
½ cup dry sherry
1 cup minced wild mushrooms, such as chanterelles
1 cup minced mushrooms
4 cups chopped tomatoes
2 tablespoons tomato paste
1 teaspoon herbal salt substitute
1 tablespoon honey
½ teaspoon dried basil
½ teaspoon dried oregano
    ground black pepper (to taste)

Thick and tasty, this salt-free sauce gets its flavor from a slow sauté of domestic and wild mushrooms in sherry. Most of the alcohol evaporates during the cooking process, eliminating calories and leaving a virtually fat-free sauce.

Makes 4 to 5 cups.

In a 3- or 4-quart saucepan over medium-high heat, sauté the onions and garlic in the sherry for 10 minutes, stirring frequently to prevent browning. Add the wild mushrooms and mushrooms. Cook for 15 minutes, or until the mushrooms exude moisture.

Add the tomatoes, tomato paste, salt substitute, honey, basil, and oregano.

Reduce the heat to medium. Cook, stirring occasionally, for 25 minutes. Season with pepper.

Tomato and Green-Olive Sauce

2 tablespoons minced garlic
1/4 cup dry sherry
3 cups chopped fresh tomatoes
1/2 cup pitted chopped green olives
1 tablespoon minced fresh parsley
1 tablespoon dried oregano
1 teaspoon olive oil

In a 2-quart saucepan over medium-high heat, sauté the garlic in the sherry for 2 minutes. Add the tomatoes, olives, parsley, oregano, and oil. Cook, stirring frequently, for 5 minutes.

Let cool, cover, and refrigerate overnight to blend flavors. Reheat before serving.

Green olives give this rich sauce a tart bite, which complements the sweetness of garden-ripe tomatoes. Be sure to make extra sauce to freeze for a summer taste during the winter months.

Makes about 3 1/2 cups.

Salt-Free Southern Italian Pasta Sauce

1/2 cup dry red wine
1 teaspoon olive oil
1 tablespoon flour
1 cup minced onions
2 teaspoons minced garlic
5 cups chopped tomatoes
2 tablespoons tomato paste
2 tablespoons minced fresh parsley
1/2 teaspoon herbal salt substitute
1/2 teaspoon honey
1/4–1/2 teaspoon dried basil
1/4–1/2 teaspoon dried thyme
1/4 teaspoon ground black pepper

This traditional recipe has been altered to fit modern healthy-cooking criteria—less oil and no salt.

Makes 3 to 4 cups.

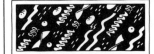

In a 3-quart saucepan over medium-high heat, heat the wine and oil. Whisk in the flour and cook, whisking constantly, for 2 minutes. Add the onions and garlic. Cook, stirring frequently, for 5 minutes.

Add the tomatoes, tomato paste, parsley, salt substitute, honey, basil, thyme, and pepper.

Cover, reduce the heat to low, and simmer for 40 minutes, stirring occasionally. Let cool, then puree in a blender.

EGGPLANT-TOMATO SAUCE

³/₄ cup dry sherry
1 teaspoon olive oil
1 small onion, finely chopped
1 cup cubed unpeeled eggplant
½ cup minced sweet red peppers
¼ cup chopped celery
2 cloves garlic, minced
3 cups Italian tomatoes, coarsely chopped
1 tablespoon chopped fresh basil
½ teaspoon ground nutmeg
    herbal salt substitute (to taste)
    ground black pepper (to taste)

In a 3-quart saucepan over medium-high heat, heat the sherry and oil until bubbling. Add the onions and cook, stirring frequently, until soft but not browned, about 5 minutes. Add the eggplant, red peppers, celery, and garlic. Cover and cook for 2 minutes.

Add the tomatoes, basil, and nutmeg. Bring to a boil, then reduce the heat to medium. Simmer, uncovered, for 20 minutes. Season with salt substitute and black pepper.

Sautéed eggplant, nutmeg, and sherry give this sauce a thickness and rich flavor often missing from plain tomato sauces. This sauce is excellent over cooked pasta. It also freezes well and will keep for up to 3 months.

Makes about 5 cups.

Green-Tomato Sauce

¼ cup chopped onions
1 teaspoon minced garlic
1 tablespoon olive oil
2 cups chopped green tomatoes or tomatillos
1 tablespoon minced fresh cilantro
1 teaspoon minced jalapeño peppers
1 teaspoon herbal salt substitute
½ teaspoon ground black pepper

In a 2-quart saucepan over medium-high heat, sauté the onions and garlic in the oil for 10 minutes, stirring frequently to prevent browning.

Add the tomatoes or tomatillos, cilantro, jalapeños, salt substitute, and pepper. Cook, stirring, for 15 minutes. Let cool, then puree in a blender.

You can also make this unusual tomato sauce with tomatillos, the citrusy Mexican vegetable available year-round in supermarkets and gourmet stores. Serve the sauce over grains or pasta, or use it as a dipping salsa for chips.

Makes about 2 cups.

Pasta Sauce Provencale

¼ cup olive oil
6 large tomatoes, coarsely chopped (about 5 cups)
2 tablespoons chopped black olives
1 clove garlic, minced
1 teaspoon herbal salt substitute
½ teaspoon honey
½ teaspoon chopped fresh parsley
½ teaspoon ground black pepper
¼ teaspoon dried thyme

In a 2- or 3-quart saucepan over medium-high heat, heat the oil until it almost smokes, about 4 or 5 minutes. Carefully add the tomatoes, olives, and garlic. Cook, stirring frequently, until the tomatoes are soft, about 8 to 10 minutes. Add the salt substitute, honey, parsley, pepper, and thyme. Reduce the heat to low and cook, uncovered, for 30 minutes.

Olives, thyme, and other seasonings of southern France provide an aroma of the herb-covered hillsides around Provence.

Makes about 5 cups.

CHAPTER 9

THE JOY OF
Soy
TOFU, TEMPEH, MISO, AND TAMARI DISHES

B ack in the days when tofu was a household word only in Tokyo, my next-door neighbors, the Noonan family, invited me to dinner. The mood was pretty much the same as it always was at the Noonans' around dinnertime: expectant. You see, everyone in the family was what used to be called "pleasantly plump," and eating was quite a big event over there. Plump Dick Noonan and his three plump sons would often be seated at the dinner table a half-hour early, just in case.

On this particular night, Marge Noonan had fixed a fairly typical menu—spaghetti topped with a meaty Bolognese sauce plus garlic bread and a green salad. The flavor was far above "typical," however. The sauce tasted just like my favorite Italian recipe, which always simmered for hours and was thick with sausage and spices. After the meal, the five Noonans had such contented smiles on their faces that it was obvious that Marge's spaghetti was a family favorite.

After dinner, I asked for the recipe. Marge handed me a neatly typed index card, which I quickly scanned for secret ingredients. "Wait a minute, Marge," I said. "You're missing something here. Where's the meat? And what's this *tofu* stuff?"

Marge smiled and told me that what I had just eaten was a meatless sauce, and tofu was her secret ingredient. She explained that she had discovered tofu quite by accident when the family doctor warned her husband, a confirmed carnivore, to lose weight or risk serious health problems. Immediately, Marge took it upon herself to formulate a workable strategy. Dick was no easy nut to crack. He had been wolfing down bacon for breakfast, ham and cheese for lunch, and steak for dinner since he was a calf. He was not about to change his grazing patterns without a fight.

Weeks went by with only minimal success in the dieting department. Then Marge picked up one of those small "calorie/recipe" booklets next to the supermarket checkout counter. This one, strangely enough, mentioned the benefits of a relatively unknown soybean cake called tofu. "Looks and tastes just like meat" said the booklet, which was all Marge needed to hear. She bought pounds of the stuff that day and immediately set to the task of incorporating it into every meal she made.

It turned out that the booklet was right: Firm tofu, crumbled and soaked in spices and tomato sauce, was a perfect substitute for ground beef. Marge began using it in sauces, lasagna, chili, scrambled eggs, pot pies, burritos, you name it. And no one knew the difference. Dick's weight began to plummet, along with his cholesterol count, and the boys still showed up at the dinner table a half-hour early.

Those who think that tofu—or tempeh or any soy product—is just a bit too, well, *foreign* should recall their initial perception of yogurt. It wasn't very long ago that yogurt was considered an ethnic health food strictly for the wheat-germ set. Now yogurt is almost as mainstream and popular as cottage cheese and ice cream.

Tofu, right out of its carton, *is* rubbery and unpalatable. But as a no-cholesterol substitute for meat and other high-fat protein foods (and used in the right recipes), it has no peer. Even if you have tried fermented soy products—tofu, tempeh, miso, and tamari—and are not crazy about them, you should consider giving them another chance just because of their nutritional benefits. They provide a low-fat, cholesterol-free source of protein for less money than meat and contribute a hefty amount of calcium—as much as an equivalent amount of milk—to boot.

Tofu's for You

If Lon Chaney was "the Man of a Thousand Faces," tofu is certainly "the Food of a Thousand Faces." Depending on your whim, tofu can simulate beef, chicken, eggs—even tuna.

Once an esoteric oddity, tofu is now distributed to most supermarkets

BETTER THAN SOUR CREAM

If you think no-cholesterol cooking means giving up the creamy taste and texture of dairy sour cream, here's a pleasant surprise. This sour cream substitute makes a healthy topping for baked potatoes and other dishes as well as a perfect base for dips. This blend keeps nicely for about 1 week.

MOCK SOUR CREAM

4 ounces soft tofu, crumbled
1 teaspoon chopped chives
1 teaspoon lemon juice

· In a blender or food processor, combine the tofu, chives, and lemon juice. Puree until smooth. Transfer to a jar, cover tightly, and store in the refrigerator.

Makes ½ cup.

and can typically be found in the produce section. Packaged tofu resembles a block of white cheese. It's made from cooked soybeans that are pureed with water and then strained into a milky liquid that is curded like dairy cheese.

Two kinds of tofu are available: soft and firm.

Soft tofu can be blended to a rich, creamy consistency; it is ideal as a replacement for more expensive and fat-rich ingredients like sour cream and cream cheese. I use it in creamy salad dressings and desserts.

Firm tofu holds its shape better and can be crumbled like ground beef or sliced like cheese. It's good for stir-frying and general cooking. Avoid firm tofu for creamy dishes, since it will remain gritty even if you puree it.

Tofu will keep for ten days if refrigerated and stored in fresh water. When I buy tofu, I remove it from the package, place it in a covered container filled with water, and change the water every two days to keep it fresh.

You can also freeze it; in fact, many people think tofu tastes better after freezing. To freeze, take the block of tofu out of its package, rinse it well, and then place it in a freezer bag. When you remove it from the freezer, thaw it, then squeeze out the excess moisture. You will notice that your rubbery block of white soy cheese now has texture! At this point you can crumble the thawed block into a bowl and marinate it with a variety of sauces.

Before cooking, tofu has very little flavor (unless it is old), which is actually its biggest advantage. It will absorb whatever flavors you marinate, bake, steam, puree, or sauté into it.

TOFU QUICKIES

Here are some fast-prep ideas for using tofu at the spur of the moment in your daily routine.

Tofu Cream-Cheese Icing. Puree 8 ounces of soft tofu until smooth and creamy. Add 2 tablespoons maple syrup, 1 teaspoon vanilla extract, 1 teaspoon grated orange rind, and a dash of grated nutmeg. Adjust the sweetener to your taste.

Baked Potato Topping. Puree 4 ounces of soft tofu with 1 teaspoon lemon juice. Stir in 1 teaspoon freeze-dried or snipped fresh chives. The results are very similar to sour cream and chives.

Lasagna Filling. To make a nondairy cheese filling for lasagna, crumble firm tofu and marinate it in vegetable stock seasoned with dried oregano and basil. Combine with your regular lasagna ingredients.

Now, Now . . . Tempeh, Tempeh!

Tempeh (pronounced *tem*-pay) is a primary protein source in Indonesia and some Southeast Asian countries. Though tempeh is also derived from soybeans, it is made very differently from tofu.

In tempeh manufacturing, partially cooked, cracked soybeans are inoculated with a culture called *Rhizopus oligosporus*. No, this is not a prehistoric beast but rather a culturing process similar to that used in making Brie cheese or wine. The soybeans take 24 hours to turn into tempeh in a strictly controlled environment with a temperature kept constant at 88°. When the tempeh is ready, it looks like a small slab of textured cheese.

Because tempeh contains significant amounts of vitamin B_{12}, which is difficult to obtain in a vegan (dairyless vegetarian) diet, it has been receiving considerable attention from vegetarians and low-fat dieters alike. The vitamin B_{12}, by the way, comes from a friendly bacterium called *Klebsiella pneumoniae*, a companion of the tempeh mold that produces about 5 micrograms of vitamin B_{12} for every 3.5 ounces of tempeh.

As health-conscious America discovered tempeh, entrepreneurial food manufacturers began to make it from other grains besides the traditional soybean. Today you can buy seven varieties of tempeh in the frozen-food section of many supermarkets. Frozen tempeh can be thawed and used right out of the package, but I like to cut it into cubes and steam it for 20 minutes. I find tempeh absorbs the flavors of a marinade or sauce better if it is warm.

Tempeh is a fine low-calorie substitute for ground beef or turkey. It's delicious in chili, lasagna, and stuffed peppers. It crumbles easily and absorbs flavors very fast; it also has a chewy texture very much like that of meat.

Store tempeh in the refrigerator or freezer. It keeps for 10 to 14 days refrigerated and up to two months frozen.

Miso and Tamari

Long esteemed in Asian cultures for their culinary and health qualities, miso and tamari are two additional products of the salted soybean. *Tamari* is soy sauce before it is diluted and salted. *Miso* is the paste left behind in the tamari kegs when the liquid drips out. Both contain healthful nutrients.

Miso and tamari are high in protein and calcium, but they tend to have a lot of sodium. The smooth texture of miso resembles peanut butter or firm cottage cheese. The Japanese make over 16 varieties of miso; some, like *natto miso,* are sweet enough to use by themselves as a spread or sandwich filler.

As both miso and tamari have a tendency to turn bitter when cooked, many Japanese cooks add them to soups or sauces at the last minute.

Tofu Dishes

Tofu is much like the chameleonesque hero in the Woody Allen film *Zelig:* It adopts the character and appearance of whatever it is standing next to at the moment. Tofu is equally comfortable in spreads and sautés, pies and casseroles, puddings and tarts, absorbing flavor from the other ingredients so thoroughly you'll never recognize it as tofu.

VEGETARIAN BURRITOS

Try this burrito filling for an easy Mexican meal. Make sure you plan ahead (5 to 6 hours) to allow the tofu to freeze solid and then thaw.

Serves 8.

1 pound tofu, frozen and thawed
2 cups Mexican salsa
8 flour tortillas, warmed
1 cup shredded part-skim soy mozzarella cheese
2 cups Refried Mexican Beans (page 149), warmed
1 cup shredded lettuce
½ cup chopped tomatoes

Squeeze the tofu to remove all excess moisture. Place in a small bowl and mash with a fork. Stir in 1 cup of the salsa. Let marinate at room temperature for 30 minutes.

To assemble the burritos, place a large spoonful of tofu on each tortilla. Top with the cheese, beans, lettuce, and tomatoes. Serve with the remaining salsa.

Charlie's Favorite Peanut Butter and Banana Sandwiches

1 pound soft tofu
2/3 cup chunky peanut butter
2 tablespoons lemon juice
1 tablespoon honey
4 slices Oatmeal-Raisin Bread (page 204)
1/2 cup sliced bananas
1/4 cup raisins

In a blender or food processor, puree the tofu, peanut butter, lemon juice, and honey until smooth. Spread thickly on each slice of bread. Top with bananas and raisins. Serve open-faced.

Meatless Tomato Sauce

2 cloves garlic, minced
1/3 cup dry red wine
1 teaspoon olive oil
1 cup minced onions
1 cup chopped mushrooms
8 ounces tofu, frozen and thawed
2 cups chopped Italian tomatoes
2 tablespoons tomato paste
1 tablespoon minced fresh basil
1/2 teaspoon dried oregano

In a 2- or 3-quart saucepan over medium-high heat, sauté the garlic in the wine and oil for 2 minutes. Add the onions and mushrooms; sauté for 2 minutes.

Squeeze the tofu to remove excess moisture. Crumble and add to the pan. Cook for 5 to 8 minutes, stirring frequently. Add the tomatoes, tomato paste, basil, and oregano. Reduce the heat and simmer for 20 minutes.

This recipe can be a special treat for the teenager or little ones in the family. My younger brother became a vegetarian at an early age and discovered this delicious spread, which he shared with me. The pureed tofu makes the fat-rich peanut butter go farther with fewer calories.

Serves 4.

You'll fool everybody with this meatless tomato sauce—the frozen tofu tastes just like ground beef. Use this versatile sauce over cooked pasta, lasagna, or stuffed shells.

Serves 4.

VEGETARIAN GOLDEN POT PIE

Though onions, carrots, and peas are specified for this satisfying vegetarian pot pie, you can use whatever vegetables you have on hand. The gravy is made from yellow-flake nutritional yeast, which is much more delicious than brewer's yeast.

Serves 6 to 8.

Pot Pie

- ½ cup whole wheat pastry flour
- 2 tablespoons nutritional yeast
- 2 teaspoons herbal salt substitute
- ½ teaspoon garlic powder
- 1 pound firm tofu, cut into 1″ cubes
- 1 tablespoon olive oil
- ½ cup dry sherry or water
- 1 onion, thinly sliced
- 1 carrot, thinly sliced
- 1 cup fresh peas
- 2 teaspoons minced garlic
- 2 tablespoons low-sodium soy sauce or tamari

Gravy

- ⅓–½ cup nutritional yeast
- ¼ cup whole wheat pastry flour
- 2 tablespoons safflower oil
- 1½ cups water
- 2 teaspoons low-sodium soy sauce or tamari
- ¾ teaspoon herbal salt substitute
- ¼ teaspoon ground pepper

To make the pot pie: In a paper bag, combine the flour, yeast, salt substitute, and garlic powder. Add the tofu and shake well to coat the pieces.

In a large frying pan over medium heat, heat the oil. Add the tofu and lightly brown on all sides, about 10 minutes. Transfer to a 1-quart casserole dish.

Add the sherry or water and onions to the pan. Sauté over medium heat until the onions are soft but not browned, about 5 minutes.

Add the carrots. Cover and cook for 5 minutes, or until tender. Add the peas and cook for 1 minute. Add the garlic and cook for 1 minute. Stir in the soy sauce or tamari.

Transfer the vegetables to the casserole and stir to combine with the tofu.

Preheat the oven to 350°.

To make the gravy: Wash and dry the frying pan. Add the yeast and flour. Stir over low heat for 3 minutes, or until fragrant. Add the oil and whisk until the mixture is smooth.

Stir in the water, soy sauce or tamari, salt substitute, and pepper. Raise the heat to medium-high and whisk until the gravy thickens, about 2 to 3 minutes. Pour over the tofu and vegetables. Bake for 15 to 20 minutes or until bubbling.

CHINESE SUPPER STIR-FRY

1 tablespoon low-sodium soy sauce or tamari
2 teaspoons dark sesame oil
1 teaspoon grated fresh ginger
6 ounces firm tofu, cut into 1/2" cubes
1 tablespoon safflower oil
1/4 cup sake or rice wine
1 cup thinly sliced scallions
1/2 cup cubed sweet potatoes
3 small beets, julienned
1 zucchini, thinly sliced
4 stalks bok choy, thinly sliced
2 cups mung bean sprouts
2 cups cooked brown rice
   herbal salt substitute (to taste)
   ground red pepper (to taste)

In a small bowl, combine the soy sauce or tamari, sesame oil, and ginger. Add the tofu and stir to combine. Let marinate, stirring occasionally, for 20 minutes.

In a wok or large frying pan over medium-high heat, heat the safflower oil and sake or rice wine. Add the scallions and stir-fry for 1 minute. Add the sweet potatoes and beets; stir-fry for 3 minutes. Add the zucchini and bok choy; stir-fry for 5 minutes, or until the sweet potatoes are tender.

Add the tofu (with marinade), sprouts, and rice. Stir-fry for 5 minutes. Season to taste with salt substitute and pepper.

Chunks of firm tofu, marinated in a delicious combination of Chinese seasonings, are stir-fried with bok choy, sweet potatoes, and other vegetables to make this colorful supper dish.

Serves 4 to 6.

SAN FRANCISCO JAPANTOWN SALAD SPREAD

Hijiki, a curly brown sea vegetable that looks like palm fronds underwater, is the secret seasoning in this salad. Look for it in health-food stores.

Serves 4 to 6.

½ cup dried hijiki
16 ounces firm tofu
 2 stalks celery, thinly sliced
 2 carrots, shredded
 6 scallions, thinly sliced
⅓ cup chopped fresh parsley
 3 tablespoons nutritional yeast
¼ cup dark sesame or olive oil
 2 tablespoons low-sodium soy sauce or tamari
 1 tablespoon lemon juice
 2 cloves garlic, minced
¼ teaspoon dried dill
½ teaspoon paprika

Place the hijiki in a small bowl with water to cover. Let soak for 10 minutes. Drain well. Dry the hijiki between paper towels, then chop coarsely. Place in a large bowl.

Crumble the tofu into the bowl. Using a potato masher, mash together the hijiki and tofu. Add the celery, carrots, scallions, parsley, and nutritional yeast.

In a small bowl, whisk together the oil, soy sauce or tamari, lemon juice, garlic, dill, and paprika. Pour over the salad and toss well.

STUFFED MUSHROOMS

This recipe is a great tofu version of veal- or beef-stuffed mushrooms. If you have leftover filling, you can freeze it for later use in casserole loaves, croquettes, or stuffed bell peppers.

Serves 6.

 4 ounces tofu, frozen and thawed
12 large mushrooms
¼ cup minced onions
 1 teaspoon safflower oil
½ cup fine whole wheat bread crumbs
¼ cup finely chopped almonds
 2 tablespoons dry sherry
 1 tablespoon low-sodium soy sauce or tamari
    pinch of dried marjoram

Squeeze the tofu to remove excess moisture. Crumble and set aside.

Preheat the broiler.

Twist or wiggle the mushroom stems to separate them from the caps. Mince the stems and set aside. Place the caps, open side down, on an ungreased baking sheet and broil for 1 minute. Remove from the oven and let cool.

In a large frying pan over medium-high heat, sauté the onions and minced mushroom stems in the oil, stirring frequently, for 3 minutes. Add the bread crumbs and stir well. Cook for 2 minutes, until lightly browned.

Add the tofu, almonds, and sherry to the pan. Cook for 1 minute, then remove from the heat.

Stir in the soy sauce or tamari and the marjoram. Mound the mixture in the mushroom caps. Broil for 1 to 2 minutes, or until lightly browned.

ANAHEIM-CHILI CASSEROLE

  1 cup finely chopped Anaheim chili peppers
1½ cups tomato sauce
14 ounces low-salt corn chips, broken into crumbs
  1 pound firm tofu, mashed
  2 cups shredded soy cheese
  ½ cup sliced scallions
1½ cups sliced black olives
  1 large bunch fresh cilantro, chopped

Preheat the oven to 350°.

In a 9″ × 13″ baking dish, spread half of the peppers. Top with half of the sauce, half of the chips, and half of the tofu. Sprinkle with ¾ cup of the cheese. Top with half of the scallions, olives, and cilantro.

Repeat to make a second set of layers. Sprinkle with the remaining cheese. Cover the casserole with foil. Bake for 30 minutes. Remove the foil and bake until the top is brown, about 15 minutes.

Another rich example of tofu's versatility, this delicious casserole was a gift from a cooking teacher in Los Angeles. It can be made ahead and refrigerated for two days before reheating and serving. Anaheim chilies are long green peppers with a very mild flavor.

Serves 6 to 8.

A cholesterol-free breakfast treat, this scrambled-egg look-alike should be served with a toasted slice of homemade Oatmeal-Raisin Bread (page 204). The crumbled tofu adopts a golden color much like eggs when it is scrambled with turmeric and other spices.

Serves 2.

Vegetable Breakfast Scramble

¼ cup hot water
1 tablespoon miso
1 tablespoon low-sodium soy sauce or tamari
¼ teaspoon turmeric powder
¼ teaspoon dried basil
¼ teaspoon dried dill
1 sweet red pepper, diced
6 large mushrooms, thinly sliced
1 small onion, minced
¼ cup safflower oil
8 ounces firm tofu

In a small bowl, combine the water, miso, soy sauce or tamari, turmeric, basil, and dill. Set aside.

In a large frying pan over medium-high heat, sauté the peppers, mushrooms, and onions in the oil, stirring frequently, for 10 minutes, or until the onions soften.

Crumble the tofu into small chunks and add to the pan. Cook, stirring frequently, for 5 minutes.

Pour the liquid mixture over the tofu and sauté for 2 minutes.

Baked Marinated Cutlets

Firm tofu is sliced into thin cutlets and marinated in a soy-ginger sauce before baking to a veal-like consistency. A great no-cholesterol recipe for the meat lovers in your family.

Serves 4 to 6.

1 pound firm tofu
3 tablespoons low-sodium soy sauce or tamari
1 tablespoon dark sesame oil
1 tablespoon grated fresh ginger
1 teaspoon raw sesame seeds
1 cup thinly sliced onions
2 cups thinly sliced mushrooms
2 tablespoons olive oil

Cut the tofu into cutlets about ⅓" thick and 3" square.

In a large shallow pan, combine the tofu, soy sauce or tamari, sesame oil, ginger, and sesame seeds. Let marinate at room temperature for 2 hours, turning the slices occasionally.

Preheat the oven to 375°.

Lightly oil a large baking sheet. Place the tofu pieces on the sheet and bake for 15 minutes, flipping the pieces after 7 minutes. If desired, brush the pieces with leftover marinade once or twice as they bake.

While the tofu is baking, in a large frying pan over medium-high heat, sauté the onions and mushrooms in the olive oil until the mushrooms exude moisture, about 15 minutes. Serve hot over the tofu.

VEGETARIAN SWEET-AND-SOUR TOFU

    1 cup diced green peppers
    1 cup diced sweet red peppers
    2 tablespoons safflower oil
    2 tablespoons arrowroot powder
 ¼ cup low-sodium soy sauce or tamari
 ½ cup apple cider vinegar
 ½ cup pineapple juice
 ½ cup lemon juice
¼–½ cup honey
 ½ teaspoon herbal salt substitute
 ½ teaspoon grated fresh ginger
    8 ounces firm tofu, cut into 1″ cubes
 ½ cup pineapple chunks
    4 cups hot cooked basmati rice

In a large frying pan over medium-high heat, sauté the green and red peppers in the oil for 10 minutes, stirring frequently to prevent browning.

In a large bowl, dissolve the arrowroot in the soy sauce or tamari. Add the vinegar, pineapple juice, lemon juice, honey, salt substitute, and ginger.

Add the liquids to the pan and bring to a boil. Simmer until the sauce thickens, about 8 to 10 minutes. Add the tofu and pineapple. Heat through. Serve over the rice.

Chunks of firm tofu are paired with bell peppers, pineapple, and onions in a sweet-and-sour sauce that tastes like it's right off your favorite Chinese restaurant menu.

Serves 4.

Mock Tuna Salad

14 ounces firm tofu
½ cup cholesterol-free mayonnaise
½ cup chopped celery
⅓ cup nutritional yeast
1 scallion, chopped
1 tablespoon lemon juice
1 tablespoon low-sodium soy sauce or tamari
1 teaspoon herbal salt substitute
½ teaspoon minced garlic

Crumble the tofu into a colander placed over a bowl. Let drain for 15 minutes. Transfer the tofu to a large bowl.

Add the mayonnaise, celery, yeast, scallions, lemon juice, soy sauce or tamari, salt substitute, and garlic. Mix well. Chill for 1 hour.

In this recipe our chameleon friend turns into tuna salad with the help of subtle seasonings—nutritional yeast, onions, and lemon—which fool the palate with a mock fish flavor. Serve this salad on crackers or bread.

Serves 4 to 6.

Dairyless Spinach Tarts

1 Light and Flaky No-Cholesterol Piecrust (page 226), unbaked
1 cup thinly sliced onions
2 tablespoons safflower oil
3 cups chopped spinach
2 cups thinly sliced mushrooms
2 cloves garlic, minced
3 cups firm tofu, mashed or pureed
½ cup chopped fresh parsley
2 tablespoons dried dill
2 tablespoons low-sodium soy sauce or tamari

Preheat the oven to 350°.

Bake the crust for 10 minutes. Remove from the oven and let cool for 10 minutes. Keep the oven hot.

While the crust is baking, in a large frying pan over medium-high heat, sauté the onions in the oil for 10 minutes, stirring frequently to prevent browning.

Lower the heat to medium, then add the spinach, mushrooms, and garlic. Sauté for 10 minutes, stirring

Who says you have to give up quiche on a no-cholesterol diet? This savory pie is made with creamy tofu, spinach, and spices. Enjoy it warm or cold with a green salad.

Serves 6 to 8.

frequently, until the mushrooms exude moisture. Add the tofu, parsley, dill, and soy sauce or tamari. Remove from the heat and pour into the baked pie shell.

Bake for 30 minutes, or until the top is browned.

Tempting Tempeh

Always a prime ingredient in Indonesian kitchens, tempeh has made significant inroads in American cuisine as well. Tempeh gives you cholesterol-free protein and plenty of vitamins and minerals—one reason it's become a popular substitute for meat.

BARBECUED VEGETARIAN BURGERS

16 ounces soy tempeh
 2 cups low-calorie Russian dressing
 1 cup medium-hot Mexican salsa
 8 whole wheat hamburger buns
    lettuce
    sprouts
    red onion rings

Tempeh is slowly baked in a zesty, homemade barbecue sauce, piled into whole wheat buns and topped with all the traditional hamburger trimmings. Serve with potato salad or coleslaw.

Serves 8.

Preheat the oven to 200°.

Cut the tempeh into 8 equal pieces. Cover a large baking sheet with aluminum foil and add the tempeh in a single layer.

In a small bowl, combine the dressing and salsa. Spread half of the sauce liberally over the tempeh.

Bake for 30 minutes. Flip the pieces, spread with the remaining sauce and bake for 30 minutes, or until the sauce thickens and sticks to the tempeh.

Warm the buns in the oven for 5 minutes. Fill each with a piece of tempeh. Top with lettuce, sprouts, and onions.

Dilled Party Spread

6-8 ounces soy tempeh, cut into ½″ cubes
1 teaspoon safflower oil
2 tablespoons low-sodium soy sauce or tamari
¼ cup minced celery
¼ cup chopped black olives (optional)
3 tablespoons cholesterol-free mayonnaise
2 tablespoons minced fresh parsley
1 tablespoon minced scallions
½ teaspoon minced fresh dill
pinch of ground red pepper

Steam the tempeh over boiling water for 15 minutes. Drain.

In a large frying pan, sauté the tempeh in the oil for 3 minutes, or until lightly browned. Remove the pan from the heat. Add the soy sauce or tamari, stir to coat the tempeh, then mash with a fork. Transfer to a large bowl.

Add the celery, olives (if using), mayonnaise, parsley, scallions, dill, and pepper.

When I served this spread at a fancy party, I drew plenty of recipe requests for the "fabulous chicken salad." It does taste like a deli salad and is delicious as sandwich filler or spread. Or serve it on whole grain crackers or with raw vegetable sticks.

Serves 4 to 6.

French Mushroom Salad with Tempeh

8 ounces soy tempeh
2 teaspoons olive oil
2 cups chopped Romaine lettuce
1 cup thinly sliced mushrooms
½ cup diagonally sliced green beans
½ cup thinly sliced cucumbers
¼ cup safflower oil
¼ cup tomato juice
¼ cup lemon juice
1 teaspoon Dijon mustard
½ teaspoon herbal salt substitute

Steamed tempeh is thinly sliced and then marinated in a mustardy French vinaigrette dressing. Combined with mushrooms and other fresh vegetables, it makes an elegant light meal or high-protein side dish.

Serves 4.

Steam the tempeh over boiling water for 20 minutes. Let cool, then slice into ½″ cubes.

In a large frying pan over medium-high heat, sauté the tempeh in the olive oil, turning once, for 5 minutes, or until lightly browned. Set aside.

Place the lettuce on a large platter or in a salad bowl. Top with the tempeh, mushrooms, beans, and cucumbers.

In a small bowl, combine the safflower oil, tomato juice, lemon juice, mustard, and salt substitute. Pour over the salad and let marinate at room temperature for 30 minutes. Toss well before serving.

Wheat Berry and Tempeh Salad with Curry Dressing

6 ounces 5-grain tempeh, cut into thin strips
2 cups cooked wheat berries
½ cup halved cherry tomatoes
⅓ cup thinly sliced radishes
⅓ cup diagonally sliced green beans
½ cup thinly sliced cucumbers
¼ cup cholesterol-free mayonnaise
¼ cup nonfat yogurt
3 tablespoons minced fresh parsley
2 tablespoons minced onions or shallots
1 teaspoon curry powder
½ teaspoon lemon juice
¼ teaspoon salt (optional)

Serve this exotic recipe as a side dish to Thai or Vietnamese entrées. Buy wheat berries in the health-food store and cook them like brown rice.

Serves 4.

Steam the tempeh over boiling water for 15 minutes. Drain and place in a large bowl.

Add the wheat berries, tomatoes, radishes, beans, cucumbers, mayonnaise, yogurt, parsley, onions or shallots, curry powder, lemon juice, and salt (if using). Toss well and let marinate at room temperature for 20 minutes before serving.

SPICY INDONESIAN CUTLETS WITH PEANUT SAUCE

An authentic Indonesian recipe, perfect for friends or family members who love spicy food.

Serves 4.

Cutlets

8 ounces soy tempeh, cut into 3″ squares
¾ cup water
2 tablespoons low-sodium soy sauce or tamari
2 tablespoons grated fresh ginger
1 tablespoon minced fresh cilantro
1 teaspoon minced garlic
¼ teaspoon ground red pepper
½ cup coarse cornmeal
½ cup whole wheat pastry flour
1 teaspoon dried basil
½ teaspoon dried oregano
¼ teaspoon curry powder
2 teaspoons safflower oil

Peanut Sauce

¼ cup peanut butter
3 tablespoons low-sodium soy sauce or tamari
1 tablespoon rice wine vinegar
1 tablespoon honey
1 teaspoon ground cumin
1 teaspoon ground coriander

To make the cutlets: In a large shallow baking dish, combine the tempeh, water, soy sauce or tamari, ginger, cilantro, garlic, and pepper. Let marinate at room temperature for 1 hour, turning frequently. Remove from the marinade with a slotted spoon.

In a small bowl or flat plate, combine the cornmeal, flour, basil, oregano, and curry powder. Dredge the tempeh in the mixture, coating well.

In a large frying pan over medium-high heat, fry the tempeh in the oil for 5 to 10 minutes, turning once, until golden brown. Transfer to a platter and keep warm.

To make the peanut sauce: In a 1-quart saucepan, whisk together the peanut butter, soy sauce or tamari, vinegar, honey, cumin, and coriander. Heat through. Pour over the tempeh and serve hot.

ONIONS STUFFED WITH TEMPEH, TOMATOES, AND PEPPERS

4 large sweet onions, such as Vidalia
2 teaspoons olive oil
6 ounces crumbled soy tempeh
2 cups coarsely chopped Italian tomatoes
½ cup diced canned mild chili peppers
⅓ cup diced sweet red peppers
¼ cup raisins
2 tablespoons tomato paste
2 cloves garlic, minced
1 tablespoon apple cider vinegar
1 teaspoon herbal salt substitute
1 teaspoon ground black pepper
¼ teaspoon ground cinnamon
⅛ teaspoon ground cloves
2 cups Garlic Broth (page 113)
¼ cup minced fresh parsley

With a melon baller, scoop the centers out of the onions, leaving a sturdy shell, about ½″ thick. Chop enough of the centers to equal 1 cup. Set aside.

Steam the shells over boiling water for 5 minutes. Drain and set aside.

Preheat the oven to 350°. Lightly oil a 9″ × 13″ baking dish. Place the shells in the dish, hollow sides up.

In a large frying pan over medium-high heat, sauté the chopped onions in the oil for 5 minutes, stirring frequently to prevent browning. Add the tempeh, tomatoes, chili peppers, red peppers, raisins, tomato paste, and garlic. Lower the heat to medium and cook, stirring often, for 15 minutes.

Add the vinegar, salt substitute, black pepper, cinnamon, and cloves. Cook for 5 to 10 minutes, or until most of the liquid has cooked away.

Spoon the filling into the reserved shells. Add the broth to the dish. Cover with foil and bake for 1 hour, or until the onions are very tender. Sprinkle with the parsley before serving.

These sweet onions are filled with a spicy mixture of tempeh, peppers, and tomatoes. Then they're baked, creating a delicious blend of flavors.

Serves 4.

Crumbled tempeh tastes just like ground beef in this mildly spiced vegetarian chili. You can increase the jalapeño peppers and chili powder for hot-food lovers in your family.

Serves 10 to 12.

MEATLESS CHILI WITH CORN CHIPS

1 cup dried kidney beans
8 ounces soy tempeh, crumbled
½ cup red wine
½ cup low-sodium soy sauce or tamari
1 teaspoon ground cumin
1 teaspoon dried basil
1 teaspoon chili powder
1 cup coarsely chopped onions
¼ cup dry sherry
2 tablespoons olive oil
2 cups sliced mushrooms
8 tomatoes, coarsely chopped
1 cup minced green peppers
1 cup minced carrots
1 cup minced celery
½ cup minced canned mild chili peppers
2 tablespoons minced jalapeño peppers
4 cloves garlic, minced
4 cups Vegetable Stock (page 113)
3 tablespoons tomato paste
   herbal salt substitute (to taste)
2 cups crushed corn chips (garnish)

Soak the beans in cold water to cover for 8 hours or overnight. Drain and set aside.

In a large bowl, combine the tempeh, wine, soy sauce or tamari, cumin, basil, and chili powder. Let marinate at room temperature for 2 hours.

Meanwhile, in a 4- to 6-quart pot over medium-high heat, sauté the onions in the sherry and oil for 10 minutes, stirring to prevent browning. Add the mushrooms and cook for 10 minutes, or until the mushrooms exude moisture.

Add the tomatoes, green peppers, carrots, celery, chili peppers, jalapeños, and garlic. Sauté, stirring frequently, for 5 minutes.

Add the beans, stock, and tomato paste. Bring to a boil, cover, and lower the heat. Simmer for 2 to 3 hours, or until the beans are tender and the chili is thick.

Add the tempeh and its marinade. Cook for 10 minutes. Season with salt substitute. Serve garnished with the corn chips.

Rancho Bernadino Salad with Green Sauce

8	ounces soy tempeh
1	tablespoon safflower oil
2	scallions, thinly sliced
3	cups chopped spinach
1	cup thinly sliced cucumbers
1	cup alfalfa sprouts
1	cup chopped romaine lettuce
½	cup sliced celery
¼	cup minced fresh parsley
3	tablespoons olive oil
1	tablespoon rice wine vinegar
1	tablespoon curry powder
2-3	teaspoons herbal salt substitute
2	teaspoons low-sodium soy sauce or tamari

A savory parsley sauce enhances slices of steamed tempeh and fresh vegetables in this Los Angeles favorite—a great salad to take on a beach picnic.

Serves 6.

Steam the tempeh over boiling water for 20 minutes. Let cool, then slice into ½″ cubes.

In a large frying pan over medium-high heat, sauté the tempeh in the safflower oil for 10 minutes, turning the pieces once.

Add the scallions and cook for 2 minutes. Transfer to a large bowl. Add the spinach, cucumbers, sprouts, lettuce, and celery.

In a blender or food processor, puree the parsley, olive oil, vinegar, curry powder, salt substitute, and soy sauce or tamari. Pour over the salad and toss well. Let marinate for 1 hour at room temperature.

CALIFORNIA TEMPEH SPREAD

To me, this is as good as foie gras. I hope you'll agree. With much less fat and none of the cholesterol of traditional pâté, this tasty spread is wonderful on crackers or vegetable spears or as a sandwich filler.

Serves 8.

4 ounces soy tempeh
1/4 cup dry sherry
2 tablespoons safflower oil
2 cups chopped mushrooms
1 cup minced onions
1/2 cup coarsely chopped almonds
1/2 cup walnuts
2 cloves garlic, minced
2 tablespoons herbal salt substitute
1 tablespoon low-sodium soy sauce or tamari
1/4 teaspoon dried thyme
1/8 teaspoon dried sage

Steam the tempeh over boiling water for 20 minutes. Let cool, then slice into 1/2″ cubes.

In a large frying pan over medium-high heat, sauté the tempeh in the sherry and oil for 10 minutes, stirring frequently.

Add the mushrooms, onions, almonds, walnuts, and garlic. Sauté, stirring, for 15 minutes, or until the onions soften. Add the salt substitute, soy sauce or tamari, thyme, and sage.

Transfer the mixture to a food processor. Blend with on/off turns to a thick pastelike consistency.

Cooking with Miso and Tamari

Introduce yourself to miso and tamari gradually, choosing the low-sodium varieties of tamari, or "shoyu" as it is sometimes labeled, and the lighter versions of miso. Remember to blend the miso with hot liquid before adding to soup or sauces. Add both miso and tamari close to serving time to avoid bitter flavors.

Miso Onion Soup

4 large sweet onions, such as Vidalia, thinly sliced
1/4 cup safflower oil
3 cloves elephant garlic, minced
3 tablespoons whole wheat pastry flour or unbleached
     flour
5 cups Garlic Broth (page 113)
5 slices round party-size rye bread
1/2 cup miso
2 teaspoons low-sodium soy sauce or tamari

In a 4-quart saucepan over medium heat, sauté the onions in the oil for 25 minutes, stirring frequently to prevent browning. Add the garlic and cook for 10 minutes. Stir in the flour and cook for 2 minutes, stirring constantly.

Add the broth and increase the heat to medium-high. Bring to a boil, then cover, reduce the heat to low, and simmer for 40 minutes.

Meanwhile, preheat the oven to 250°.

Place the bread in a single layer on a large ungreased baking sheet. Bake for 20 minutes per side, or until crisp. Set aside.

In a small bowl, combine the miso with 1 cup of the hot soup. Remove the soup from the heat and stir in the miso mixture and soy sauce or tamari. Serve hot, topped with the croutons.

> Season your onion soup to perfection with miso and tamari; the secret to this soup is sweet Vidalia onions and elephant garlic. Serve it French-style, with toasted rye croutons.
>
> Serves 5.

Eve's Miso-Tahini Dip

1/4 cup tahini
3 tablespoons rice wine vinegar
2 tablespoons miso
2 tablespoons Vegetable Stock (page 113)
2 teaspoons honey
2 teaspoons dark sesame oil
2 teaspoons low-sodium soy sauce or tamari

In a food processor or blender, puree the tahini, vinegar, miso, stock, honey, oil, and soy sauce or tamari until smooth.

> Tahini, a smooth spread made from sesame seeds, blends with miso into this delicious dip that's equally at home with vegetables or as a sandwich spread.
>
> Serves 4.

Over 16 varieties of miso are made, and 8 are sold commercially. This vegetarian soup uses a red miso and a white miso, which are made from different grains added to the salted soybeans. The broth is also seasoned with *kombu,* a sea vegetable also known as kelp. Dried kombu is available in health-food stores.

Serves 4 to 6.

Sushi bar miso soup

6 cups Vegetable Stock (page 113)
3″ piece of dried kombu
½ cup red miso
½ cup white miso
6 ounces firm tofu, cut into ½″ cubes
1 scallion, minced
1 teaspoon dark sesame oil
   low-sodium soy sauce or tamari (to taste)

In a 3-quart saucepan over medium-high heat, bring the stock and kombu to a boil. Lower the heat to medium-low and simmer for 10 minutes. Remove the kombu and discard.

In a small bowl, mix the red miso, white miso, and 1 cup of the hot stock to form a smooth paste. Add this mixture to the pan. Turn the heat to low. Add the tofu and cook for 1 minute.

Remove the pan from the heat. Stir in the scallions, oil, and soy sauce or tamari.

A friend's favorite topping for steamed vegetables.

Serves 4.

John's special sauce for vegetables

3 tablespoons lemon juice
2 tablespoons red miso
1 tablespoon dry sherry
1 tablespoon tahini
1 teaspoon grated fresh ginger
1 teaspoon minced garlic
1 teaspoon honey

In a small bowl, combine the lemon juice, miso, sherry, tahini, ginger, garlic, and honey. Pour over steamed vegetables and toss to combine.

CHAPTER 10

BREADS

Oven-Fresh

In the minds of many people, bread baking is tantamount to needlepoint or knitting—an activity reserved solely for grandmothers with nothing else to do and lots of time on their hands. 'Tain't necessarily so. Bread baking can be an ageless and soothing retreat—an island of serenity for anyone caught in the white water rapids of modern life.

My cousin Gill taught me to bake bread—using a woodstove—when I was a mere stripling of 12. Gill, it turned out, had learned the art from (who else?) our grandmother, who made a loaf of whole wheat every Wednesday of her life. A special mill in the northwoods country ground grain while Grandma waited, and she drove there every week to pick some up.

Sometimes she let Gill stir the dough; always Gill watched, amazed that the flaccid lump in the bowl could turn into something as savory and steamy as the slices she served for dinner. (My grandmother's recipe for whole wheat bread, Wednesday Bread, is on page 211.)

Gill could produce loaves that were so perfect and identical it seemed as if they were popped out of a mold or had the same chromosomes. She even ground the grain herself when necessary. For my first lesson, Gill handed me a tattered copy of her primer, *The Tassajara Bread Book* by Edward Espe Brown, and we started in on a batch of oatmeal bread.

Gill informed me that there was really no secret to bread baking except nurturing the yeast. In her eyes, yeast granules were like puppies. If you fed them properly and provided a warm environment and a little TLC, they would grow into the beautiful "show-dog" loaves for which she was well known. Years later, bread is also my signature item. I arrive at dinner parties or potlucks proudly bearing a loaf—still hot from the oven and effusing wonderful aromas—wrapped preciously in a swaddling cloth.

Unless you cook with a woodstove, you won't have to overcome the same obstacles as I did, not that I am trying to impress you with my frontier fortitude. I simply want to point out that if a 12-year-old rookie can bake bread using Pleistocene Age equipment, you can succeed in a modern kitchen.

Bread baking is a boon to any no-cholesterol dieter. Whole grain bread, for example, turns out quite well without eggs or dairy products and is full of insoluble fiber, which is beneficial for colon health. All in all, a loaf of homemade bread is a staple that rounds out the squarest of menu plans. The old saying about paradise being "a loaf of bread, a jug of wine, and thou" is not far from the truth. Paired with a salad and a simple dessert, a wholesome loaf of fresh bread can be the centerpiece of many a meal in your house.

"Ahem, this is all very nice," you may be saying, "but you still haven't explained where I'm going to find the time for all this bread baking. Few people have an entire morning to set aside for baking *anything*."

Well, sometimes neither do I. Which is why I've developed a method of overnight rising for most of the yeast breads in this chapter, *saving you about 3 hours of kitchen time*. The idea is to divide your bread-baking sessions in two: In the evening, you prepare the dough and pack it away in the fridge. The next day, you assemble and bake the loaves. (See "Bread Baking on a Busy Schedule" on page 197 for details.) To make your bread baking even quicker, you can use the new quick-rising yeasts available in supermarkets and health-food stores.

Now that you have a little confidence that you, too, can master bread baking, we can go on. But before you open your own bakery, a few important concepts must be addressed: First, you must understand the chemistry of your leavening ingredients.

Yeast: Don't Leaven Bread without It

One way of classifying breads is according to their rising methods. *Yeasted breads* are usually made with baker's yeast and a combination of flours, liquids, and sweetener, plus any number of extra flavorings and seasonings. Baker's yeast is most commonly sold as little packets of active dry yeast. But it also comes in small cakes of compressed fresh yeast, which tends to be more perishable.

When yeast is mixed with warm water and a little honey, maple syrup, or other sweetener, it produces small bubbles of carbon dioxide (CO_2). As it "proofs," it digests the sugar in the sweetener. Once added to the flour, the proofed yeast works hand in hand with the gluten, or protein, in the flour. When you knead or stir a bread dough, the gluten is developed into long strands. Yeast ingests the starch in flour and emits CO_2; the little bubbles of CO_2 push against the rubbery threads of gluten and expand them. Voilà, the bread rises. As long as you provide your yeast with warmth and good food, it will rise like the sun. I often add a little bit of salt to certain bread recipes because it keeps the yeast from working too fast and overraising the dough.

Fitting this slow-paced, satisfying activity into a fast-paced, 1990s life-style is no easy chore, but it can be done. Yeasted breads take about three to five hours total time, from mixing bowl to finished loaf. But most of this time—about four of those five hours—the dough is rising by itself in a corner. I try to plan bread making for a rainy Saturday afternoon, when I'm going to be home anyway. And I usually make double batches of bread each time; most breads freeze beautifully.

Sourdough breads also use yeast to make dough rise, but the technique is different. Yeast, water, and flour are combined, then allowed to ferment just like beer or wine over a period of weeks or months. A portion of this starter or "mother culture"—about 1 to 2 cups—is used per loaf of bread. It takes about six months to develop a truly sour culture.

Quick breads are the simplest to bake because baking powder and baking soda, not yeast, create the rise, so there's no need for the kneading or lengthy

SOURDOUGH STARTER

If you'd like to try your hand at making sourdough, here's a basic recipe.

BASIC SOURDOUGH STARTER

2 cups rye or whole wheat flour
1½ cups warm water (98°–110°)
1 tablespoon active dry yeast

In a 2- to 3-quart bowl, combine the flour, water, and yeast. Stir well to dissolve the yeast and make a smooth batter. Cover the bowl with a dish towel and place it in a warm spot for 1 day. It's important that the temperature be moderate (68° to 75°); if it's too hot, the starter may mold. On the morning of the second day, stir the starter with a wooden spoon. Let stand for 2 more days.

The first day the starter will foam and come close to overflowing the bowl. The second day it will begin to recede and turn dark brown. The third day it will separate into a watery liquid and a thick mass. The starter is ready to refrigerate at this point.

Pour it into a quart jar and cap tightly. Refrigerate for 6 days.

Remove 1 cup of the starter and replace with ½ cup rye or whole wheat flour and ½ cup water. (You can use this cupful of starter for a bread recipe or just discard it.) Stir well, let the jar stand at room temperature overnight and then refrigerate again. This is called "replenishing the starter."

If you repeat this process every week, the sourdough will begin to taste truly sour after about 6 months, and you will be able to use it in your recipes for years. Simply replenish according to the ratios given above: equal parts flour and water. It's not necessary to add any more yeast.

rising time that yeasted breads demand. That means you can turn out a loaf of quick bread in about 1½ hours versus three to five hours for yeasted bread. There's only one drawback: Quick breads usually depend on fat- and cholesterol-rich foods, such as milk, egg yolks, and butter, to rise high. Although I've managed to create some wonderful recipes for cholesterol-free quick breads, you have much more versatility with yeasted breads on a no-cholesterol diet.

Much like yeast, baking powder and baking soda react with the liquid in the batter to create CO_2 bubbles that cause the batter to rise. Ideally, this process occurs while your bread is in the oven, where the heat will hold the rise created by the bubbles. That way your finished loaf will be light and airy. If the baking powder and baking soda react in the bowl *before* the batter gets to the oven, the bread will not rise as well. In fact, it may turn out so heavy you'll have to cart it away in a wheelbarrow.

You can avoid this problem by following several guidelines: Always preheat your oven. Ready your loaf pan (by oiling it or coating it with no-stick spray) before mixing the batter. Mix the wet ingredients in one bowl and the dry ones in another bowl. Combine the two, then *immediately* pour the batter into the pan and whisk it into the hot oven.

Sponging Off the Host

Every baker has a favorite method for combining ingredients and kneading dough. In most methods, you mix everything simultaneously, which works just fine for doughs lightened with white flour, eggs, and buttermilk. But whole grain, cholesterol-free breads demand a different treatment because you can't rely on featherlight ingredients such as white flour and sugar. Whole wheat flour is simply heavier than white.

But, not to worry—the *sponge method* will save you. With this old-fashioned technique, you add one extra step: You let the yeast, water, sweetener, and half of the flour rise as a batter in a warm place for 30 minutes before adding the rest of the ingredients. This head start allows the yeast to grow fast and make more bubbles, which in turn makes the bread rise higher. Yeast can flourish in this lightweight solution without other ingredients (salt, oil, and the full amount of flour) to slow it down. The gluten strands become longer and more elastic—in baker's lingo, this means a more stable and higher-rising dough.

The name "sponge method" derives from the appearance of the dough after its initial (batter) rising. When you pull a wooden spoon through the batter, the exposed trough looks like a cut sponge, full of holes made by the yeast as it bubbled.

Because all the yeasted bread recipes in this chapter use the sponge method, you might try one of them to get the hang of the method before applying the technique to your favorite bread recipes. Here's the process in a nutshell.

1. Proof the yeast by dissolving it in a bowl with the warm water or other liquid (whatever your recipe calls for) and sweetener. The yeast should lightly foam or bubble within 10 minutes.
2. Stir in half of the flour and let the mixture stand for 30 minutes to rise as a batter.
3. Add the oil, salt (if using), and other seasonings. Then stir in enough of the remaining flour to make a firm, kneadable dough.
4. Lightly flour a bread board or kitchen counter, turn the dough onto the surface and knead it for 8 to 10 minutes, or until the dough is no longer sticky and feels elastic.
5. Place the dough in a clean, lightly oiled bowl. Turn the dough to lightly coat it on all sides with oil. Cover the bowl with a clean dish towel and set it in a warm, draft-free spot. Let the dough rise for 45 minutes.
6. Punch the air out of the dough with your fist. This step is important: As the yeast rises in the dough, the CO_2 bubbles become trapped and begin to suffocate the yeast. As the yeast die, they give off an alcoholic odor that affects the taste of your bread. If you punch the dough three times with your fist, you'll hear an expulsion of air and the dough will deflate, releasing the trapped CO_2. Now flip the dough, cover the bowl with the towel again, and let the dough rise for 30 minutes.
7. Coat your baking pans with no-stick spray or a little oil. Form the dough into loaves, place the loaves in their pans and let them rise for 10 to 20 minutes. (If you're making free-form loaves—round ones or baguettes, for example—they don't actually need extra rising at this time, although it wouldn't harm them.)
8. During the last few minutes of the final rising time, preheat the oven. Bake the bread for the length of time specified in the recipe.

You'll notice that the sponge method does not change the total rising time. It merely separates the rising into two short periods rather than one long. Because you're providing the yeast with such a congenial atmosphere, it grows faster. The same is true for the gluten strands, which develop longer and are more elastic. Over the years, I've found that I don't have to knead as much for the same reason.

We All Knead the Dough

Kneading is the most physically satisfying part of bread baking, the step where you can really "get your hands into it." Though some bread cookbooks devote whole chapters to the topic, I'll try to condense it for you in this one.

Kneading is like a massage for the bread dough. As you knead, you push and pull the developing gluten strands, stretching them like muscles. Long, elastic gluten strands seem to produce lighter loaves than short stubby strands.

Using our sponge method, you convert the initial batter into a dough by adding oil, seasonings and only enough of the remaining flour to make a kneadable mass. Many beginning bakers overflour the dough at this stage, producing heavy bread. So you should add flour by half-cupfuls until the dough is firm enough to work with your hands. You'll know you've reached this stage when you can no longer easily stir the dough with your wooden spoon.

To begin kneading, prepare your counter or bread board by lightly sprinkling it with flour. Then place the dough on the board. This is a good time to wash your hands so that they won't stick to the dough and to wash the bowl so that you have a clean place to put the dough after it is kneaded. Then, lightly dust your hands with flour. Essentially, kneading comprises four steps.

1. Sprinkle flour on the dough.
2. Flatten the ball of dough into a pancake shape—any size, just so it's about 1/2″ thick and fairly flat.
3. Fold the pancake in half.
4. Repeat the process.

Experienced bread bakers get into a rhythm with these steps. As the gluten strands elongate, the amount of starch decreases and the dough becomes less sticky—hopefully you will not have to sprinkle on more flour before each kneading cycle. You'll feel the dough getting more elastic and smooth in texture. When you press the dough and it bounces back completely, it is ready to put back into the bowl and let rise. The sponge method shortcuts the entire kneading; it usually takes about 8 to 10 minutes, but experienced sponge-method bakers can get away with 5.

Getting a Rise
out of Your Bread

As the dough rises, some bakers take the opportunity to loaf (so to speak), but you can use the time wisely by preparing your pans or baking sheets (coat them with no-stick spray or oil—I like to use safflower oil) and setting them near the dough.

In all bread-baking recipes, sponge method or not, the yeasted dough rises twice and gets punched down between the two stages. When it has completed these stages, it is ready to be formed into loaves. Using a sharp knife, divide the dough into equal sections according to the number of loaves yielded by your recipe. Lightly flour your work surface again. Flatten each ball of dough into a rectangle, then roll it into a tight cylinder. It's important to roll tightly enough to expel any air bubbles, preventing the loaf from separating in the oven.

Pinch along the seam of your cylinder and then fold the two ends under and pinch them, too. Place the roll, seam side down, in the prepared loaf pan or on the baking sheet. Let the loaf rise for 15 to 20 minutes to develop its shape, then bake it.

Your loaves are completely baked when they begin to recede from the sides of the pan and sound hollow when tapped on the top. Remove from the pan and let them cool on a wire rack before slicing.

BREAD BAKING
ON A BUSY SCHEDULE

One way to make yeast breads fit *your* schedule is to control the rising time. Although it's difficult to speed up the process, you can easily slow it down to accommodate your needs. A cool environment considerably slows the yeast's growth and extends the rising time. Placing the dough in the refrigerator overnight, for example, can lengthen the rising time by 6 hours. (And that's time you can use to your advantage, spelled s-l-e-e-p.) Because an hour of working time is needed the next morning, this shortcut method is ideal for starting on a Friday or Saturday night. You can also use this method to start a loaf in the morning and then finish it late in the day. Here are the steps.

1. Prepare your recipe through the sponge stage. Knead the dough and place it in a clean bowl.
2. Cover the bowl with a clean dish towel. On top of the towel place a tray, then a weight, such as a phone book. This will keep the dough from rising over the sides of the bowl.
3. Place the bowl in the refrigerator. Instead of being ready to punch down in 1½ hours, it can be left for 8 to 10 hours in the refrigerator without needing to worry about it.
4. When you are ready to proceed, take the bowl out of the refrigerator. Punch down the dough and let it stand at room temperature to warm up. It should be ready to form into loaves and bake within an hour.

Yeasted Breakfast Breads

Homemade breakfast breads supply an early dose of protein, fiber, and other nutrients to get you through a busy morning. The following recipes were chosen for their ease of slicing and toasting.

This recipe comes from a
Czech friend, although
I've reduced the fat con-
tent considerably. This
bread is wonderful for
morning coffee breaks.

Makes 1 roll; 16 slices.

Walnut Poteca

2 cups warm water (98°–110°)
½ cup honey
1 tablespoon active dry yeast
5–6 cups unbleached or whole wheat pastry flour
2 tablespoons safflower oil
1½ cups date sugar
1 cup ground walnuts
½ cup raisins
¼ cup maple syrup

In a large bowl, combine the water, honey, and yeast.
Let stand in a warm place until the mixture foams, about 10
minutes. Stir in 2 cups of the flour, mixing well with a
wooden spoon. Let this batter rise in a warm place for 30
minutes. Stir in the oil and enough of the remaining flour to
form a kneadable dough.

Turn onto a lightly floured surface and knead for 5 to 8
minutes, or until the dough becomes elastic and less sticky.
Place in a clean, lightly oiled bowl. Cover and let rise in a
warm, draft-free place for 1 hour. Punch down and let rise
again for 30 minutes.

While the dough is rising, in a medium bowl combine
the date sugar, walnuts, and raisins.

Lightly oil a large baking sheet.

Roll the dough into a large rectangle, about 8″ × 12″.

In a 1-quart saucepan, warm the maple syrup for 1 to 2
minutes. Brush it over the dough. Sprinkle with the walnut
mixture, leaving a scant ½″ border all the way around. Roll
up, starting with a short edge; the finished roll will measure
about 8″ long × 3″ wide. Place, seam side down, on the
baking sheet. With a sharp knife, cut 3 diagonal slits about
¼″ deep in the top of the roll for steam to escape. Let rise 10
minutes.

Preheat the oven to 375°.

Bake the roll for 30 to 45 minutes, or until golden. Cut
into slices and serve warm.

Minnesota Christmas Stollen

½ cup warm water (98°–110°)
¼ cup maple syrup
2 tablespoons active dry yeast
2 cups unbleached flour
1 cup chopped dried fruit (such as raisins, apricots, prunes, or dates)
¼ cup finely chopped almonds
3 tablespoons safflower oil
1 tablespoon ground cardamom
1½ cups whole wheat flour
2 tablespoons poppy seeds

In a large bowl, combine the water, maple syrup, and yeast. Let stand in a warm place until the mixture foams, about 10 minutes. Stir in the unbleached flour, mixing well with a wooden spoon. Let this batter rise in a warm place for 30 minutes.

Stir in the fruit, almonds, oil, and cardamom. Add enough of the whole wheat flour to form a workable dough.

Turn the dough out onto a lightly floured surface and knead for 5 to 8 minutes, or until the dough becomes elastic and less sticky. Place in a clean, lightly oiled bowl. Cover and let rise in a warm, draft-free place for 1 hour. Punch down and let rise again for 30 minutes.

Preheat the oven to 350°.

Lightly oil a large baking sheet. Divide the dough in thirds. With your hands, roll each piece into a rope about 12″ to 14″ long. Place the ropes on the counter parallel to each other. Braid into a fat loaf. Pinch the ends together and tuck them under. Transfer the loaf to the baking sheet.

Lightly brush the top of the loaf with a little water. Sprinkle with the poppy seeds.

Bake for 45 minutes, or until the loaf is golden and sounds slightly hollow when tapped on the top. Let cool on a wire rack before slicing.

Stollen is a Scandinavian and German treat—a sweet torpedo-shaped loaf studded with raisins, nuts, and candied orange peel. The cardamom-seed flavoring is the signature ingredient of traditional stollen. Every Christmas Eve, my father would buy a loaf at a German bakery and we would devour it Christmas morning. You can make this into a traditional braided bread, or simply form it into a round loaf.

Makes 1 large loaf; about 10 slices.

Commercial bakeries are discovering the benefits —financial and otherwise —of adding oat bran to English muffins. It makes the muffins chewier and richer tasting, as well as healthier. Here's my favorite recipe for Saturday morning breakfast.

Makes 14 muffins.

ENGLISH MUFFINS WITH OAT BRAN

1¼ cups warm water (98°–110°)
1 tablespoon active dry yeast
1 tablespoon honey
4–5 cups unbleached or whole wheat flour
3 tablespoons farina
3 tablespoons oat bran
2 tablespoons olive oil
1 tablespoon herbal salt substitute
½ cup coarse cornmeal

In a large bowl, combine the water, yeast, and honey. Let stand in a warm place until the mixture foams, about 10 minutes. Stir in 1 cup of the flour, mixing well with a wooden spoon. Let this batter rise in a warm place for 30 minutes. Stir in the farina, oat bran, oil, salt substitute, and enough of the remaining flour to form a kneadable dough.

Turn onto a lightly floured surface and knead for 5 to 8 minutes, or until the dough becomes elastic and less sticky. Place in a clean, lightly oiled bowl. Cover and let rise in a warm, draft-free place for 1 hour. Punch down.

Halve the dough, roll out each half ¼″ thick on a lightly floured surface. Cut using a 3″ biscuit cutter. Lightly dredge each round in the cornmeal to coat both sides. Set the rounds on a piece of plastic and let rise for 30 minutes.

Heat a griddle or cast-iron skillet over medium-high heat until hot. Using a metal spatula, transfer several of the muffins to the pan and cook for 3 minutes on each side until lightly set and pale in color. Transfer to a wire rack. Repeat until all the muffins have received a preliminary cooking.

Again working in batches, return the muffins to the pan and cook for 5 minutes more on each side, or until they are golden brown on both sides and cooked through.

To serve, split with a fork and toast as desired.

ALMOND-CHIVE BREAD

1 tablespoon active dry yeast
1 tablespoon honey
1 cup warm water (98°–110°)
½ cup chopped almonds
1 cup whole wheat pastry flour
2 cups unbleached flour
2 tablespoons minced fresh chives
1½ teaspoons herbal salt substitute

In a large bowl, combine the yeast, honey, and ½ cup of the water. Let the bowl stand in a warm spot until the yeast mixture bubbles, about 10 minutes.

In a blender, combine the almonds and remaining ½ cup of water. Puree, then strain through a fine sieve. Add the liquid to the yeast mixture; reserve the solids.

Stir the pastry flour and ½ cup of the unbleached flour into the yeast mixture. Mix well with a wooden spoon. Let this batter rise in a warm place for 30 minutes.

Stir in the reserved almonds, chives, salt substitute, and enough of the remaining flour to form a kneadable dough.

Turn onto a lightly floured surface and knead for 5 to 8 minutes, or until the dough becomes elastic and less sticky. Place in a clean, lightly oiled bowl. Cover and let rise in a warm, draft-free place for 1 hour. Punch down and let rise again for 30 minutes.

Preheat the oven to 350°.

Lightly oil a large baking sheet. Form a large round loaf from the dough and place in the center of the sheet.

Bake for 45 to 60 minutes, or until the loaf is golden and sounds slightly hollow when you tap it on the top. Transfer to a wire rack to cool before slicing.

Almonds ground with water to a milky liquid take the place of milk in this recipe and make an equally milk-light (and cholesterol-free) loaf. Fresh chives sprinkled throughout the batter give this bread color and an onion flavor.

Makes 1 large loaf; 12 to 15 slices.

I generally slice this bread very thinly. It's especially good at parties, topped with California Tempeh Spread (page 186).

Makes 2 loaves; about 20 very thin slices.

Dark Rye with Molasses

1½ cups warm water (98°-110°)
2 tablespoons molasses
2 tablespoons honey
1 tablespoon active dry yeast
3-4 cups whole wheat flour
1½ cups dark rye flour
2 tablespoons minced garlic
2 tablespoons olive oil
1 tablespoon ground caraway
1 tablespoon dried sage

In a large bowl, combine the water, molasses, honey, and yeast. Let stand in a warm place until the mixture foams, about 10 minutes.

Stir in 2 cups of the whole wheat flour, mixing well with a wooden spoon. Let this batter rise in a warm place for 30 minutes. Stir in the rye flour, garlic, oil, caraway, sage, and enough of the remaining whole wheat flour to form a kneadable dough.

Turn onto a lightly floured surface and knead for 8 to 10 minutes, or until the dough becomes elastic and less sticky. Place in a clean, lightly oiled bowl. Cover and let rise in a warm, draft-free place for 1 hour.

Lightly oil a large baking sheet. Divide the dough into two equal balls and form each ball into a round. Let rise for 30 minutes.

Preheat the oven to 350°.

Bake the loaves for 45 to 60 minutes, or until they sound slightly hollow when you tap them on the top. Let cool before slicing.

Lunch Sandwich Breads

These breads will complement any sandwich filling, and you can even toast them for croutons to sprinkle over lunchtime soups. They are more savory and less rich than the dinner breads that follow in "Family Dinner Breads."

ITALIAN TOMATO-HERB BREAD

3 cups warm water (98°–110°)
2 tablespoons honey
1 tablespoon active dry yeast
6-7 cups whole wheat flour
½ cup oil-packed sun-dried tomatoes, drained and diced
¼ cup olive oil
1 tablespoon tomato paste
2 teaspoons herbal salt substitute

Sun-dried tomatoes give these loaves a rosy color and—paired with the olive oil—a distinct Mediterranean flavor.

Makes 2 loaves; about 20 slices.

In a large bowl, combine the water, honey, and yeast. Let stand in a warm place until the mixture foams, about 10 minutes. Stir in 2 cups of the flour, mixing well with a wooden spoon. Let this batter rise in a warm place for 30 minutes.

Stir in the tomatoes, oil, tomato paste, salt substitute, and enough flour to form a kneadable dough.

Turn onto a lightly floured surface and knead for 5 to 8 minutes, or until the dough becomes elastic and less sticky. Place in a clean, lightly oiled bowl. Cover and let rise in a warm, draft-free place for 1 hour. Punch down and let rise again for 30 minutes.

Lightly oil 2 (9″ × 5″) loaf pans. Divide the dough in half, form each half into a loaf, and place in the pans. Let rise for 20 minutes.

Preheat the oven to 375°.

Bake the loaves for 40 minutes, or until lightly browned. Turn out onto wire racks and let cool before slicing.

I've treasured this recipe since my first bread-baking lesson with cousin Gill. The oatmeal contributes soluble fiber—a benefit in reducing blood cholesterol levels—and a wonderfully smooth texture to each bite.

Makes 2 loaves; about 20 slices.

OATMEAL-RAISIN BREAD

    1 cup warm water (98°–110°)
 1/2 cup molasses
    2 tablespoons active dry yeast
 5-6 cups whole wheat flour
    2 cups boiling water
    1 cup rolled oats
    1 cup raisins
 1/2 teaspoon salt
 1/4 teaspoon grated fresh ginger

In a large bowl, combine the warm water, molasses, and yeast. Let stand in warm place until the mixture foams, about 10 minutes. Stir in 2 cups of the flour, mixing well with a wooden spoon. Let this batter rise in a warm place for 30 minutes.

Meanwhile, in a small bowl, combine the boiling water and oats. Let stand until lukewarm, about 20 minutes.

Stir the oats into the yeast mixture. Add the raisins, salt, and ginger. Stir in enough of the remaining flour to form a kneadable dough.

Turn onto a lightly floured surface and knead for 5 to 8 minutes, or until the dough becomes elastic and less sticky. Place in a clean, lightly oiled bowl. Cover and let rise in a warm, draft-free place for 1 hour. Punch down and let rise again for 30 minutes.

Lightly oil 2 large baking sheets. Divide the dough in half. Form each half into a smooth ball. Place 1 ball in the center of each baking sheet. Let rise for 20 minutes.

Preheat the oven to 375°.

Bake the loaves for 40 to 45 minutes, or until the loaves sound hollow when tapped on the bottom.

ALFALFA SPROUT BREAD

    2 small baking potatoes, chopped
    4 cups water
    ¾ cup honey
    2 tablespoons active dry yeast
8-10 cups whole wheat flour
    4 cups alfalfa sprouts
    ¼ cup olive oil
    ½ teaspoon salt or 1½ tablespoons herbal salt substitute

In a 2-quart saucepan over medium-high heat, cook the potatoes in the water until soft, about 10 to 15 minutes. Let cool for 5 minutes. Transfer the potatoes and water to a blender and puree.

Pour into a large bowl and let stand until lukewarm (98° to 110°). Add the honey and yeast. Let stand for 10 minutes.

Stir in 4 cups of the flour. Mix well, then let rise for 30 minutes. Stir in the sprouts, oil, salt or salt substitute, and enough of the remaining flour to form a kneadable dough. Turn onto a lightly floured surface and knead for 5 to 8 minutes, or until the dough becomes elastic and less sticky.

Place in a clean, lightly oiled bowl. Cover and let rise in a warm, draft-free place for 1 hour. Punch down and let rise again for 30 minutes.

Lightly oil 3 (9″ × 5″) loaf pans. Divide the dough into 3 equal balls and form into loaves. Place in the pans. Let rise for 15 to 20 minutes.

Preheat the oven to 350°.

Bake for 45 to 55 minutes, or until the loaves are golden and sound slightly hollow when tapped on the top. Turn out onto wire racks and let cool before slicing.

Potatoes—cooked and blended into a thick puree—give this old-fashioned recipe a wonderfully light texture. The sprouts are a 1990s addition for extra greenery and flavor.

Makes 3 loaves; about 30 slices.

A flat Italian bread, focaccia is all the rage in upscale restaurants these days. Instead of being formed into a high, rounded loaf, focaccia is pancake shaped, often baked on baking sheets or pizza tiles. Even if you don't have a traditional brick oven, you can make focaccia at home. This version is flavored with marjoram, dill, and oregano, but you can try other herbs and flavorings.

Makes about 8 to 10 pieces.

Focaccia

  ½ cup warm water (98°–110°)
  1 tablespoon active dry yeast
  1 teaspoon honey
2-3 cups unbleached or whole wheat pastry flour
  ½ teaspoon salt or 1 teaspoon herbal salt substitute
  ¼ cup olive oil
  1 tablespoon red wine vinegar
  2 teaspoons dried marjoram
  1 teaspoon dried dill
  1 teaspoon dried oregano
  ¼ teaspoon ground black pepper

In a large bowl, combine the water, yeast, and honey. Let stand in a warm place until the mixture foams, about 10 minutes. Stir in half of the flour, mixing well with a wooden spoon. Let this batter rise in a warm place for 30 minutes. Stir in the salt or salt substitute and enough of the remaining flour to form a kneadable dough.

Turn onto a lightly floured surface and knead for 5 to 8 minutes, or until the dough becomes elastic and less sticky. Place in a clean, lightly oiled bowl. Cover and let rise in a warm, draft-free place for 1 hour. Punch down.

Lightly oil a 15″ × 10″ baking sheet or jelly-roll pan. Roll the dough into a rectangle and fit it into the pan.

In a small bowl, whisk together the oil, vinegar, marjoram, dill, oregano, and pepper. Brush over the surface of the dough. Let rise for 30 minutes.

Preheat the oven to 350°.

Bake the focaccia for 20 to 25 minutes, or until golden brown. Cut into pieces and serve warm.

Family Dinner Breads

Designed for dinnertime—because of richer-tasting ingredients or elegant presentation—the breads in this section will elicit plenty of contented evening purrs. Serve them hot from the oven. Or make them ahead and freeze; heat just before serving.

DILLY BREAD

2 cups warm water (98°-110°)
2 tablespoons active dry yeast
2 tablespoons honey
5-6 cups whole wheat flour
2 tablespoons olive oil
1½ tablespoons dried dill
2 teaspoons herbal salt substitute

In a large bowl, combine the water, yeast, and honey. Let stand in a warm place until the mixture foams, about 10 minutes. Stir in 2 cups of the flour, mixing well with a wooden spoon.

Let this batter rise in a warm place for 30 minutes. Stir in the oil, dill, salt substitute, and enough of the remaining flour to form a kneadable dough.

Turn onto a lightly floured surface and knead for 5 to 8 minutes, or until the dough becomes elastic and less sticky. Place in a clean, lightly oiled bowl. Cover and let rise in a warm, draft-free place for 1 hour. Punch down and let rise again for 30 minutes.

Lightly oil 2 (1- to 1½-quart) casserole dishes. Divide the dough in half, form into balls and place in the casseroles. Let rise for 10 minutes.

Preheat the oven to 350°.

Bake the loaves for 45 minutes, or until the tops and sides sound hollow when tapped. Turn out onto wire racks and let cool before slicing.

Almost every bread book has a recipe for dilly bread—a green-flecked loaf with a pungent herb flavor. In experimenting with this recipe, I loved the combination of whole wheat flour (instead of the usual white) and honey to complement the dill.

Makes 2 loaves; about 15 slices.

This rich mixture of honey-sweetened dough and cinnamon-raisin filling was voted the tastiest bread in my bread-baking classes in California. You'll get rave reviews when you make these buns at home for family and friends.

Makes about 12 to 15 buns.

CALIFORNIA STICKY BUNS

1½ cups warm water (98°–110°)
¼ cup honey
2 tablespoons active dry yeast
3½–4 cups whole wheat flour
¼ cup safflower oil
1 cup chopped walnuts
¾ cup raisins
¾ cup maple syrup
⅓ cup orange juice
2 tablespoons ground cinnamon
1 tablespoon grated orange rind
1 teaspoon ground cardamom

In a large bowl, combine the water, honey, and yeast. Let stand in a warm place until the mixture foams, about 10 minutes. Stir in 2 cups of the flour, mixing well with a wooden spoon. Let this batter rise in a warm place for 30 minutes.

Stir in the oil and enough of the remaining flour to form a kneadable dough.

Turn onto a lightly floured surface and knead for 5 to 8 minutes, or until the dough becomes elastic and less sticky. Place in a clean, lightly oiled bowl. Cover and let rise in a warm, draft-free place for 1 hour. Punch down and let rise again for 30 minutes.

In a medium bowl, combine the walnuts, raisins, ½ cup of the maple syrup, orange juice, cinnamon, orange rind, and cardamom. Set aside.

Lightly oil a 9″ × 13″ baking dish. Pour in the remaining ¼ cup maple syrup to coat the bottom of the pan.

Roll the dough into a large rectangle, about 24″ × 14″. Spread with the cinnamon mixture to within a scant ½″ of the borders. Roll up, starting at a short edge. Cut into segments about 2″ long.

Place the rolls, cut side up and sides touching, in the baking dish. Let rise for 10 minutes.

Preheat the oven to 350°.

Bake the buns for 25 to 30 minutes, or until browned.

CELERY BISCUITS

1½ cups warm water (98°–110°)
½ cup honey
1½ tablespoons active dry yeast
6 cups whole wheat flour
1 cup minced onions
½ cup olive oil
⅓ cup minced celery leaves
1½ teaspoons dried sage
1 teaspoon celery seed
1 teaspoon dried thyme
1 teaspoon dried basil
½ teaspoon salt or 2 teaspoons herbal salt substitute
½ teaspoon ground black pepper

In a large bowl, combine the water, honey, and yeast. Let stand in a warm place until the mixture foams, about 10 minutes. Stir in 2 cups of the flour, mixing well with a wooden spoon. Let this batter rise in a warm place for 30 minutes.

Stir in the onions, oil, celery leaves, sage, celery seed, thyme, basil, salt or salt substitute, and pepper. Add enough of the remaining flour to form a kneadable dough.

Turn onto a lightly floured surface and knead for 5 to 8 minutes, or until the dough becomes elastic and less sticky. Place in a clean, lightly oiled bowl. Cover and let rise in a warm, draft-free place for 1 hour. Punch down and let rise again for 30 minutes.

Lightly oil 2 baking sheets.

Turn the dough onto a floured work surface and roll to a thickness of about 1″. Using a floured 2″ biscuit cutter, cut circles of the dough. Place on the sheets, either ½″ or 2″ apart (depending on whether you want the finished biscuits to be touching). Cover and let rise for 20 minutes, or until doubled in bulk.

Preheat the oven to 350°.

Bake the biscuits for about 25 minutes, or until browned and the bottoms sound hollow when tapped.

My grandmother loved these biscuits, especially at holiday time. The flavor is reminiscent of turkey stuffing—celery leaves, plus familiar herbs such as sage, thyme, and basil. Because they're made from a yeasted dough, these biscuits have less than a third of the fat of regular biscuits. And of course they have no cholesterol!

Makes 40 biscuits.

These miniature baguettes, perfect accessories for streamlined family dinners, also transport well for picnics.

Makes 16 miniature baguettes.

Onion Baguettes

  1 cup finely chopped onions
  2 tablespoons olive oil
2¼ cups warm water (98°–110°)
 ¼ cup honey
  2 tablespoons active dry yeast
5–6 cups whole wheat flour
  1 tablespoon chopped fresh rosemary or 1 teaspoon
      dried
  1 teaspoon dried thyme
  1 teaspoon dried basil

In a small frying pan over medium-low heat, sauté the onions in the oil until limp, about 10 minutes, stirring frequently to prevent browning. Remove from the heat and set aside.

In a large bowl, combine the water, honey, and yeast. Let stand in a warm place until the mixture foams, about 10 minutes. Stir in 2 cups of the flour, mixing well with a wooden spoon. Let this batter rise in a warm place for 30 minutes.

Stir in the onions, rosemary, thyme, basil, and enough of the remaining flour to form a kneadable dough.

Turn onto a lightly floured surface and knead for 5 to 8 minutes, or until the dough becomes elastic and less sticky. Place in a clean, lightly oiled bowl. Cover and let rise in a warm, draft-free place for 1 hour. Punch down and let rise again for 30 minutes.

Lightly oil 2 large baking sheets. Divide the dough into 16 equal balls and roll each ball into a cylinder no more than 5″ long. Place on the baking sheets. Using a sharp knife, cut 3 diagonal slits about ¼″ deep in the top of each cylinder. Let rise for 10 minutes.

Preheat the oven to 375°.

Bake the baguettes for 25 to 30 minutes, or until golden.

WEDNESDAY BREAD

2 cups warm water (98°–110°)
1 cup honey
2 tablespoons active dry yeast
4 cups stone-ground whole wheat flour
3 cups unbleached flour
¼ cup safflower oil
1 tablespoon ground cinnamon
½ teaspoon salt

In a large bowl, combine the water, honey, and yeast. Let stand in a warm place until the mixture foams, about 10 minutes. Stir in 2 cups of the whole wheat flour, mixing well with a wooden spoon. Let this batter rise in a warm place for 30 minutes.

Stir in the unbleached flour, oil, cinnamon, and salt. Stir in enough of the remaining flour to form a kneadable dough.

Turn onto a lightly floured surface and knead for 5 to 8 minutes, or until the dough becomes elastic and less sticky. Place in a clean, lightly oiled bowl. Cover and let rise in a warm, draft-free place for 1 hour. Punch down and let rise again for 30 minutes.

Lightly oil 2 (9″ × 5″) loaf pans. Divide the dough in half. Form each piece into a loaf and place in a pan, seam side down. Let rise for 10 minutes.

Preheat the oven to 350°.

Bake the loaves for 45 minutes, or until the top and sides sound hollow when tapped. Turn out onto wire racks and let cool before slicing.

Inheriting its name from the day my grandmother traditionally baked it, this bread uses stone-ground whole wheat for the sweet dough, rich with honey and cinnamon. We especially enjoyed it as an after-school snack, spread with homemade apple butter.

Makes 2 loaves; about 20 slices.

All the savory aroma of Thanksgiving—without the cholesterol! The secret is the thyme and sage, two richly flavored herbs that blend well with the wheat flour and honey in this recipe.

Makes 1 loaf; 10 to 12 slices.

THYME, SAGE, AND OLIVE LOAF

1 cup warm water (98°–110°)
⅓ cup honey
2 tablespoons active dry yeast
3 cups whole wheat flour
¾ cup buckwheat flour
½ cup chopped Kalamata or other black olives
2 tablespoons olive oil
1 teaspoon dried thyme
1 teaspoon ground black pepper
½ teaspoon dried sage

In a large bowl, combine the water, honey, and yeast. Let stand in a warm place until the mixture foams, about 10 minutes. Stir in 1 cup of the whole wheat flour, mixing well with a wooden spoon. Let this batter rise in a warm place for 30 minutes.

Stir in the buckwheat flour, olives, oil, thyme, pepper, and sage. Add enough of the remaining flour to form a kneadable dough.

Turn onto a lightly floured surface and knead for 5 to 8 minutes, or until the dough becomes elastic and less sticky. Place in a clean, lightly oiled bowl. Cover and let rise in a warm, draft-free place for 1 hour. Punch down and let rise again for 30 minutes.

Lightly oil a 1½-quart casserole. Form the dough into a ball and press into the casserole. Let rise for 10 minutes.

Preheat the oven to 350°.

Bake the bread for 35 to 45 minutes, or until the top and sides sound hollow when tapped. Let cool on a wire rack before slicing.

Sprouted and Sourdough Breads

Sourdough breads have been famous since the California gold rush. But doughs containing sprouted grains—added to increase protein and fiber contents—have become popular only over the last decade. Sprouted breads are made with very simple ingredients: water and wheat, which is sprouted, then ground into doughy submission.

HOW TO MAKE SPROUTED BREADS

If you want to prepare sprouted breads, you'll need to grow some sprouts. Start with wheat or rye berries and soak them in water overnight. Then sandwich the berries between layers of dampened kitchen towels and keep them moist until tiny shoots begin to form. After 48 hours the berries should have sprouted enough for you to grind them.

If you let the sprouts grow too long— more than the standard 48 hours—an enzyme called *diastase* will form, giving the dough a gluelike consistency. That in turn will make the bread dense and un-palatable. If you do neglect the sprouts, use them in salads rather than trying to salvage them for bread.

Once the sprouts are ready, you can grind them to a smooth, sticky paste in a food processor, blender, or food mill. At this point, they're ready to add to yeasted bread, such as Sprouted Two-Grain Bread (page 214).

Another way to make sprouted bread is to incorporate sprouts of different grains into your regular wheat dough.

Makes 1 loaf; about 10 slices.

SPROUTED TWO-GRAIN BREAD

1½ cups rye berries
1½ cups red winter-wheat berries
½ cup warm water (98°–110°)
¼ cup maple syrup or honey
1 tablespoon active dry yeast
4-5 cups whole wheat flour
1 tablespoon safflower oil
½ teaspoon salt or 2 teaspoons herbal salt substitute

Sprout the rye and wheat berries for 24 to 48 hours according to the directions given in "How to Make Sprouted Breads" on page 213. Rinse the emerging sprouts and drain well. Coarsely grind in a food processor, food mill, or blender. Set aside.

In a large bowl, combine the water, maple syrup or honey, and yeast. Let stand in a warm place until the mixture foams, about 10 minutes.

Stir in 2 cups of the flour, mixing well with a wooden spoon. Let this batter rise in a warm place for 30 minutes.

Stir in the sprouts, oil, salt or salt substitute, and enough of the remaining flour to form a kneadable dough.

Turn onto a lightly floured surface and knead for 5 to 8 minutes, or until the dough becomes elastic and less sticky. Place in a clean, lightly oiled bowl. Cover and let rise in a warm, draft-free place for 1 hour. Punch down and let rise again for 30 minutes.

Lightly oil a 9″ × 5″ loaf pan. Turn the dough onto a floured work surface and shape into a loaf. Place in the prepared pan and let rise for 20 minutes.

Preheat the oven to 350°.

Bake the loaf for 45 to 60 minutes, or until lightly browned and the bottom sounds hollow when tapped. Turn out onto a wire rack and let cool before slicing.

DARK RYE SOURDOUGH BREAD

1 cup warm water (98°–110°)
¼ cup molasses
1 tablespoon active dry yeast
1 cup Basic Sourdough Starter (page 192), at room
    temperature
3–4 cups whole wheat flour
2 cups rye flour
3 tablespoons safflower oil
1 tablespoon caraway seeds
½ teaspoon salt or 1 tablespoon herbal salt substitute
2 tablespoons coarse cornmeal

In a large bowl, combine the water, molasses, and yeast. Let stand in a warm place until the mixture foams, about 10 minutes. Stir in the starter and 2 cups of the whole wheat flour, mixing well with a wooden spoon. Let this batter rise in a warm place for 30 minutes.

Stir in the rye flour, oil, caraway, salt or salt substitute, and enough of the remaining flour to form a kneadable dough.

Turn onto a lightly floured surface and knead for 5 to 8 minutes, or until the dough becomes elastic and less sticky. Place in a clean, lightly oiled bowl. Cover and let rise in a warm, draft-free place for 1 hour. Punch down and let rise again for 30 minutes.

Lightly oil a large baking sheet and dust with the cornmeal. Roll the dough into a cylinder about 12″ to 14″ long. Place on the baking sheet. Let rise for 25 minutes.

Preheat the oven to 375°.

With a sharp knife, make 3 diagonal slits in the top of the loaf about 1/4″ deep. Bake until golden, about 40 minutes.

This very pungent bread reminds me of German beer halls and sauerkraut. It's perfect for sandwiches and for homemade croutons.

Makes 1 large loaf; 10 to 12 slices.

I like to use this beautiful loaf for elegant dinner parties.

Makes 1 loaf; 10 to 15 slices.

Sourdough Wheat Baguette

1½ cups Basic Sourdough Starter (page 192), at room
       temperature
1½ cups warm water (98°–110°)
  5 tablespoons honey
  1 tablespoon active dry yeast
4–5 cups whole wheat flour
  2 tablespoons safflower oil
  1 teaspoon herbal salt substitute
  2 tablespoons coarse cornmeal

In a large bowl, combine the starter, water, honey, and yeast. Let stand in a warm place until the mixture foams, about 10 minutes.

Stir in 2 cups of the flour, mixing well with a wooden spoon. Let this batter rise in a warm place for 30 minutes.

Stir in the oil, salt substitute, and enough of the remaining flour to form a kneadable dough.

Turn onto a lightly floured surface and knead for 5 to 8 minutes, or until the dough becomes elastic and less sticky. Place in a clean, lightly oiled bowl. Cover and let rise in a warm, draft-free place for 1 hour. Punch down and let rise again for 30 minutes.

Lightly oil a large baking sheet and dust with the cornmeal.

Roll the dough into a cylinder about 12″ to 14″ long. Place on the sheet. Let rise for 25 minutes.

Preheat the oven to 350°.

With a sharp knife, make 3 diagonal slits in the top of the loaf about ¼″ deep. Bake until golden, about 35 to 40 minutes.

Quick Breads

Baking time for these breads is less than 1 hour—with less than 30 minutes preparation time—so they're perfect for occasions when you can't take the time for a yeasted dough.

IRISH RAISIN BREAD

⅓ cup raisins
¼ cup chopped dried apricots
2 tablespoons brandy or apricot nectar
1 cup warm water (98°-110°)
2 tablespoons honey
2 tablespoons safflower oil
3½-4 cups unbleached or whole wheat pastry flour
1½ teaspoons baking soda
1½ teaspoons baking powder

In a medium bowl, combine the raisins, apricots, and brandy or apricot nectar. Let stand for 1 hour, then drain. Add the water, honey, and oil.

Preheat the oven to 375°. Lightly oil a large baking sheet.

Into a large bowl, sift 3 cups of the flour with the baking soda and baking powder.

Pour the liquid ingredients over the flour mixture. Mix well and knead lightly to combine, adding enough of the remaining flour to keep the dough from sticking.

Pat the dough into a 7″ round and place on the baking sheet. Cut a shallow X in the top with a sharp knife.

Bake for 45 to 50 minutes, or until lightly browned. Transfer to a wire rack and let cool before slicing thinly.

A perfect bread for slicing and toasting, Irish Raisin Bread is full of raisins and other dried fruit. It's crumbly and sweet like its Irish soda bread cousin.

Makes 1 loaf; about 15 slices.

Blue cornmeal, available in health-food stores, originated in Hopi Indian territory in northeastern Arizona. The corn kernels are actually blue, by the way, and lend a sweeter taste to the dough than their yellow cousins.

Makes 12 to 16 pieces.

BLUE CORNBREAD WITH FRESH SWEET AND HOT PEPPERS

2 sweet red peppers, finely diced
3 jalapeño peppers, finely diced
2 tablespoons dry sherry
3 cloves garlic, minced
1 cup water
½ cup egg substitute
¼ cup olive oil
2 tablespoons honey
1¼ cups blue cornmeal
1 cup unbleached flour
1 tablespoon baking powder
1 teaspoon herbal salt substitute
¼ teaspoon baking soda

In a 1-quart saucepan over medium-high heat, simmer the red peppers, jalapeños, sherry, and garlic, stirring constantly, for 10 minutes. Transfer to a medium bowl and let cool.

Preheat the oven to 400°.

Lightly oil a 9" × 13" baking dish. Place the dish in the oven to heat for 5 minutes.

Add the water, egg substitute, oil, and honey to the bowl with the peppers.

Into a large bowl, sift the cornmeal, flour, baking powder, salt substitute, and baking soda.

Pour the liquid ingredients over the cornmeal mixture. Mix well. Pour the batter into the hot dish. Bake for 25 to 30 minutes, or until lightly browned. Let cool before cutting into pieces.

ORANGE, CRANBERRY, AND DATE BREAD

1 cup orange juice
½ cup chopped dates
½ cup raisins
½ cup cranberries
½ cup honey
1-2 tablespoons grated orange rind
¼ cup safflower oil
2½ cups whole wheat pastry or unbleached flour
1 tablespoon baking powder
1 teaspoon baking soda

In a 2-quart saucepan over medium heat, cook the orange juice, dates, raisins, cranberries, honey, and orange rind for 10 minutes, or until the cranberries pop. Remove from the heat and let cool. Stir in the oil.

Preheat the oven to 375°. Lightly oil a 9″ × 5″ loaf pan.

In a large bowl, combine the flour, baking powder, and baking soda. Add the cranberry mixture and stir well to combine.

Pour the batter into the pan and bake for 40 to 45 minutes, or until a knife inserted in the center of the loaf comes out clean. Let cool before slicing thinly.

Cranberries and orange rind give this sweet bread a tart taste and jewel-like colors when sliced. It's our household's favorite bread for tea parties or as a sweet treat in a lunch-box. You may use fresh or frozen cranberries.

Makes 1 loaf; about 15 slices.

CHAPTER 11

SWEET

Treats

t is a rare cook who can stay away from desserts too long—they are just too enticing to the creative spirit. Well, I wasn't so much *enticed* into making desserts as *recruited*. After the birth of my younger siblings, life got a little hectic for my mother, and homemade desserts became one the first casualties of the new order. Between the diapers, the dishes, and the doctors, she didn't have much time left over for baking apple pie. With my mother temporarily out of the dessert business, my father found a 12-year-old in-house replacement in yours truly.

My training period was long and intense. My mom's piecrusts took months of practice to duplicate. Too much water and the dough stuck to the rolling pin like a stucco patch; too much flour and the crust turned into baked plywood. I felt like a chemist searching desperately for a formula that was just beyond my grasp. But finally the apprentice was ready to enter the ring alone, and I was given the dubious honor of making apple pie for one of our Thanksgiving dinners.

So there I was, working in nervous but methodical solitude in the kitchen, when my hand slipped and a measuring cup filled with water tilted into the bowl of dough. Suddenly an ocean of water was submerging my beautiful island of dough like the Lost Continent of Atlantis.

Praying that no one would suddenly appear at the kitchen door, I quickly piled a mound of flour onto the countertop and scooped the sodden dough onto it. Working the flour into the watery mass was a sticky job, but several cupfuls of flour later I was able to roll out the dough and fit it into the pan. Filled with sliced apples, cinnamon, and sugar, then topped with another stiff slice of dough, my pie was looking passable, even attractive. Thinking I had saved the day, I shoved it into the oven and a few hours later presented my first creation to a large tableful of Carrolls.

"What delicious-looking pie," my grandmother exclaimed. "And Mary made it all by herself?"

I blushed with satisfaction as she took up her fork. In a few seconds I was blushing for another reason. No matter how hard she pressed, my grandmother could not cut through the crust. Looking back now, I feel a great deal of gratitude to my grandmother for her persistence: She pressed on, so to speak, only out of pure loyalty to me, changing the angle of her fork, puttering with her plate, clearing her throat, all to stall for time until some act of God got her out of this predicament. Meanwhile, Grandfather, never one to stand on ceremony, had immediately abandoned his fork when he saw what was happening and began to chop methodically at his piece with a butter knife.

"Anybody got an ice pick?" he asked.

Well, after many years and many mistakes, I finally learned how to make my favorite piecrust, Light and Flaky No-Cholesterol Piecrust (page 226), and now you can make it, too.

Sweet Choices

Though homemade desserts are such fulfilling foods, reminding us of family gatherings or special occasions, a *real* homemade dessert is a rare bird these days. So why is dessert the first course to get scratched when we change to a healthier diet? Perhaps we think that sugar and fat are inevitable ingredients in desserts. Sweets, however, can be based on simpler foods, such as fresh fruit, just as they are in many foreign cuisines. A year in Paris convinced me that it takes just as much skill to bring out the essence of a pear or a strawberry with very little sweetener as to cover it with marzipan or chocolate.

If you know the right techniques, you can even make many pastries with cholesterol-free ingredients, such as egg whites and whole wheat pastry flour. In short, you don't have to give up desserts—just relearn how to make them.

To do this you must first know the functions of various dessert ingredients. Ignorance may be bliss, but not when it comes to dessert preparation. Being unaware of how various ingredients differ and interact can result in culinary catastrophe.

Flour

All flours are not created equal. Regular whole wheat flour is ideal for the breads in chapter 10, but its high gluten content creates heavy and unpalatable pastries. Luckily, another version—whole wheat pastry flour—is available for baking desserts. Made from a durum wheat grown in the short northern summer, whole wheat pastry flour has all the nutrients of whole wheat bread flour but little of its gluten. Instead it has a higher starch content, which gives it a flaky lightness that's perfect for pastries.

Whole wheat pastry flour, available in health-food stores and some well-stocked supermarkets, has a short shelf life, so I recommend double-bagging it in freezer bags and storing it in the freezer. Pastries usually demand cold ingredients anyway, so frozen flour for dessert baking is not a problem.

Sweeteners

The choice of sweeteners is also important. You might choose honey for a peanut butter cookie but maple syrup or date sugar to sweeten a fruit crisp or cobbler. The chart on the opposite page gives conversion amounts for various sweeteners plus tips on using them.

Most healthful low-sugar sweeteners are liquid rather than solid or granular. That means they work best in a liquid mixture, such as a fruit pie filling, that is heated so excess liquid can evaporate. In recipes where the balance of liquid and dry ingredients is crucial—cakes or cookies, for example—you should use a combination of liquid sweeteners and dry sweeteners like maple sugar and date sugar.

Oils

In pastry, oils or fats serve two important functions: They provide moistness and flakiness to prevent crumbling. It's easy to make a layer cake with a lot of high-cholesterol ingredients, such as egg yolks and butter. Traditional bakers prize butter mainly because its fat contains small pockets of moisture that expand as the heat increases, causing the pastry to rise in flaky layers.

Contrary to popular belief, achieving this same flakiness from no-cholesterol oils is not impossible, just more difficult. One alternative is choosing recipes (for example, fruit muffins) that don't need to rise much to be successful.

In most recipes, safflower oil substitutes beautifully for butter or shortening—you can generally use the same amount. It's more successful than other oils because it adds very little flavor of its own to the batter.

You can bypass oil entirely by making a recipe that requires a yeasted dough, such as Blueberry Turnover Pastries (page 230). Egg yolks and cream can be eliminated or replaced with fruit purees, which also give moistness to a recipe.

"BYE, SUGAR!"

Working with new sweeteners in baked goods can sometimes produce half-baked cakes or soggy cookies. Use this chart to mix and match sweeteners in your dessert recipes. Substitute the conversion amount of each sweetener for *1 cup* of white sugar.

Sweetener	Flavor	Conversion Amount (cups)
All-fruit jam	Fruity	1
Apple juice	Fruity	³/₄–1
Apple juice concentrate	Very fruity	¹/₄–¹/₂
Barley malt syrup	Malty	1¹/₂
Clover honey	Usually neutral	¹/₂
Date sugar	Fruity	1
Maple sugar	Neutral, fruity	³/₄
Maple syrup	Neutral, fruity	¹/₂
Molasses	Strong, especially blackstrap	¹/₃
Orange juice concentrate	Fruity	¹/₃
Pureed raisins	Fruity	1¹/₄
Rice bran syrup	Heavy grain taste	¹/₂

Tips

Here are some pointers to keep in mind when working with alternative sweeteners.

• When using a liquid sweetener in place of white sugar: For every 1 cup of liquid sweetener, increase the amount of flour by ¹/₄ cup and decrease the amount of other liquid (such as water or oil) by ¹/₄ cup. Use your judgment when only a small amount of oil is called for in the recipe—you may not want to eliminate it all; you may prefer to add extra flour to compensate for the liquid sweetener.

• When measuring honey or any other sticky sweetener: Coat the inside of the measuring cup or spoon with oil before adding the honey. The honey will slide right out of the measure.
• The sweeteners that are "fruity" or "neutral" in flavor—such as all-fruit jam or date sugar—may be substituted easily for white sugar without altering the original flavor much. These sweeteners also tend to taste sweeter than barley malt syrup, rice bran syrup, or molasses, so you may want to choose them when cooking for anyone with a sweet tooth.

MY FAVORITE PIECRUST

The two unusual ingredients in this recipe—egg white and vinegar—help increase the crust's flakiness. Vinegar also helps keep the gluten from developing, which would toughen the dough. Be sure to use flours that are naturally lower in gluten, such as whole wheat pastry or unbleached instead of whole wheat bread flour. Although I think this crust is at its flaky best using ¼ cup of oil, you can cut the oil to 2 tablespoons if you're worried about your fat intake.

This recipe makes 1 (9″) crust. Make a double recipe if you need a top and a bottom crust, as in Heavenly Rhubarb Pie (page 234).

LIGHT AND FLAKY NO-CHOLESTEROL PIECRUST

1 cup plus 2 tablespoons whole wheat
        pastry or unbleached flour
    pinch of salt (optional)
¼ cup safflower oil, chilled
1 egg white, lightly beaten
1 teaspoon apple cider vinegar
    ice water (as needed)

To mix the dough by hand: In a medium bowl, mix together the flour and the salt (if using). Make a well in the center of the flour and add the oil. Lightly mix it in with your fingertips until you have a cornmeal-like texture. Do not let the dough become warm from overmixing, especially if you have hot hands, because the crust will turn out tough.

Add the egg white and vinegar to the bowl. Mix lightly with your fingertips or a fork until incorporated. Try to form the dough into a ball. If it is still dry and crumbly (and this will vary depending on the weather and other factors), add the water, 1 tablespoon at a time, until you get a slightly sticky dough that holds together. Proceed to the dough-rolling step.

To mix the dough with a food processor: Place the steel blade into the workbowl, pushing it down until it fits snugly in the bowl. Add the flour and salt; mix for 1 second.

Add the oil, egg white, and vinegar. Use on/off turns to mix lightly. With the machine running, dribble in as much water as needed for the dough to form a ball.

Liquids and Thickeners

Most pastries use egg yolks to thicken or bind the batter as it bakes. I have found arrowroot powder and ground kuzu, both from dried vegetable roots, to be excellent substitutes. I use them to thicken custards, cake batters, and pie fillings. They are similar to cornstarch but cloud and flavor the sauce much less. Agar-agar, a seaweed gelatin, is another good choice, especially for

(This may only take a tiny bit of water and a few seconds, so don't overwork the dough by mixing too long.) Proceed to the dough-rolling step.

To roll the dough: Using your hands, form the dough into a flattened circle about ½″ thick. If the dough is still cold, you can roll it out immediately or press it into an ungreased pie pan. Otherwise, wrap it in plastic wrap or waxed paper and refrigerate for at least 20 minutes.

Working on a very lightly floured surface, roll the dough into an 11″ circle. Carefully ease the dough into a 9″ pie plate, being careful not to stretch it. Trim the excess dough, leaving a ½″ overhang. Form the overhang into a fluted edge.

Cover the dough with plastic wrap and place in the freezer while you prepare the filling. When the filling is ready, discard the plastic and add the filling to the crust. Either freeze the unbaked pie (tightly wrapped) at this point or bake it according to your recipe directions.

To bake the crust without a filling: Roll out the dough and fit it into a pie plate as directed above. Line the shell with aluminum foil and place in the freezer for at least 20 minutes. Set the pie plate on a baking sheet and bake the crust at 400° for 8 to 12 minutes. Remove it from the oven, discard the foil, and let the crust cool.

Makes 1 crust.

To make a double-crust pie: Double the basic dough recipe. Divide the ball of dough in half and roll each half into an 11″ circle. Fit 1 circle into your pie plate and cover with plastic wrap. Sandwich the second circle of dough between 2 layers of plastic wrap. Place both pieces in the freezer while you prepare your filling.

When the filling is ready, remove the dough from the freezer, discard the plastic wrap from both pieces, and immediately place the filling in the bottom crust. Lay the second piece of dough over the filling. Trim the edges and pinch them together to seal the gaps and form a fluted edge. Cut 3 slits in the top crust to allow steam to escape during baking. (This helps lessen the chances of the filling bubbling over onto the floor of your oven as the pie bakes.) You can either freeze your unbaked pie (tightly wrapped) at this stage or bake it according to your recipe directions.

Makes 1 top crust and 1 bottom crust.

mousses and soufflés. It works like gelatin but jells much more quickly.

In baked goods, liquid ingredients must be carefully balanced with the dry—the ratio must be maintained for cakes to bake all the way through and for cookies to crisp. But it makes little difference to the recipe whether you choose whole milk or a no-cholesterol "milk" made from blended zucchini, cashews, or almonds, all of which taste as rich as buttermilk, whole milk, or skim milk.

SELECTING FALL AND WINTER FRUITS

Many people add fresh fruit to their diets in summertime, this being the prime time for juicy fruits like peaches, berries, plums, and nectarines. But winter offers its own choice selections: apples, pears, bananas, citruses, cranberries, and persimmons. Use the handy chart below for up-to-date information on selecting and storing fresh fruits for desserts from September through February.

Fruit	Characteristics	Storage Time
Apples[1]	Smooth skin, free of blemishes	Several weeks
Avocados	Soft, black (if Haas), no spots	Several days after ripening
Cranberries	Small, dark berries	Months (in freezer)
Grapefruit[2]	Firm, heavy	Several weeks
Lemons[3]	Fine-textured skin, bright yellow color	1 week
Limes	Bright green, heavy	Several weeks
Melons[4]	Fragrant, heavy	1 week
Nectarines	Smooth, fragrant, heavy, good color	5–7 days
Oranges[5]	Smooth, heavy, fragrant	Several weeks
Peaches	Firm, blush-colored	5–7 days
Pears[6]	Firm, but not hard	1 week
Persimmons	Bright orange, soft, shriveled	Several days
Pomegranates[7]	Mottled red/pink color	2 months (in refrigerator) or 1 month (in cool, dark place)
Tangerines	Bright orange, shiny skin	Several weeks

[1]Tart apples, such as Granny Smith, McIntosh, Winesap, Jonathan, and Northern Spy are best for baking since they retain much of their tart flavor and natural sugar. Red and Golden Delicious are best for eating out of hand or for uncooked desserts.

[2]If a grapefruit is heavy, it often contains a lot of juice. Beware of spongy or lightweight grapefruit.

[3]Slightly green lemons are more acidic and are good for marinades; deep yellow lemons are sweeter. Thick- or bumpy-skinned lemons tend to yield less juice.

[4]Watermelons and cantaloupes are summer melons, while honeydews, casabas, Crenshaws, and Persian melons are all grown under irrigation in the winter in western states and are available year-round.

[5]Valencia oranges are good for juice; navels are best for eating out of hand. Oranges often turn orange before they're fully ripe, so color is not indicative of sweetness. Oranges are a good source of pectin, fiber, and potassium.

[6]Choose Bosc pears for poaching or baking, since they retain both shape and flavor under heat. Comice, Bartlett, and Anjou are good for fruit salads or eating out of hand.

[7]Pomegranates that have been sliced open should be stored in cold water.

A Word to Experimentalists

Baking demands a certain devotion to detail and precision. Unlike a soup, for example, where throwing in an extra ¼ cup of chopped onion alters the final result very little, adding an extra ¼ cup of flour to a cake can produce a dramatically different dessert. Take piecrust. Many cooks attempt their first healthy piecrust using whole wheat flour and safflower oil instead of white flour and butter. Not knowing much about how these new ingredients interact, they add a little extra oil, then compensate with more flour—resulting in a tough crust. Or they work the dough too long so it gets warm and doesn't rise in the oven.

In short, baking is an exact science. Don't let this scare you off; just follow the recipes carefully until you get the hang of the techniques before you begin experimenting.

Perfect Pies, Tarts, and Pastries

Whole grain flours flavor pastries and piecrusts more richly than white flour. Read the instructions for Light and Flaky No-Cholesterol Piecrust (page 226) before starting, to make sure you understand the vagaries of working with whole wheat flour.

Tofu Whipped Cream

4 ounces soft tofu
2 tablespoons maple syrup
½ teaspoon vanilla

In a food processor or blender, puree the tofu, maple syrup, and vanilla until very smooth.

Tastes like high-fat, cholesterol-rich dairy whipped cream. Be sure to use soft tofu.

Makes ½ cup.

Using yeasted dough lets you avoid the butter in most turnover recipes. This recipe doesn't use pastry flour because it needs the development of gluten to rise. The blueberry filling is sweet and slightly tart with lemon juice and grated lemon rind.

Serves 8.

BLUEBERRY TURNOVER PASTRIES

Dough

1 cup warm water (98°–110°)
¼ cup honey
1 tablespoon active dry yeast
3 cups whole wheat or unbleached flour
3 tablespoons safflower oil

Filling

2 cups thinly sliced tart apples, such as Granny Smith
1½ cups fresh or frozen blueberries
½ cup apple juice
¼ cup currants
1 cup plus 2 tablespoons maple syrup
3 tablespoons arrowroot powder
1 tablespoon lemon juice
1 tablespoon grated lemon rind
½ teaspoon ground cinnamon

To make the dough: In a large bowl, combine the water, honey, and yeast. Stir well, then let rise for 10 minutes, or until the mixture foams. Stir in 1½ cups of the flour, mixing well to form a loose batter. Let rise in a warm place for 40 minutes. Add the oil and enough of the remaining flour to form a sticky dough.

Lightly flour a clean countertop or breadboard and knead the dough for 10 minutes, or until the dough becomes elastic and less sticky (if necessary, incorporate extra flour into the dough as you go). Place in a clean, lightly oiled bowl. Cover and let rise in a warm, draft-free place for 45 minutes.

To make the filling: While the dough is rising, combine the apples, blueberries, apple juice, and currants in a 2-quart saucepan. Simmer over medium-high heat for 10 minutes, or until the apples soften.

In a small bowl, combine 1 cup of the maple syrup with the arrowroot and lemon juice. Add to the apple mixture and cook, stirring constantly, until the mixture thickens, about 8 to 10 minutes. Remove from the heat and stir in the

lemon rind and cinnamon. Let cool for 10 minutes while you roll out the dough.

Preheat the oven to 350°.

Lightly oil a large baking sheet. Divide the dough into 8 portions and roll each into a very thin circle about 5″ in diameter. Place ⅓ cup filling in the center of each circle. Brush a thin line of water around the edge of each circle and fold each piece in half to form a half-moon shape. Press the edges together to seal. Reserve any remaining filling.

Transfer the turnovers to the baking sheet. Brush the tops with the remaining 2 tablespoons maple syrup. Bake for 20 minutes, or until browned.

If desired, puree any reserved filling and serve as a sauce over the turnovers.

FRENCH APPLE PIE

  1 Light and Flaky No-Cholesterol Piecrust (page 226)
1½ cups thick unsweetened applesauce
 ½ cup honey
  3 tablespoons apple brandy (optional)
  1 tablespoon vanilla
     grated rind of 1 lemon
  3 green apples, thinly sliced
 ½ cup all-fruit apricot jam

Prepare and bake the crust; set aside.

Preheat the oven to 375°.

In a 2-quart saucepan over medium-high heat, simmer the applesauce, honey, brandy (if using), vanilla, and lemon rind until quite thick, about 10 to 15 minutes.

Pour the mixture into the prepared crust. Arrange the apples in concentric circles on top of the sauce.

In a 1-quart saucepan over medium-high heat, melt the apricot jam, then press it through a sieve. Use a pastry brush to glaze the apples with the jam.

Bake the pie for 30 minutes. Let cool before slicing.

Imagine layers of brandy-flavored applesauce and sliced baked apples, glazed with apricot jam. This pie will make you a fount of nostalgia for anyone who has sampled the aromas of a Parisian bakery.

Serves 8 to 10.

If you weren't concerned about cholesterol—or fat—you'd probably serve this dessert topped with a dollop of regular whipped cream. But it's equally delicious with no-cholesterol Tofu Whipped Cream (page 229) as the topping.

Serves 4.

Apple Dumplings

2⅓ cups whole wheat pastry or unbleached flour
½ teaspoon finely ground date sugar
½ cup safflower oil, chilled
¼ cup cold water
¼ cup honey
1 teaspoon ground cinnamon
4 tart apples, thinly sliced
1½ cups apple juice
⅔ cup maple syrup
1 tablespoon lemon juice
¼ teaspoon ground nutmeg

Preheat the oven to 425°.

In a large bowl, combine the flour and date sugar. Add the oil and incorporate it with a pastry blender or your fingertips until the dough resembles coarse cornmeal. Sprinkle lightly with the water and blend it in with a fork to make a dough that you can form into a ball. Divide into 4 equal portions.

Lightly flour a clean countertop or breadboard. Roll each portion of the dough into a 7″ square. In the center of each, place 1 tablespoon of honey and sprinkle with ¼ teaspoon of cinnamon. Top with ¼ of the apple slices. Fold up the corners of each square to meet in the center and seal the edges with water. Place each dumpling in a small baking or gratin dish large enough to hold the dumpling and about ½ cup of syrup.

In a 1-quart saucepan over medium-high heat, simmer the apple juice, maple syrup, lemon juice, and nutmeg for 10 minutes, stirring frequently. Pour the syrup over the dumplings. Bake for 40 minutes (if the syrup starts to scorch, add a little water to each dish).

Apple, Kiwifruit, and Berry Tart

1 Oat-Almond Piecrust (page 234)
2 cups apple juice
1 tablespoon agar-agar flakes
3 kiwifruit, peeled and sliced
1 cup fresh raspberries
2 tablespoons all-fruit apricot jam

Prepare and bake the crust; set aside.

In a 1-quart saucepan, combine 1 cup of the apple juice with the agar. Cook over medium heat, stirring constantly, until the flakes dissolve, about 15 minutes. Remove from the heat and stir in the remaining 1 cup of apple juice. Place the pan in the refrigerator and let stand until the mixture cools and begins to thicken to the consistency of unbeaten egg whites, about 25 to 30 minutes.

Pour the juice mixture into the prepared crust. Top with the kiwis and berries in a decorative pattern. Place the tart in the refrigerator and chill for 45 minutes, or until the filling is set.

In a 1-quart saucepan over low heat, melt the apricot jam, stirring constantly. Press the jam through a fine sieve to remove any bits of peel. Brush over the fruit. Refrigerate for 15 minutes to set the glaze.

Sweet
Treats

This stunningly beautiful dessert is worthy of your most elegant dinner party. The Oat-Almond Piecrust is an excellent complement to the filling of jelled fruit juice, fresh kiwifruit, and berries.

Serves 8.

Though some people have an unreasonable bias against rhubarb—especially those who haven't eaten it—this tart, tasty member of the buckwheat family glows like a ruby when it's cooked as a pie filling. Because it is so tart, it has to be heavily sweetened. In this recipe, maple syrup is used for that purpose.

Serves 8 to 10.

As an alternative to an all whole wheat piecrust, this recipe gets its crunch from ground dry oatmeal and almonds—a good way to add cholesterol-lowering fiber to your dessert recipes. I like to use safflower oil, but canola or any other mild vegetable oil would also work.

Makes 1 (9'') crust.

Heavenly Rhubarb Pie

pastry for 2 Light and Flaky No-Cholesterol Piecrusts
    (page 226)
6 cups chopped fresh or frozen rhubarb
1½ cups maple syrup
⅓ cup arrowroot powder
7 tablespoons whole wheat pastry flour

Prepare the piecrust dough according to the recipe directions. Roll half of the dough into an 11″ circle and fit it into a 9″ pie plate. Roll the remainder into an 11″ circle and set aside.

Preheat the oven to 350°.

In a large bowl, combine the rhubarb, maple syrup, arrowroot, and flour. Pour into the bottom piecrust. Top with the remaining dough. Trim, seal, and crimp the edges. Cut 3 steam slits in the top crust.

Bake for 60 to 70 minutes, or until the filling bubbles out of the steam slits and the top is lightly browned. Let cool before serving.

Oat-Almond Piecrust

½ cup rolled oats
¼ cup blanched almonds
¾ cup whole wheat pastry flour
2-3 tablespoons oil
1-2 tablespoons ice water

In a blender or food processor, combine the oats and almonds and grind to a coarse powder. Transfer to a large bowl. Add the flour and mix well.

Drizzle on the oil and incorporate it with a pastry blender or your fingertips until the mixture resembles coarse cornmeal. Sprinkle in enough of the water (mixing it lightly with a fork) to moisten all the flour and make a dough that you can form into a ball.

Flatten the dough into a circle about ½″ thick. On a lightly floured board or a sheet of waxed paper, roll the dough into a thin (about ⅛″) circle about 11″ in diameter. Line a 9″ pie pan with the dough and trim the edges to leave a ½″ overhang all around. Use the overhang to form a fluted edge.

Place the crust in the freezer for at least 20 minutes.

Fill the shell and bake it according to the directions of your specific recipe.

To bake the crust without a filling: Preheat the oven to 425°.

Line the prepared piecrust with aluminum foil and place it on a baking sheet. Bake for 8 minutes. Remove it from the oven and discard the foil. Bake for 7 minutes. Let the crust cool before filling.

Fresh-Fruit Crisps

Traditional crisps are usually combinations of lightly sweetened fruit—apples, pears, peaches, or plums, for example—in a deep dish with a crumb topping. In most crisps, the crumb topping is a rich mixture of flour, oats, and butter. But cholesterol-free toppings are easy to make and just as delicious.

Toppings bound with butter or lightened with baking powder rise like biscuits, but a cholesterol-free topping—composed of whole wheat flour, oats, spices, and apple juice—bakes into a crunchy crust.

Begin your crisp with fresh or frozen fruit that has a rich color and will produce plenty of juice while baking. If you choose unsweetened frozen raspberries or strawberries, pair them with apples or other high-pectin fruit to give body to the crisp. Or add arrowroot powder to the uncooked fruit to help thicken the juices as the crisp bakes.

Raspberry-Apple Crisp

6 cups thinly sliced tart apples
2 cups fresh or frozen raspberries
1/2 cup honey
1 tablespoon lemon juice
1 tablespoon arrowroot powder
3/4 cup apple juice
3/4 cup whole wheat pastry or unbleached flour
1/2 cup rolled oats
3 tablespoons yellow cornmeal
1/2 teaspoon ground nutmeg
1 teaspoon vanilla

Preheat the oven to 350°.

In a 3-quart saucepan, combine the apples, raspberries, honey, lemon juice, and arrowroot. Stir in 1/2 cup of the apple juice. Bring to a boil over medium-high heat. Reduce the heat and simmer, stirring frequently, until the apples begin to soften, about 5 to 10 minutes.

Lightly oil a 9″ × 13″ baking dish. Add the apple mixture.

In a medium bowl, combine the flour, oats, cornmeal, and nutmeg. Sprinkle with the remaining 1/4 cup of apple juice and the vanilla. Mix well. Sprinkle this mixture over the apples. Bake for 20 minutes, or until lightly browned. Serve hot.

Vermont Maple Crisp

10 small tart apples
1 teaspoon ground cinnamon
1/2 cup apple juice
1/3 cup maple syrup
1/4 cup raisins
1/4 cup boiling water
1 cup rolled oats
1 cup whole wheat pastry flour
1/2 teaspoon salt (optional)
1/2 cup safflower oil

Perfectly matched for sweetness and color, the raspberries and apples in this crisp are lightly sweetened with honey and enhanced with lemon juice. Be sure to use tart apples that will hold together well as they cook, such as Pippin or Granny Smith.

Serves 6 to 8.

Enjoy the cholesterol-lowering benefits of apple pectin in this Vermont treat that's flavored with maple syrup and raisin puree.

Serves 6 to 8.

Lightly oil a 9" × 13" baking dish.

Core the apples, but do not peel them. Slice into thin rings and place in the baking dish. Sprinkle with the cinnamon. Add the apple juice and maple syrup.

In a blender, puree the raisins and boiling water. Pour over the apples.

In a medium bowl, combine the oats, flour, and salt (if using). Add the oil and mix into a crumbly dough. Spread over the apples. Let stand 30 for minutes.

Preheat the oven to 400°.

Bake for 45 minutes, or until the filling bubbles and the top crust is evenly browned.

PEAR CRISP
WITH OAT BRAN CRUST

     7 cups thinly sliced pears, such as Bosc
   ½ cup plus 2 tablespoons date sugar
   ¼ cup pear juice or brandy
     1 tablespoon lemon juice
     1 tablespoon arrowroot powder
     1 cup whole wheat pastry or unbleached flour
   ⅔ cup oat bran
  1½ teaspoons baking powder
   ⅓ cup apple juice
     2 tablespoons safflower oil
     1 teaspoon vanilla

Preheat the oven to 375°.

In a large bowl, combine the pears, ½ cup of the date sugar, the pear juice or brandy, lemon juice, and arrowroot.

Lightly oil a 9" × 13" baking dish. Add the pear mixture.

In a medium bowl, combine the flour, oat bran, baking powder, and remaining 2 tablespoons of date sugar. Add the apple juice, oil, and vanilla. Stir just until a dough forms. Drop by spoonfuls on top of the pears. Bake for 20 to 30 minutes, or until the top is browned.

Serve this crisp at your next dinner party. The oat bran adds chewy texture; the date sugar (simply ground dried dates) enhances even off-season pears.

Serves 6 to 8.

CAPE COD CRANBERRY-BLUEBERRY CRISP

Cranberry lovers who do not get enough of this tart fruit during the holidays will find this dish from Cape Cod, where the best cranberries grow, a delicious new way to serve them. It freezes well after it is baked and adds cholesterol-lowering oats to your diet.

Serves 6 to 8.

2 cups fresh or frozen blueberries
1¾ cups fresh or frozen cranberries
1 cup maple syrup
¼ cup currants
3 tablespoons arrowroot powder
2 tablespoons lemon juice
¾ cup whole wheat pastry or unbleached flour
½ cup rolled oats
¼ cup blanched almonds, ground
1 teaspoon toasted sesame seeds
¼ teaspoon ground cinnamon
¼ cup apple juice

Preheat the oven to 350°.

In a large bowl, combine the blueberries, cranberries, maple syrup, currants, arrowroot, and lemon juice.

Lightly oil a 9″ × 13″ baking dish. Add the fruit mixture.

In a medium bowl, combine the flour, oats, almonds, sesame seeds, and cinnamon. Sprinkle with the apple juice and mix well. Spoon over the fruit. Bake about 40 minutes, or until lightly browned.

Ices and Parfaits

Fresh, frosty, and cholesterol-free, these desserts will become year-round favorites in your household. Pureeing the frozen desserts twice—once when they've frozen to the slush point and again before serving—will make them smooth as silk.

SUMMER FRUIT PARFAITS

8 ounces soft tofu
2 tablespoons almonds
½ teaspoon vanilla
1 cup fresh or frozen blueberries
1 cup sliced fresh peaches
1 cup sliced fresh strawberries

In a blender, puree the tofu, almonds, and vanilla until smooth. Divide among 4 parfait glasses.

In the blender, puree the blueberries and peaches. Pour over the tofu layer in the parfait glasses.

Rinse the blender jar, then puree the strawberries. Pour over the blueberry layer in the parfait glasses. Chill for 20 minutes.

CAROB-DATE POPS

1 cup chopped dates
1 ripe banana, sliced
½ cup almonds
½ cup apple juice
4 ounces soft tofu
¼ cup raisins
¼ cup roasted carob powder
1 teaspoon vanilla
½ teaspoon ground cinnamon
¼ teaspoon ground nutmeg

In a food processor or blender, combine the dates, bananas, almonds, apple juice, tofu, raisins, carob, vanilla, cinnamon, and nutmeg. Puree until very smooth.

Pour into 5 (6-ounce) paper cups and place a wooden or plastic ice-pop stick in the center of each. Freeze solid. To serve, tear off the paper cup.

One sophisticated five-year-old neighbor told me this was his favorite "ice cream"—even though it's not frozen. What better praise for a cholesterol-free dessert? Be sure to use soft tofu—the firm style makes the dessert gritty.

Serves 4.

You'll never see the local ice-cream vendor selling these out of his truck, but they do taste like old-fashioned fudge pops —with no chocolate or dairy products.

Serves 5.

Thump a watermelon for ripeness (it should sound dense and heavy) and tote it home to puree into this rose-colored sherbet. Agar-agar helps jell the sherbet into a creamy consistency. I always try to freeze an extra batch for out-of-season desserts.

Serves 8.

Layered with slices of bright green kiwifruit, this parfait is perfect as a palate cleanser between courses or as a light dessert.

Serves 6.

Watermelon Sherbet

8 cups seeded, chopped watermelon
1 cup honey (or to taste)
1½ tablespoons lemon juice
1½ teaspoons agar-agar flakes

Place the watermelon in a fine sieve set over a large bowl. Using a large spoon, press the chunks against the sieve to extract as much liquid as possible. Reserve the juice and remaining pulp separately.

In a 3-quart saucepan, combine the watermelon juice, honey, lemon juice, and agar. Bring to a simmer over medium heat and cook, stirring frequently, for 5 minutes. Remove from the heat and let cool in the pan for 10 minutes.

Transfer the reserved watermelon pulp to a blender or food processor. Process until smooth. Add to the agar mixture and mix well. Pour into a large shallow pan and freeze for 2 hours.

Cut into cubes and place in a blender or food processor, then puree to a slushy consistency. Pour back into the pan and freeze for 2 hours. Cut into cubes and puree until smooth. Serve in chilled bowls.

Cranberry Sherbet Parfait

3 cups fresh or frozen cranberries
2 cups apple juice
½ cup honey (or to taste)
¼ cup orange juice concentrate
¼ cup maple syrup
2 cups sliced kiwifruit

In a 3-quart saucepan, combine the cranberries, apple juice, honey, orange juice concentrate, and maple syrup. Cover and cook over medium-high heat until the berries pop, about 5 minutes. Let the mixture cool slightly, then

puree in a blender or food processor. Taste for sweetness and add additional honey if needed.

Press the mixture through a sieve into a large bowl, using the back of a wooden spoon to extract as much liquid as possible. Pour into a large shallow pan and freeze for 2 hours.

Cut into cubes and place in a blender or food processor, then puree to a slushy consistency. Pour back into the pan and freeze for 2 hours. Cut into cubes and puree until smooth. Pour into parfait glasses, alternating with layers of kiwi.

Mousses and Puddings

The same light and airy effects characteristic of egg yolks and whipped cream can be duplicated in no-cholesterol dishes using pureed fruit and quick-cooking tapioca or agar-agar.

Mocha Mousse

4 cups apple juice
3 tablespoons agar-agar flakes
3 tablespoons maple syrup
2 tablespoons almond butter
1 tablespoon roasted carob powder
1 tablespoon roasted-grain coffee substitute

In a blender, combine the apple juice, agar, maple syrup, almond butter, and carob. Puree until smooth.

Transfer to a 2-quart saucepan and cook over medium heat for 10 minutes, stirring constantly. Remove from the heat and let cool for 10 minutes. Add the coffee substitute and stir to dissolve it. Pour into 6 dessert goblets. Refrigerate until firm, about 30 minutes.

Flavored with roasted-grain coffee substitute and roasted carob powder, Mocha Mousse will satisfy your cravings for something rich (as well as something fun to say).

Serves 6.

Born of the British sense of thrift, this recipe uses leftover bread or pastry covered with berries and wine. The mixture is left to soak until it becomes a thick, delicious pudding. You can change the type of wine and increase the amount if you desire; I've used only a modest amount here.

Serves 8.

Kanten is the Japanese name for agar-agar, an all-purpose vegetable gelatin that thickens to a creamy consistency reminiscent of dairy-rich puddings. This form of it comes in compressed bars and is sold in health-food stores.

Serves 8.

English Summer Pudding

6 cups mixed berries
¼ cup honey
¼ cup sauterne
3 cups cubed Minnesota Christmas Stollen (page 199) or
        Oatmeal-Raisin Bread (page 204)
    Tofu Whipped Cream (page 229)

In a 3-quart saucepan, combine the berries, honey, and sauterne. Bring to a boil and simmer for 5 minutes.

Place the bread cubes in a large heatproof bowl. Add the berry mixture. Cover with plastic wrap and refrigerate overnight. Serve with the whipped cream.

Berry and Banana Kanten

4 cups apple juice
1 ripe banana, sliced
2 cups sliced fresh or frozen strawberries
1 cup fresh or frozen raspberries
1 (0.5 ounce) bar kanten, broken into small pieces
¼ cup maple syrup
1 teaspoon lime juice
1 teaspoon vanilla

In a blender or food processor, process the apple juice and bananas until smooth. Transfer to a 3-quart saucepan.

Add the strawberries, raspberries, kanten, maple syrup, lime juice, and vanilla. Cook over medium-high heat, stirring constantly, until the kanten dissolves, about 12 to 15 minutes. Let cool slightly.

Pour into 8 individual bowls. Chill until set, about 2 hours.

Maple-Cashew Mousse

2 cups cashew Nut Milk (page 244)
¼ cup maple syrup
3 tablespoons agar-agar flakes
1 tablespoon vanilla
2 tablespoons tahini
2 tablespoons cashews

In a 2-quart saucepan, combine the nut milk, maple syrup, agar, and vanilla. Cook over medium heat, stirring constantly, until the agar dissolves, about 5 minutes. Stir in the tahini.

Pour into a medium bowl and refrigerate until firm, about 50 minutes. Transfer to a blender or food processor and process until creamy. Spoon into 6 dessert goblets.

In a small frying pan over medium heat, toast the cashews until a nutty aroma emerges, about 3 to 5 minutes. Chop coarsely and sprinkle over the mousse. Chill and serve.

Cashew milk takes the place of dairy in this creamy light mousse. You can serve this dessert in goblets or pour it into a precooked piecrust for an elegant ending to a no-cholesterol meal.

Serves 6.

Fresh Peach Pudding

8 large ripe peaches, sliced
2 teaspoons lemon juice
2 tablespoons agar-agar flakes
1 tablespoon honey
  grated rind of ½ orange
½ teaspoon ground cinnamon
  Sweet Cherry Sauce (page 251)

In a blender or food processor, combine the peaches, lemon juice, agar, honey, orange rind, and cinnamon. Puree until smooth. Transfer to a 2-quart saucepan.

Simmer over medium heat, stirring constantly, for 5 minutes, or until the agar dissolves. Pour into 6 to 8 custard cups or ramekins and refrigerate until firm. Serve with the cherry sauce.

This delicious pudding was invented in one of my cooking classes during the peak of summer. The tartness of the lemon juice and orange peel brings out the sweetness of perfectly ripe peaches.

Serves 6 to 8.

FRESH BERRY TAPIOCA

In June, when the U-Pick farms open with fresh strawberries, making this dessert is high on my "to-do" list.

Serves 6.

4 cups sliced fresh or frozen strawberries
1 cup apple juice
3 tablespoons quick-cooking tapioca
3 tablespoons honey
1 cup raspberries

Puree the strawberries in a blender or food processor. In a 2-quart saucepan over medium-high heat, bring the strawberries, apple juice, tapioca, and honey to a boil, stirring constantly.

Remove the pan from the heat. Stir in the raspberries. Pour into 6 dessert goblets and chill in the refrigerator until set, about 1 hour.

NO-CHOLESTEROL MILK

I've found that nut "milks" are excellent substitutes for regular dairy milk. They're easy to make and are delicious on cereals, in baked goods, and as the base for creamy sauces. Depending on the intended use, you can either sweeten the milk or leave it plain. This recipe makes 2 cups, but you can easily double it. Store your nut milk in a sealed container in the refrigerator, where it will keep for about three or four days. If you'd like, you can save the resulting nut pulp to add to breads, pastries, or even casseroles.

NUT MILK

2 cups water
1 cup raw almonds or cashews
1 tablespoon molasses or honey
    (optional)

In a blender, puree the water and almonds or cashews on high speed for about 3 minutes, or until the nuts are very finely chopped. Pour into a fine sieve and strain into a bowl. Press on the nut pulp with the back of a spoon to extract as much liquid as possible.

If desired, stir in the molasses or honey. If not using immediately, transfer to a container with a tight lid and store in the refrigerator.

Makes 2 cups.

CAROB PUDDING

16 ounces soft tofu, cut into cubes
 3 medium bananas
¼ cup carob powder
 1 teaspoon vanilla
 1 tablespoon honey or maple syrup

In a blender, puree the tofu, bananas, carob, vanilla, and honey or maple syrup until smooth and creamy. Pour into dessert glasses and chill for 30 minutes.

Carob might not satisfy chocoholics, but for everyone else it has a rich flavor, color, and texture. Maybe that's why this pudding is such a big hit with kids—as well as parents who know that it's much healthier than sugar- and fat-laden chocolate desserts.

Serves 4 to 6.

Easy Fruit Desserts

For those evenings when you arrive home from the shopping mall with little money and even less time for cooking, you can prepare most of these thrifty recipes in a jiffy (translated: less than 20 minutes).

PEACHES WITH MELBA SAUCE

4 large ripe peaches, peeled and sliced
1 cup fresh or frozen raspberries
¼ cup honey
1 tablespoon vanilla

Divide the peaches among 4 dessert dishes.
In a blender or food processor, puree ½ cup of the raspberries with the honey and vanilla. Pour into a small bowl and stir in the remaining ½ cup berries. Spoon over the peaches. Serve at room temperature or chilled.

Melba sauce traditionally combines a puree of sweetened raspberries with kirsch or other liqueur. In this version we use pureed berries, vanilla, and honey over sliced fresh peaches—a simple yet delicious dessert for busy evenings.

Serves 4.

Here's a twist on traditional rice pudding—this one's sweetened with vanilla and honey and thickened with almond milk. Contrary to what your kids might think when they eat this creamy pudding, almonds do not have udders, nor do you have to milk them at 5:00 A.M.

Serves 4.

When winter produce reaches its February low, I often make this dried-fruit dessert. It's also a good choice for a holiday finale, since the sugary figs make plain apples taste sinfully sweet.

Serves 4 to 6.

ALMOND RICE PUDDING

3–4½   cups cooked short-grain brown rice
   ½   cup currants
   2   cups apple juice
   ½   cup almonds
   ⅓   cup honey
   1   teaspoon vanilla
   ½   teaspoon ground cinnamon
   ¼   teaspoon ground nutmeg

Preheat the oven to 350°.

Lightly oil a 9″ × 5″ loaf pan. Combine the rice and currants in the pan and set aside.

In blender, puree the apple juice, almonds, honey, vanilla, cinnamon, and nutmeg. Pour over the rice.

Bake for 45 minutes, or until all liquid has been absorbed. Serve warm or cold.

PINEAPPLE-FIG BAKE

   3   cups pineapple juice
   2   cups chopped tart apples
1½   cups chopped dried figs
   ¾   cup chopped dried pineapple
   ⅓   cup chopped dates
   ¾   teaspoon ground cinnamon
   ½   teaspoon ground nutmeg

Preheat the oven to 300°.

In a 3-quart saucepan, combine the pineapple juice, apples, figs, pineapple, dates, cinnamon, and nutmeg. Bring to a boil over medium-high heat. Reduce the heat and simmer for 5 minutes, stirring frequently.

Transfer the fruit to a 9″ × 13″ baking dish. Bake for 1 hour, or until the fruit is very soft. Serve hot or cold.

CHINESE MELON DESSERT

4 cups cantaloupe balls
1 cup pineapple chunks
1 cup canned litchi nuts, rinsed and drained
1 cup canned mandarin orange slices, rinsed and drained
1 cup orange juice
¼ cup maple syrup
¼ cup date sugar
1 teaspoon chopped fresh mint leaves

In a large bowl combine the cantaloupe, pineapple, litchi nuts, and oranges.

In a small bowl, combine the orange juice, maple syrup, date sugar, and mint. Pour over the fruit and toss well. Let marinate at room temperature for 1 hour before serving.

MAPLE-APPLE BAKE

2 large tart apples, such as Granny Smith
¼ cup maple syrup
1 teaspoon ground cinnamon
1 teaspoon ground nutmeg
½ ripe banana, thinly sliced
½ cup apple juice concentrate

Preheat the oven to 350°.

With an apple corer, core each apple to within ⅛″ from the bottom, leaving a small amount of skin intact. Place apples in a 9″ × 9″ baking dish. Place 1 tablespoon of maple syrup in each cavity. Sprinkle with the cinnamon and nutmeg. Pack the cavities with the bananas.

In a cup, mix the apple juice concentrate and the remaining 2 tablespoons maple syrup. Pour around the apples in the dish. Bake for 20 minutes. Serve hot.

Canned litchi nuts and mandarin orange slices bring a touch of the Orient into this simple fruit dessert. You can find date sugar at health-food stores — it's an essential ingredient to bring out the delicate flavors of the melon and oranges.

Serves 6 to 8.

These baked apples are a twist on the traditional: They're stuffed with bananas, maple syrup, and spices. The bananas add a fruity sweetness that's unusual and very tasty.

Serves 2.

Poached-Fruit Desserts and Fruit Sauces

The simplest all-fruit dessert is poached fresh fruit. Poaching requires a strong-flavored liquid that permeates the fruit as it softens. Wines are my favorite poaching medium: Because the alcohol cooks off within 10 minutes, calories in most wine-poached desserts are minimal. Besides adding flavor, red wines make fruit shine like jewels. White wines lend a sweet, flowery aroma and a pale golden hue.

Ruby apples

You can make these apples ahead and keep them in the refrigerator for up to six days. They make great hostess and holiday gifts —place a few in a beautiful serving dish and wrap with a nice bow.

Serves 6.

6 medium tart apples
2 cups red zinfandel
1 cinnamon stick
1 tablespoon honey
2 tablespoons grated orange rind

Peel the apples, leaving them whole and keeping the stems intact, if possible. Using a sharp knife or melon baller, core the apples from the bottom. Place the apples, right side up, in a large pot. Add the zinfandel, cinnamon, and honey.

Bring to a boil over medium-high heat. Then reduce the heat to medium and simmer, uncovered, for 25 to 30 minutes, or until the apples are soft but not ready to collapse.

Transfer the apples to small dessert dishes and spoon some of the poaching liquid over them. Sprinkle with the orange rind.

Sweet GOLDEN PEARS

6 Bosc or other firm pears
1 cup Riesling or other white wine
1 cup apple juice
   juice of 1 large lemon
5 whole cloves

Peel the pears, leaving them whole. Using a sharp knife or melon baller, core the pears from the bottom.

Place them upright in a large pot. Add the wine, apple juice, lemon juice, and cloves. Bring to a boil over medium-high heat. Reduce the heat to medium and simmer, uncovered, for 25 to 30 minutes, or until the pears are soft but not ready to collapse.

Transfer to small dessert dishes. Discard the cloves and spoon some of the poaching liquid over the pears. Serve hot.

This is one of my favorite elegant—yet very simple—desserts. These pears keep in the refrigerator for about 3 weeks if stored in their own syrup; simply reheat to serve. Just-underripe, brown-skinned pears, such as Bosc, are best because they hold together in the hot poaching liquid.

Serves 6.

Low-Sugar Fruit Sauces

Giving up whipped cream toppings is easier said than done. But one of the best ways is to replace them with something just as good—maybe better: fruit sauces. Because fruit sauces can be made up to 10 days ahead and stored in the refrigerator, I often have two varieties on hand.

PEACH SAUCE WITH GRAND MARNIER

4 large peaches, sliced
½ cup honey
2 tablespoons lemon juice
1 tablespoon Grand Marnier liqueur

In a 3-quart saucepan over medium-high heat, simmer the peaches, honey, and lemon juice, stirring often, for 20 minutes, or until the peaches soften. Add the liqueur.

Transfer the sauce to a blender or food processor and puree until smooth. Serve warm.

The tang of orange (from the liqueur), lemon, and peach makes this a tasty topping for sherbet, pudding, or a slice of pie. If you don't have Grand Marnier, you may substitute orange juice or orange-juice concentrate.

Makes about 3 cups.

BLUEBERRY SAUCE WITH NUTMEG

2 cups fresh or frozen blueberries
⅓–½ cup honey
1 tablespoon arrowroot or kuzu powder
1 teaspoon ground nutmeg
1 teaspoon grated lemon rind

In a blender combine the blueberries, ⅓ cup honey, arrowroot or kuzu, nutmeg, and lemon rind. Transfer to a 1-quart saucepan. Cook over medium-high heat, whisking frequently, until the sauce thickens, about 10 to 12 minutes. Taste and adjust the sweetener, if necessary. Let cool slightly before serving.

The sweet flavor of grated nutmeg enhances the blueberries in this easy sauce. Serve it over slices of angel food cake or poached fruit.

Makes 1½ to 2 cups.

Sweet CHERRY SAUCE

2½ cups pitted sweet cherries
1 cup apple juice
⅓ cup rice bran syrup or maple syrup
3 tablespoons arrowroot powder

In a blender, combine 1 cup of the cherries, apple juice, rice bran syrup or maple syrup, and arrowroot. Process for 1 minute.

Pour into a 2-quart saucepan. Add the remaining cherries. Bring to a boil over medium-high heat, stirring constantly, and cook until thick. Let cool slightly before using.

My favorite topping for rice pudding features rice bran syrup—an interesting alternative to traditional sweeteners that also happens to go well with cherries.

Makes about 3½ cups.

Fresh RASPBERRY SAUCE

¼ cup all-fruit raspberry or currant jelly
3 tablespoons cold water
1 tablespoon arrowroot powder
2 cups fresh raspberries

In a 1-quart saucepan over medium-low heat, melt the jelly.

In a small bowl, combine the water and arrowroot, stirring until smooth. Add to the jelly and cook, stirring constantly, until clear and thick. Add the berries. Cook over low heat until the sauce is slightly thickened, about 5 minutes. Serve warm or cold.

An elegant sauce that works well over Blueberry Turnover Pastries (page 230) or Almond Rice Pudding (page 246).

Makes about 2½ cups.

A MONTH'S
WORTH OF
No-Cholesterol
MEALS

When my friend Mollie wanted to lower her cholesterol, she asked me to help revamp her diet. She knew that without a clear-cut plan she might slip back into the high-fat, high-cholesterol eating habits that got her into dietary trouble in the first place. Moreover, she worried that she might fall into a rut eating a few favorite no-cholesterol dishes day after day. And she realized that boredom with any diet dooms it to failure.

So I created four weeks of daily menus for Mollie to follow. And then I gave her recipes for all but the most basic items—recipes that I have included in this book. Now at first glance, the menus might seem ambitious. The very first day below, for example, calls for preparing seven different recipes. I don't expect you to follow these plans religiously, cooking completely new meals each day. Rather my intent is to show the variety possible on an essentially no-meat diet. And I also want to give you a sense of which foods you can mix or match to keep your interest piqued—and your taste buds satisfied.

One way to get a lot of variety into your menus is to prepare dishes that freeze well. Serve a portion of the recipe immediately and freeze the rest in single-serving containers. Another trick I use to minimize daily kitchen chores is to spend a few hours over the weekend preparing food for the week ahead. I boil up some grains or beans, make a quick bread, bake a casserole, stir up a salad dressing, and simmer a pot of soup. Later, it's quick work to get a meal on the table.

Here are your meal plans. I hope you enjoy them as much as Mollie does.

WEEK ONE

Day 1

Breakfast
Morning-Glory Fruit Shake (page 64)
Walnut Poteca (page 198)

Lunch
Red Pepper Cornbread (page 63)
Southwestern Red-Bean Chili (page 61)

Dinner
Baked Marinated Cutlets (page 176)
Mushroom-Essence Soup (page 126)
Carob-Date Pops (page 239)

Day 2

Breakfast
Sprouted Two-Grain Bread (page 214),
    toasted
Apple butter
Sliced fresh fruit
Sweet Cherry Sauce (page 251)

Lunch
Spiced Tempeh Sandwiches (page 64)
Refrigerator Pickled Vegetables (page 56)
Almond Rice Pudding (page 246)

Dinner
Vegetarian Golden Pot Pie (page 172)
Steamed broccoli and snow peas
Tossed green salad

Day 3

Breakfast
Sweet Golden Pears (page 249)
English Muffins with Oat Bran (page
    200), toasted
Eve's Miso-Tahini Dip (page 187)

Lunch
Simple Bean Spread on Rye Croutons
    (page 65)
Warm Chopped-Vegetable Salad (page
    92)

Dinner
Grilled-Eggplant Salad with Teriyaki
    Marinade (page 85)
Barbecued Vegetarian Burgers (page 179)

Day 4

Breakfast
Hot cereal with sliced bananas and
    strawberries
Dark Rye Sourdough Bread (page 215),
    toasted
Orange juice

Lunch
Red Pepper Cream Soup with Thyme
    (page 118)
Miniature Stuffed Vegetables (page 58)
Steamed red chard and spinach

Dinner
French Mushroom Salad with Tempeh
    (page 180)
Chilled Leek and Potato Soup (page
    128)
Grilled Vegetables en Papillote (page 70)

Day 5

Breakfast
Apple Dumplings (page 232)
Sliced fresh fruit
Papaya and pineapple juice

Lunch
California Pizza Toasts (page 55)
Green and White Bean Salad (page 98)

Dinner
Vegetarian Burritos (page 170)
Refried Mexican Beans (page 149)
Tossed green salad

Day 6

Breakfast
California Sticky Buns (page 208)
Orange and grapefruit sections with
    cinnamon

Lunch
Ann's Sweet Potato Soup (page 120)
Grilled Vegetables en Papillote (page 70)
Lemon-Rice Salad (page 95)

Dinner
Stuffed Mushrooms with Parsley Pesto
    (page 60)
Focaccia (page 206)
Pasta
Meatless Tomato Sauce (page 171)

Day 7

Breakfast
Orange, Cranberry, and Date Bread
    (page 219)
Vegetable Breakfast Scramble (page 176)

Lunch
Spicy Chinese Noodles (page 95)
Orange-Carrot Soup with Ginger (page
    125)
Steamed kale and spinach

Dinner
Hot Tomato Toddies (page 66)
Baked New Potatoes with Assorted Dips
(page 57)
Onions Stuffed with Tempeh, Tomatoes,
and Peppers (page 183)
Pineapple-Fig Bake (page 246)

WEEK TWO

Day 1

Breakfast
Sliced apples with maple syrup and
nutmeg
Sprouted Two-Grain Bread (page 214),
toasted

Lunch
Southwestern Bread Wraps (page 70)
Pasta and Corn Salad with Red Sauce
(page 89)
Oil-Free Potato Chips (page 66)

Dinner
Caper and Garlic Dip with Fresh
Vegetables (page 56)
Tomato-Cilantro Soup (page 124)
Vermont Maple Crisp (page 236)

Day 2

Breakfast
Mushroom Ragout on Rye Toast
Triangles (page 71)
Hot herbal tea

Lunch
Rice-Paper Vegetarian Spring Rolls
(page 69)
Szechuan Hot-and-Sour Soup (page 121)
Steamed greens
Tossed green salad with lemon juice and
olive oil dressing

Dinner
Vegetarian Sierra Stew (page 146)
Blue Cornbread with Fresh Sweet and
Hot Peppers (page 218)

Day 3

Breakfast
Hot cereal with fresh fruit
English Muffins with Oat Bran (page
200), toasted

Lunch
Escarole Soup with Orzo (page 120)
Harvest Salad (page 68)
Onion Baguettes (page 210)

Dinner
Red and Green Pasta with Walnut Sauce
(page 158)
Gingered Cucumber and Squash Salad
(page 86)
Carob Pudding (page 245)

Day 4

Breakfast
Morning-Glory Fruit Shake (page 64)
Red Pepper Cornbread (page 63),
toasted
Simple Bean Spread (page 65)

Lunch
Warm Cauliflower Salad (page 62)
Steamed kale or Swiss chard
Sweet Onion Soup (page 126)
Garlic bread

Dinner
Sprouted Bean Burgers (page 144)
Oil-Free Potato Chips (page 66)
French Apple Pie (page 231)

Day 5

Breakfast
Hot cereal with peaches and strawberries
Orange, Cranberry, and Date Bread
(page 219)
Hot tea

Lunch
Chili Tortilla Strips (page 67)
Mock Tuna Salad (page 178)
Alfalfa Sprout Bread (page 205)
Hungarian Cream of Potato Soup (page
114)

Dinner
Dairyless Spinach Tarts (page 178)
Cuban Black Beans and Rice (page 153)
Orange Salad with Walnuts (page 89)

Day 6

Breakfast
Maple-Apple Bake (page 247)
Irish Raisin Bread (page 217), toasted

Lunch
Meatless Chili with Corn Chips (page
184)
Three-Sprout Salad with Lemon
Dressing (page 88)

Dinner
Indian Rice Pilaf with Vegetables (page
144)
Steamed broccoli
Mango Salad with Curry Dressing (page
90)
Mocha Mousse (page 241)

Day 7

Breakfast
Blueberry Turnover Pastries (page 230)
Fresh fruit
Blueberry Sauce with Nutmeg (page
250)

Lunch
Charlie's Favorite Peanut Butter and
Banana Sandwiches (page 171)
Momma's Mock Chicken Soup (page
123)
Spinach salad

Dinner
Five-Vegetable Lasagna (page 154)
Sourdough Wheat Baguettes (page 216)
Tossed green salad

WEEK THREE

Day 1

Breakfast
Morning-Glory Fruit Shake (page 64)
Walnut Poteca (page 198)

Lunch
San Francisco Japantown Salad Spread
(page 174)
Dark Rye Sourdough Bread (page 215)
Fresh-Corn and Pepper Chowder (page
131)

Dinner
Vegetarian Sweet-and-Sour Tofu (page
177)
Brown rice
Maple-Cashew Mousse (page 243)

Day 2

Breakfast
Sprouted Two-Grain Bread (page 214),
toasted
Apple butter
Sliced fresh fruit
Sweet Cherry Sauce (page 251)

Lunch
Noodles with Miso Sauce (page 62)
Cashew and Bean Salad (page 93)
Ruby Apples (page 248)

Dinner
Carrot Bisque (page 116)
Sun-Dried-Tomato Pesto in Endive
Spears (page 58)
Baked Marinated Cutlets (page 176)

Day 3

Breakfast
Sweet Golden Pears (page 249)
English Muffins with Oat Bran (page
200), toasted
Eve's Miso-Tahini Dip (page 187)

Lunch
Beet Soup with Orange Juice and Green
Onions (page 119)
Wednesday Bread (page 211)
Green and White Bean Salad (page 98)

Dinner
Spinach Fried Rice (page 146)
Steamed root vegetables
Anaheim-Chili Casserole (page 175)

Day 4

Breakfast
Hot cereal with sliced bananas and
strawberries
Dark Rye Sourdough Bread (page 215),
toasted
Orange juice

Lunch
Sweet Grapefruit, Orange, and Kiwifruit
Salad (page 96)
Grilled Vegetables en Papillote (page
70)
Basmati or brown rice

Dinner
Butternut Squash Soup with Five Spices
(page 115)
Asian-Style Quinoa (page 150)
Cranberry Sherbet Parfait (page 240)

Day 5

Breakfast
Apple Dumplings (page 232)
Sliced fresh fruit
Papaya and pineapple juice

Lunch
Chinese Picnic Coleslaw (page 87)
Sprouted Bean Burgers (page 144)
Pear Crisp with Oat Bran Crust (page
237)

Dinner
Baked Eggplant and Tomato Pasta
Casserole (page 159)
Tossed green salad
Sourdough Wheat Baguettes (page 216)
Mocha Mousse (page 241)

Day 6

Breakfast
California Sticky Buns (page 208)
Orange and grapefruit sections with
cinnamon

Lunch
Steamed broccoli, carrots, and other
vegetables
John's Special Sauce for Vegetables (page
188)
Wild Rice with Mushrooms and Pecans
(page 149)
Fresh Peach Pudding (page 243)

Dinner
Vegetarian Burritos (page 170)
Black Beans with Cumin and Garlic
(page 150)
Orange Salad with Walnuts (page 89)

Day 7

Breakfast
Orange, Cranberry, and Date Bread
(page 219)
Vegetable Breakfast Scramble (page 176)

Lunch
Spicy Indonesian Cutlets with Peanut
Sauce (page 182)
Steamed broccoli and carrots
Mocha Mousse (page 241)

Dinner
Sweet Onion Soup (page 126)
Marinated Mushrooms (page 84)
Next-Day Pizzas with Hot Peppers (page
63)
Fresh sliced fruit
Sweet Cherry Sauce (page 251)

WEEK FOUR

Day 1

Breakfast
Sliced apples with maple syrup and
nutmeg
Sprouted Two-Grain Bread (page 214),
toasted

Lunch
Whole wheat pasta
Pasta Sauce Provençale (page 164)
Winter Pear and Spinach Salad with
Balsamic Vinegar (page 96)

Dinner
Sushi Bar Miso Soup (page 188)
Thai Noodle and Vegetable Salad (page
160)
Sliced fresh oranges

Day 2

Breakfast
Mushroom Ragout on Rye Toast
Triangles (page 71)
Hot herbal tea

Lunch
Herbed Red-Potato Salad (page 84)
California Pizza Toasts (page 55)
Dairyless Cream of Spinach Soup (page
117)

Dinner
Mediterranean Pesto Soup (page 122)
Dilly Bread (page 207), toasted
Three-Sprout Salad with Lemon
Dressing (page 88)

Day 3

Breakfast
Hot cereal with fresh fruit
English Muffins with Oat Bran (page
200), toasted

Lunch
Chick-Pea and Tomato Gazpacho (page
129)
Spiced Tempeh Sandwiches (page 64)
Chili Tortilla Strips (page 67)

Dinner
Grilled vegetables
Miso Marinade for Vegetables (page
87)
Wild Rice with Mushrooms and Pecans
(page 149)

Day 4

Breakfast
Morning-Glory Fruit Shake (page 64)
Red Pepper Cornbread (page 63),
toasted
Simple Bean Spread (page 65)

Lunch
Fresh-Corn and Pepper Chowder (page
131)
Ratatouille Salad in Lettuce Cups
(page 97)
Celery Biscuits (page 209)

Dinner
Jalapeño-Pepper and Wild-Mushroom
Risotto (page 148)
Thyme, Sage, and Olive Loaf (page 212)
Fresh Peach Pudding (page 243)

Day 5

Breakfast
Next-Day Pizzas with Hot Peppers
(page 63)

Lunch
Mexican Rice Salad with Roasted
　　Peppers (page 91)
Tomato-Cilantro Soup (page 124)
Steamed broccoli and kale
Watermelon Sherbet (page 240)

Dinner
Anaheim-Chili Casserole (page 175)
Green Rice and Avocado Salad (page
　　98)
Vermont Maple Crisp (page 236)

Day 6

Breakfast
Maple-Apple Bake (page 247)
Irish Raisin Bread (page 217), toasted

Lunch
Creamy Polenta with Roasted
　　Vegetables (page 147)
Tossed green salad
Berry and Banana Kanten (page 242)

Dinner
Southwestern Red-Bean Chili (page 61)
Red Pepper Cornbread (page 63)
Sweet Grapefruit, Orange, and Kiwifruit
　　Salad (page 96)

Day 7

Breakfast
Blueberry Turnover Pastries (page 230)
Fresh fruit
Blueberry Sauce with Nutmeg (page
　　250)

Lunch
Rancho Bernadino Salad with Green
　　Sauce (page 185)
Dark Rye Sourdough Bread (page 215)
Fennel Soup Italian-Style (page 123)

Dinner
Spicy Chinese Noodles (page 95)
Chinese Supper Stir-Fry (page 173)
Fresh Berry Tapioca (page 244)

THE
HIDDEN
CHOLESTEROL

in Your Diet

Y

ou can't tell just by looking at most foods how much cholesterol they have. It's true, of course, that all fruits, vegetables, grains, oils, and other plant-based foods are cholesterol-free. But animal products—such as meat, poultry, seafood, and dairy foods—can vary tremendously in their cholesterol content. Here's a rundown of common cholesterol-containing foods. This chart will help you to pinpoint those foods that it's wise to avoid altogether—especially those that can quickly send you over the daily 300-milligram limit recommended by the American Heart Association. It will also let you identify those items that are low enough for occasional consumption on an otherwise no-cholesterol diet. But keep in mind that some foods low in cholesterol, such as bacon, can be high in fat, so you should think twice before indulging.

Food	Portion	Cholesterol (mg)
Chicken liver	3½ oz.	631
Turkey liver	3½ oz.	626
Pork kidneys	3½ oz.	480
Ham and cheese omelet	1	446
Cheese blintz	1	436
Beef liver	3½ oz.	389
Beef kidneys	3½ oz.	387
Egg yolk	1 large	272
English muffin sandwich with egg, cheese, and bacon	1	214
Fish sandwich with cheese	1	196
Beef heart	3½ oz.	193
Shrimp	3 oz.	166
Pork picnic roast	3½ oz.	114
Pork sirloin	3½ oz.	110
Chuck blade roast	3½ oz.	106
Pork loin	3½ oz.	105
Double cheeseburger with bacon	1	104
Perch	3 oz.	98
Fried chicken breast	1	96
Goose without skin	3½ oz.	96

Food	Portion	Cholesterol (mg)
Beef brisket	3½ oz.	93
Dark meat chicken without skin	3½ oz.	93
Oysters	3 oz.	93
Pork center loin	3½ oz.	91
Crab cake	1	90
Dark meat turkey with skin	3½ oz.	89
Duck without skin	3½ oz.	89
Lean ground beef	3½ oz.	87
Dark meat turkey without skin	3½ oz.	85
Light meat chicken without skin	3½ oz.	85
Extra-lean ground beef	3½ oz.	84
Light meat chicken with skin	3½ oz.	84
Porterhouse steak	3½ oz.	80
T-bone steak	3½ oz.	80
Soft-serve French vanilla ice cream	½ cup	77
Light meat turkey with skin	3½ oz.	76
Egg custard pudding	½ cup	73
Light meat turkey without skin	3½ oz.	69
Bacon cheeseburger	1	68
Herring	3 oz.	65
Mackerel	3 oz.	64
Salmon patty	1	64
Haddock	3 oz.	63
Ricotta cheese	½ cup	63
Lobster	3 oz.	61
Clams	9 small	57
Cheese pizza	1 slice	56
Roast beef sandwich	1	56
Ham	3½ oz.	53
Bratwurst	1 link	51
Mussels	3 oz.	48
Cod	3 oz.	47
Alaskan king crab	3 oz.	45
Cheeseburger	1	45

(continued)

Food	Portion	Cholesterol(mg)
Chicken frankfurter	1	45
Coho salmon	3 oz.	42
Tuna, fresh	3 oz.	42
Snapper	3 oz.	40
Lamb loin chop	1	39
Turkey frankfurter	1	39
Part-skim ricotta cheese	½ cup	38
Chocolate shake	1	37
Beef frankfurter	1	35
Chocolate eclair	1	35
Cream puff	1	35
Halibut	3 oz.	35
Whole milk	1 cup	34
Butter	1 Tbsp.	33
Gouda cheese	1 oz.	32
Oyster stew	1 cup	32
Vanilla shake	1	32
Cream cheese	1 oz.	31
Cheddar cheese	1 oz.	30
Chocolate milk	1 cup	30
Light tuna, canned	3 oz.	30
Turkey pastrami	2 slices	30
Vanilla ice cream	½ cup	30
Brie cheese	1 oz.	28
Scallops, raw	6 large	28
American cheese	1 oz.	27
Brick cheese	1 oz.	27
Canadian bacon	2 slices	27
Colby cheese	1 oz.	27
Cream of chicken soup	1 cup	27
Chili	1 cup	26
Swiss cheese	1 oz.	26
White tuna, canned	3 oz.	26
Edam cheese	1 oz.	25

Food	Portion	Cholesterol (mg)
Cream of asparagus soup	1 cup	22
Cream of potato soup	1 cup	22
Mozzarella cheese	1 oz.	22
Neufchâtel cheese	1 oz.	22
Sausage patty	1	22
Blue cheese	1 oz.	21
Camembert cheese	1 oz.	20
Cream of mushroom soup	1 cup	20
Provolone cheese	1 oz.	20
Low-fat (2%) milk	1 cup	18
Macaroni and cheese	¾ cup	18
Banana cream pudding	½ cup	17
Chocolate pudding	½ cup	17
Creamed cottage cheese	½ cup	17
Pork and beans	1 cup	17
Bacon	3 slices	16
Part-skim mozzarella cheese	1 oz.	16
French fries	3 oz.	14
Low-fat yogurt	1 cup	14
Low-fat (2%) cottage cheese	½ cup	10
Low-fat (1%) milk	1 cup	10
Buttermilk	1 cup	9
Mayonnaise	1 Tbsp.	7
Dry-curd cottage cheese	½ cup	5
Sour cream	1 Tbsp.	5
Parmesan cheese	1 Tbsp.	4
Skim milk	1 cup	4

SOURCE: All figures are taken from *Bowes and Church's Food Values of Portions Commonly Used,* 15th edition, 1989. Unless otherwise noted, figures are for cooked foods.

INDEX

A

Almonds. *See also* Nuts
    Almond-Chive Bread, 201
    Almond Rice Pudding, 246
    Oat-Almond Piecrust, 234–35
American Heart Association (AHA) dietary
    guidelines, 17–22
Appetizers, 54–60
Apples, 74, 228
    Apple, Kiwifruit, and Berry Tart, 233
    Apple Dumplings, 232
    French Apple Pie, 231
    Maple-Apple Bake, 247
    Pineapple-Fig Bake, 246
    Raspberry-Apple Crisp, 236
    Ruby Apples, 248
    Vermont Maple Crisp, 236–37
Appliances, 45
Apricots
    Bulgur Wheat Salad with Apricots, 94
Artichokes, 76
    Vegetarian Red Pepper and Artichoke Paella,
    143
Atherosclerosis, 4, 6, 17
Avocados, 228
    Green Rice and Avocado Salad, 98

B

Baguettes
    Onion Baguettes, 210
    Sourdough Wheat Baguette, 216
Bananas
    Berry and Banana Kanten, 242
    Charlie's Favorite Peanut Butter and Banana
    Sandwiches, 171
Barley, 35, 141
    Southwestern Corn and Barley Salad, 92
Beans, 26–29, 74–75, 77, 137–41
    Basic Bean Soup, 145
    Basque Bean Salad, 90
    Black Beans with Cumin and Garlic, 150
    Boston Bean Soup, 133

Cashew and Bean Salad, 93
Cuban Beans and Rice, 153
Green and White Bean Salad, 98
Meatless Chili with Corn Chips, 184–85
Mexican Corn Stew, 142
Nona's Pasta with Beans, 158
Noodles and White Bean Salad with Low-Oil
    Vinaigrette, 152
Refried Mexican Beans, 149
Simple Bean Spread on Rye Croutons, 65
Southwestern Bread Wraps, 70
Southwestern Red-Bean Chili, 61
Vegetarian Sierra Stew, 145–46
Beef stock, substitutes for, 27
Beets, 76
    Beet Noodles, 157
    Beet Soup with Orange Juice and Green
    Onions, 119
    Red Ranch Salad Dressing, 80
Berries. *See also* Blueberries; Cranberries;
    Raspberries; Strawberries
    Apple, Kiwifruit, and Berry Tart, 233
    Berry and Banana Kanten, 242
    English Summer Pudding, 242
    Fresh Berry Tapioca, 244
    Summer Fruit Parfait, 239
Beverages
    Hot Tomato Toddies, 66
Biscuits
    Celery Biscuits, 208
Blood cholesterol, 4–7, 10, 21–22
Blueberries
    Blueberry Sauce with Nutmeg, 250
    Blueberry Turnover Pastries, 230–31
    Cape Cod Cranberry-Blueberry Crisp, 238
Breads, 190–97
    Alfalfa Sprout Bread, 205
    Almond-Chive Bread, 201
    Basic Sourdough Starter, 192
    Blue Cornbread with Fresh Sweet and Hot
    Peppers, 218
    California Sticky Buns, 208

Breads *(continued)*
    Celery Biscuits, 208
    Dark Rye with Molasses, 202
    Dark Rye Sourdough Bread, 215
    Dilly Bread, 207
    English Muffins with Oat Bran, 200
    Focaccia, 206
    Irish Raisin Bread, 217
    Italian Tomato-Herb Bread, 203
    Minnesota Christmas Stollen, 199
    Oatmeal-Raisin Bread, 204
    Onion Baguettes, 210
    Orange, Cranberry, and Date Bread, 219
    Red Pepper Cornbread, 63
    Sourdough Wheat Baguette, 216
    Sprouted Two-Grain Bread, 214
    Thyme, Sage, and Olive Loaf, 212
    Walnut Poteca, 198
    Wednesday Bread, 211
Breakfast
    breads for, 197–202
    Vegetable Breakfast Scramble, 176
Brown rice, 35–36. *See also* Rice
    Basic Brown Rice, 36
    Brown-Rice Salad with Mint in Lettuce
        Cups, 151
Bulgur, 141
    Bulgur Wheat Salad with Apricots, 94
Burgers
    Barbecued Vegetarian Burgers, 179
    Sprouted Bean Burgers, 144
Burritos
    Southwestern Bread Wraps, 70
    Vegetarian Burritos, 170
Butter, substitutes for, 27

C
Cabbage, 76
    Chinese Picnic Coleslaw, 87
    Chinese Vegetable Salad with Kiwifruit, 83
Calories, weight loss and, 23–24
Carob
    Carob Date Pops, 239
    Carob Pudding, 245
Carrots, 74, 76
    Carrot Bisque, 116
    Orange-Carrot Soup with Ginger, 125
    Red Ranch Salad Dressing, 80
    Rice-Paper Vegetarian Spring Rolls, 69

Cashews. *See also* Nuts
    Cashew and Bean Salad, 93
    Maple-Cashew Mousse, 243
Cauliflower, 76
    Warm Cauliflower Salad, 62
Celery, 77
    Ants on a Log, 68
    Celery Biscuits, 208
Cheese
    California Pizza Toasts, 55
    ricotta, substitutes for, 27
Chicken stock, substitutes for, 27
Chick-peas, 28, 140
    Chick-Pea and Tomato Gazpacho, 129
    sprouted, 86
        Sprouted Bean Burgers, 144
Chili
    Anaheim-Chili Casserole, 175
    Chili Tortilla Strips, 67
    Meatless Chili with Corn Chips, 184–85
    Southwestern Red-Bean Chili, 61
Chilled soups, 104, 127–30
Chocolate, substitutes for, 27
Cholesterol, 2–12
    children and, 23
    content of common foods, 262–65
    fruits and vegetables and, 74
    insulin and, 49
Complex carbohydrates in diet, 22
Condiments, 29–31
Cooking methods, 40–43
Cooking oils, 31, 224
Cookware, 42–43, 44–45, 139–41
Corn, 36–37
    Fresh-Corn and Pepper Chowder, 131
    Mexican Corn Stew, 142
    Pasta and Corn Salad with Red Sauce, 89
    Southwestern Corn and Barley Salad, 92
Cornbread
    Blue Cornbread with Fresh Sweet and Hot
        Peppers, 218
    Red Pepper Cornbread, 63
Corn chips
    Chili Tortilla Strips, 67
    Meatless Chili with Corn Chips, 184–85
Cornmeal, 36–37. *See also* Cornbread
    Creamy Polenta with Roasted Vegetables,
        147
Cornstarch, substitutes for, 27

Cranberries, 228
    Cape Cod Cranberry-Blueberry Crisp, 238
    Cranberry Sherbet Parfait, 240-41
    Orange, Cranberry, and Date Bread, 219
Cream, substitutes for, in soup, 104
Cream soups, 114-18
Crisps
    Cape Cod Cranberry-Blueberry Crisp, 238
    Pear Crisp with Oat Bran Crust, 237
    Raspberry-Apple Crisp, 236
    Vermont Maple Crisp, 236-37
Cucumbers, 76
    Cucumber-Dill Dressing, 81
    Gingered Cucumber and Squash Salad, 86
Currants
    Almond Rice Pudding, 246

D
Dates
    Carob Date Pops, 239
    Orange, Cranberry, and Date Bread, 219
Desserts, 222-51
Diet, 11, 17-24
Dinner parties, 52-54
Dips
    Baked New Potatoes with Assorted Dips, 57
    Caper and Garlic Dip with Fresh Vegetables, 56-57
    Eve's Miso-Tahini Dip, 187

E
Eggplant, 76
    Baked Eggplant and Tomato Pasta Casserole, 159
    Eggplant-Tomato Sauce, 163
    Grilled-Eggplant Salad with Teriyaki Marinade, 85
    Ratatouille Salad in Lettuce Cups, 97
Egg yolk substitutes, 226
Endive, 76
    Sun-Dried-Tomato Pesto in Endive Spears, 58
Entertaining, 54, 94-99
Escarole
    Escarole Soup with Orzo, 120
Exercise, 9, 11

F
Fat intake, reducing, 18
Fennel, 77
    Fennel Soup Italian-Style, 123

Fiber, blood cholesterol and, 21-22
Figs
    Pineapple-Fig Bake, 246
Flavored vinegars, 29-31
    Raspberry Vinegar, 30
Flour, 35-38, 223-24
    white, substitutes for, 27
Focaccia, 206
Food and Drug Administration survey on cholesterol awareness, 2
Foods, cholesterol content, 262-65
Framingham Heart Study, 6-7, 10-12
French bread. See Baguettes
Fruit, 42, 74, 228. See also specific fruits
    desserts, 243-51
    Morning-Glory Fruit Shake, 64
    party platters, 51
    sauces, 249-51

G
Garlic, 32, 76, 79
    Black Beans with Cumin and Garlic, 150
    Caper and Garlic Dip with Fresh Vegetables, 56-57
    Garlic Broth, 113
    Momma's Mock Chicken Soup, 123
Gelatin, substitutes for, 27, 226-27
Gender, heart disease risk and, 9
Genetics, heart disease risk and, 8
Grains, 35-38, 139-41. See also specific grains
Grapefruit, 74, 228
    Sweet Grapefruit, Orange, and Kiwifruit Salad, 96-97
Green beans
    Green and White Bean Salad, 98
Green peppers (sweet), 76, 79
    Vegetarian Sweet and Sour Tofu, 177
Greens, 76-77
    Escarole Soup with Orzo, 120
    Momma's Mock Chicken Soup, 123

H
HDL cholesterol, 4-7
Heart disease, 5, 10-12
    risk, 6, 8-9, 23
Herbal salt substitutes, 33
Herbs, 32-33, 108-10
    Herbed Red-Potato Salad, 84

Herbs *(continued)*
  Herb Noodles, 157
  Italian Tomato-Herb Bread, 203
High-density lipoproteins (HDLs), 4–6
Hors d'ouevres, 54–60
Hot peppers
  Anaheim-Chili Casserole, 175
  Blue Cornbread with Fresh Sweet and Hot
    Peppers, 218
  Jalapeño-Pepper and Wild-Mushroom
    Risotto, 148
  Next-Day Pizzas with Hot Peppers, 63
  Onions Stuffed with Tempeh, Tomatoes, and
    Peppers, 183

I
Ices
  Carob Date Pops, 239
  Cranberry Sherbet Parfait, 240–41
  Watermelon Sherbet, 240
Icing
  Tofu Cream-Cheese Icing, 168
Ingredient substitutes. *See* Substitutes for
  ingredients

K
Kiwifruit
  Apple, Kiwifruit, and Berry Tart, 233
  Chinese Vegetable Salad with Kiwifruit,
    83
  Cranberry Sherbet Parfait, 240–41
  Sweet Grapefruit, Orange, and Kiwifruit
    Salad, 96–97
Kudzu, 226

L
Lasagna
  Five-Vegetable Lasagna, 154–55
  Lasagna Filling, 168
LDL cholesterol, 4–7
Leeks, 76
  Chilled Leek and Potato Soup, 128
Leftovers as snacks, 50
Legumes, 26–29, 137–41. *See also* Beans
Lemons, 228
  Lemon-Rice Salad, 95
  Lemon-Rosemary Dressing, 80
Lentils, 28, 140
  Greek Lentil Soup, 132

Lettuce, 76, 77
  Brown-Rice Salad with Mint in Lettuce
    Cups, 151
  Ratatouille Salad in Lettuce Cups, 97
Lipoproteins, 4
Low-density lipoproteins (LDLs), 4–5

M
Mangoes
  Mango Salad with Curry Dressing, 90–91
Maple Syrup
  Maple-Apple Bake, 247
  Maple-Cashew Mousse, 243
  Vermont Maple Crisp, 236–37
Meal plans, 254–60
Melons, 228
  Chinese Melon Dessert, 247
  Two-Melon Soup, 128
  Watermelon Sherbet, 240
Milk, substitutes for, 27, 244, 227
Miso, 33, 169–70
  Eve's Miso-Tahini Dip, 187
  John's Special Sauce for Vegetables, 188
  Miso Marinade for Vegetables, 87
  Miso Onion Soup, 187
  Noodles with Miso Sauce, 62
  Sushi Bar Miso Soup, 199
Monounsaturated fats, 10, 21
Mousse
  Maple-Cashew Mousse, 243
  Mocha Mousse, 241
Mushrooms, 32, 76
  Baked Marinated Cutlets, 176–77
  French Mushroom Salad with Tempeh,
    180–81
  Jalapeño-Pepper and Wild-Mushroom
    Risotto, 148
  Marinated Mushrooms, 84–85
  Mushroom-Essence Soup, 126–27
  Mushroom Kabobs, 55
  Mushroom Ragout on Rye Toast Triangles, 71
  Salt-Free Tomato Sauce with Mushrooms,
    161
  Shiitake-Mushroom Dressing, 80
  Stuffed Mushrooms, 174
    with Parsley Pesto, 60
  Szechuan Hot-and-Sour Soup, 121
  Wild Rice with Mushrooms and Pecans,
    149

Mustard, 29, 30
    Hot and Sweet German-Style Mustard, 30
    Mild Ballpark Mustard, 30
    Mustard Dressing with Garlic, 81

N
National Cholesterol Education Program
    (NCEP), 6
National Heart, Lung, and Blood Institute
    (NHLBI), 6
    dietary guidelines, 18–22
Noodles. *See* Pasta
Nuts. *See also specific nuts*
    Asian Nut Balls, 59
    Nut Milk, 244

O
Oat bran, 11, 21–22
    English Muffins with Oat Bran, 200
    Pear Crisp with Oat Bran Crust, 237
Oats, 37, 141
    Oat-Almond Piecrust, 234–35
    Oatmeal-Raisin Bread, 204
Obesity, heart disease risk and, 9
Oils, 31, 79, 224
Olives
    Thyme, Sage and Olive Loaf, 212
    Tomato and Green-Olive Sauce, 162
Onions, 76, 79
    Miso Onion Soup, 187
    Onion Baguettes, 210
    Onions Stuffed with Tempeh, Tomatoes, and
        Peppers, 183
    Sweet Onion Soup, 126
Oranges, 228
    Orange, Cranberry, and Date Bread, 219
    Orange-Carrot Soup with Ginger, 125
    Orange Salad with Walnuts, 89
    Sweet Grapefruit, Orange, and Kiwifruit
        Salad, 96–97
Ornish, Dean, 7, 14–15, 17
Orzo
    Escarole Soup with Orzo, 120
    Saffron Orzo, 155

P
Pancreas, inflammation of, 5
Papaya
    Chilled Papaya-Pineapple Soup, 129

Parfaits
    Cranberry Sherbet Parfait, 240–41
    Summer Fruit Parfait, 239
Pasta, 156–57
    Baked Eggplant and Tomato Pasta Casserole,
        159
    Basic Pasta Dough, 156–57
    Beet Noodles, 157
    Five-Vegetable Lasagna, 154–55
    Herb Noodles, 157
    Nona's Pasta with Beans, 158
    Noodles with Miso Sauce, 62
    Noodles and White Bean Salad with Low-Oil
        Vinaigrette, 152
    Pasta and Corn Salad with Red Sauce, 89
    Peanutty Pasta Salad, 99
    Red and Green Pasta with Walnut Sauce, 158
    Saffron Orzo, 155
    Salt-Free Southern Italian Pasta Sauce, 162–63
    Spicy Chinese Noodles, 95
    Spinach Noodles, 157
    Thai Noodle and Vegetable Salad, 160
    toppings, 161–164
Pastries, 229–35. *See also* Tarts
    Apple Dumplings, 232
    Blueberry Turnover Pastries, 230–31
Peaches, 228
    Fresh Peach Pudding, 243
    Peaches with Melba Sauce, 243
    Peach Sauce with Grand Marnier, 250
    Summer Fruit Parfait, 239
Peanut butter
    Charlie's Favorite Peanut Butter and Banana
        Sandwiches, 171
    Peanutty Pasta Salad, 99
    Spicy Indonesian Cutlets with Peanut Sauce,
        182
Peanuts
    Peanutty Pasta Salad, 99
Pears, 228
    Pear Crisp with Oat Bran Crust, 237
    Sweet Golden Pears, 249
    Winter Pear and Spinach Salad with Balsamic
        Vinegar, 96
Pecans
    Wild Rice with Mushrooms and Pecans,
        149
Peppers. *See* Green peppers (sweet); Hot peppers;
    Red peppers (sweet)

Pesto
  Mediterranean Pesto Soup, 122
  Stuffed Mushrooms with Parsley Pesto, 60
  Sun-Dried-Tomato Pesto in Endive Spears, 58
Piecrust
  Light and Flaky No-Cholesterol Piecru t,
    226–27
  Oat-Almond Piecrust, 234–35
Pies, 229–35. *See also* Tarts
  French Apple Pie, 231
  Heavenly Rhubarb Pie, 234
Pineapple
  Chilled Papaya-Pineapple Soup, 129
  Chinese Melon Dessert, 247
  Pineapple-Fig Bake, 246
Pizza. *See also* Focaccia
  California Pizza Toasts, 55
  Next-Day Pizzas with Hot Peppers, 63
Plaque in arteries, 4, 5, 6, 17
Polenta, 37
  Creamy Polenta with Roasted Vegetables, 147
Polyunsaturated fats, 10, 20
Popcorn
  Savory Garlicky Popcorn, 67
Potatoes, 76
  Baked New Potatoes with Assorted Dips, 57
  Baked Potato Topping, 168
  Chilled Leek and Potato Soup, 128
  Herbed Red-Potato Salad, 84
  Hungarian Cream of Potato Soup, 114
  Oil-Free Potato Chips, 66
Presentation of foods, 52, 53, 77–78, 104, 111–12
Pudding. *See also* Mousse
  Almond Rice Pudding, 246
  Berry and Banana Kanten, 242
  Carob Pudding, 245
  English Summer Pudding, 242
  Fresh Berry Tapioca, 244
  Fresh Peach Pudding, 243

Q
Quick breads, 192–93, 217–19
Quinoa, 141
  Asian-Style Quinoa, 150–51

R
Raisins
  Irish Raisin Bread, 217
  Oatmeal-Raisin Bread, 204

Raspberries
  Apple, Kiwifruit, and Berry Tart, 233
  Fresh Raspberry Sauce, 251
  Peaches with Melba Sauce, 243
  Raspberry-Apple Crisp, 236
  Raspberry Vinegar, 30
Red peppers (sweet), 76, 79
  Blue Cornbread with Fresh Sweet and Hot
    Peppers, 218
  Fresh-Corn and Pepper Chowder, 131
  Mexican Rice Salad with Roasted Peppers, 91
  Onions Stuffed with Tempeh, Tomatoes, and
    Peppers, 183
  Red Pepper Cornbread, 63
  Red Pepper Cream Soup with Thyme, 118
  Vegetarian Red Pepper and Artichoke Paella,
    143
  Vegetarian Sweet-and-Sour Tofu, 177
Rhubarb
  Heavenly Rhubarb Pie, 234
Rice, 141. *See also* Brown rice; Wild rice
  Almond Rice Pudding, 246
  Cuban Beans and Rice, 153
  Green Rice and Avocado Salad, 98
  Indian Rice Pilaf with Vegetables, 144–45
  Jalapeño-Pepper and Wild-Mushroom
    Risotto, 148
  Lemon-Rice Salad, 95
  Mexican Rice Salad with Roasted Peppers, 91
  Spinach Fried Rice, 146
  Three-Color Rice, 152–53
  Vegetarian Red Pepper and Artichoke Paella,
    143
  Vegetarian Sweet-and-Sour Tofu, 177
  white, substitutes for, 27
Ricotta cheese, substitutes for, 27
Rye, 37–38, 141
  Dark Rye with Molasses, 202
  Dark Rye Sourdough Bread, 215
  sprouts, 213

S
Salad dressings, 78–81
  Cucumber-Dill Dressing, 81
  Lemon-Rosemary Dressing, 80
  Mustard Dressing with Garlic, 81
  Red Ranch Salad Dressing, 80
  San Francisco Japantown Salad Spread, 174
  Shiitake-Mushroom Dressing, 80

Sweet Dill Dressing, 82
Tofu-Dill Dressing, 81
Tofu-Mayonnaise Dressing, 81
Tomato-Tarragon Dressing, 81
Vinegar-Herb Dressing, 82
Salads, 74–81. *See also* Salad dressings
Basque Bean Salad, 90
Brown-Rice Salad with Mint in Lettuce
Cups, 151
Bulgur Wheat Salad with Apricots, 94
Cashew and Bean Salad, 93
Chinese Picnic Coleslaw, 87
Chinese Vegetable Salad with Kiwifruit, 83
French Mushroom Salad with Tempeh,
180–81
Gingered Cucumber and Squash Salad, 86
Green Rice and Avocado Salad, 98
Green and White Bean Salad, 98
Grilled-Eggplant Salad with Teriyaki
Marinade, 85
Harvest Salad, 68–69
Herbed Red-Potato Salad, 84
Lemon-Rice Salad, 95
Mango Salad with Curry Dressing, 90–91
Marinated Mushrooms, 84–85
Mexican Rice Salad with Roasted Peppers, 91
Miso Marinade for Vegetables, 87
Mock Tuna Salad, 178
Noodles and White Bean Salad with Low-Oil
Vinaigrette, 152
Orange Salad with Walnuts, 89
Pasta and Corn Salad with Red Sauce, 89
Peanutty Pasta Salad, 99
Rancho Bernadino Salad with Green Sauce,
185
Ratatouille Salad in Lettuce Cups, 97
Southwestern Corn and Barley Salad, 92
Spicy Chinese Noodles, 95
Sweet Grapefruit, Orange, and Kiwifruit
Salad, 96–97
Thai Noodle and Vegetable Salad, 160
Three-Sprout Salad with Lemon Dressing, 88
Warm Cauliflower Salad, 62
Warm Chopped-Vegetable Salad, 92–93
Wheat Berry and Tempeh Salad with Curry
Dressing, 181
Winter Pear and Spinach Salad with Balsamic
Vinegar, 96
Salt, substitutes for, 27, 33

Sandwiches
breads for, 203–6
Charlie's Favorite Peanut Butter and Banana
Sandwiches, 171
Spiced Tempeh Sandwiches, 64
Saturated fat, 8–10, 19–20
Sauces, 34–35
Blueberry Sauce with Nutmeg, 250
Eggplant-Tomato Sauce, 163
Fresh Raspberry Sauce, 251
Green-Tomato Sauce, 164
John's Special Sauce for Vegetables, 188
Meatless Tomato Sauce, 171
Peach Sauce with Grand Marnier, 250
Salt-Free Southern Italian Pasta Sauce, 162–63
Salt-Free Tomato Sauce with Mushrooms, 161
Spicy Indonesian Cutlets with Peanut Sauce,
182
Sweet Cherry Sauce, 251
Tomato and Green-Olive Sauce, 162
Sautéing, 42, 44–45
soup vegetables, 103, 105–7
Seasonings, 32–33, 103–4, 107–10
Serum cholesterol. *See* Blood cholesterol
Shopping tips, 43
Smoking, heart disease risk and, 8–9
Snacks, 48–51
Ants on a Log, 68
Chili Tortilla Strips, 67
Hot Tomato Toddies, 66
Oil-Free Potato Chips, 66
Savory Garlicky Popcorn, 67
Soups, 102–12
Ann's Sweet Potato Soup, 120–21
Basic Bean Soup, 145
Beet Soup with Orange Juice and Green
Onions, 119
Boston Bean Soup, 133
Butternut Squash Soup with Five Spices, 115
Carrot Bisque, 116
Chick-Pea and Tomato Gazpacho, 129
Chilled Leek and Potato Soup, 128
Chilled Papaya-Pineapple Soup, 129
Dairyless Cream of Spinach Soup, 117
Escarole Soup with Orzo, 120
Fennel Soup Italian-Style, 123
Fresh-Corn and Pepper Chowder, 131
Garlic Broth, 113
Greek Lentil Soup, 132

Soups *(continued)*
    Hungarian Cream of Potato Soup, 114
    Mediterranean Pesto Soup, 122
    Miso Onion Soup, 187
    Momma's Mock Chicken Soup, 123
    Mushroom-Essence Soup, 126-27
    Orange-Carrot Soup with Ginger, 125
    Red Pepper Cream Soup with Thyme, 118
    Simple Split-Pea Soup, 132-33
    Spinach and Wild Rice Soup, 124
    stock, 103, 104-5, 113
    Sushi Bar Miso Soup, 199
    Sweetheart Strawberry Soup, 130
    Sweet Onion Soup, 126
    Szechuan Hot-and-Sour Soup, 121
    Tahini Creamed Vegetable Soup, 116-17
    Tomato-Cilantro Soup, 124-25
    Two-Melon Soup, 128
    Vegetable Stock, 113
Sour cream
    Mock Sour Cream, 167
    substitutes for, 27
Sourdough, 192
    Basic Sourdough Starter, 192
    Sourdough Wheat Baguette, 216
Soybeans, 28-29. *See also* Miso; Tempeh; Tofu
Spices, 32-33, 108-9
Spinach, 76, 77
    Dairyless Cream of Spinach Soup, 117
    Dairyless Spinach Tarts, 178-79
    Spinach Fried Rice, 146
    Spinach Noodles, 157
    Spinach and Wild Rice Soup, 124
    Winter Pear and Spinach Salad with Balsamic
        Vinegar, 96
Split peas, 28, 140
    Simple Split-Pea Soup, 132-33
Spreads
    California Tempeh Spread, 186
    Dilled Party Spread, 180
    San Francisco Japantown Salad Spread, 174
    Simple Bean Spread on Rye Croutons, 65
Sprouts, 86
    Alfalfa Sprout Bread, 205
    in breads, 213-16
    rye berries, 213
    Sprouted Bean Burgers, 144
    Sprouted Two-Grain Bread, 214

Three-Sprout Salad with Lemon Dressing,
    88
    wheat berries, 213
Squash, 76
    Butternut Squash Soup with Five Spices, 115
    Gingered Cucumber and Squash Salad, 86
    Ratatouille Salad in Lettuce Cups, 97
Staples, 44
Stew
    Mexican Corn Stew, 142
    Mushroom Ragout on Rye Toast Triangles,
        71
    Vegetarian Sierra Stew, 145-46
Stock, 103, 104-5
    Garlic Broth, 113
    Vegetable Stock, 113
Storage tips, 43-44
    soup, 105, 112
Strawberries
    Sweetheart Strawberry Soup, 130
Stress, heart disease risk and, 9
Substitutes for ingredients, 27
    cream in soup, 103
    milk, 227, 244
    sour cream, 167
    sweeteners, 225
    thickeners, 226-27
Sugar, substitutes for, 27, 225
Sun-dried tomatoes
    Italian Tomato-Herb Bread, 203
    Sun-Dried-Tomato Pesto in Endive Spears,
        58
Sweetened condensed milk, substitutes for, 27
Sweeteners, 224-25
Sweet potatoes
    Ann's Sweet Potato Soup, 120-21

T
Tahini
    Eve's Miso-Tahini Dip, 187
    Tahini Creamed Vegetable Soup, 116-17
Tamari, 33, 169-70, 186-88
Tarts, 229-35
    Apple, Kiwifruit, and Berry Tart, 233
    Dairyless Spinach Tarts, 178-79
Tempeh, 28, 169
    Barbecued Vegetarian Burgers, 179
    California Tempeh Spread, 186

Dilled Party Spread, 180
French Mushroom Salad with Tempeh, 180-81
Meatless Chili with Corn Chips, 184-85
Miniature Stuffed Vegetables, 58-59
Onions Stuffed with Tempeh, Tomatoes, and Peppers, 183
Rancho Bernadino Salad with Green Sauce, 185
Spiced Tempeh Sandwiches, 64
Spicy Indonesian Cutlets with Peanut Sauce, 182
Wheat Berry and Tempeh Salad with Curry Dressing, 181
Thickeners, 34-35, 226-27
Tofu, 29, 79, 167-68
Anaheim-Chili Casserole, 175
Baked Marinated Cutlets, 176-77
Baked Potato Topping, 168
California Pizza Toasts, 55
Caper and Garlic Dip with Fresh Vegetables, 56-57
Carob Pudding, 245
Charlie's Favorite Peanut Butter and Banana Sandwiches, 171
Chinese Supper Stir-Fry, 173
Dairyless Spinach Tarts, 178-79
Five-Vegetable Lasagna, 154-55
Lasagna Filling, 168
Lemon-Rosemary Dressing, 80
Mango Salad with Curry Dressing, 90-91
Meatless Tomato Sauce, 171
Mock Sour Cream, 167
Mock Tuna Salad, 178
San Francisco Japantown Salad Spread, 174
Stuffed Mushrooms, 174
Summer Fruit Parfait, 239
Szechuan Hot-and-Sour Soup, 121
Tofu Cream-Cheese Icing, 168
Tofu-Dill Dressing, 81
Tofu-Mayonnaise Dressing, 81
Tofu Whipped Cream, 229
Vegetable Breakfast Scramble, 176
Vegetarian Burritos, 170
Vegetarian Golden Pot Pie, 172-73
Vegetarian Sweet-and-Sour Tofu, 177
Vinegar-Herb Dressing, 8

Tomatoes, 76. *See also* Sun-dried tomatoes
Baked Eggplant and Tomato Pasta Casserole, 159
Chick-Pea and Tomato Gazpacho, 129
Eggplant-Tomato Sauce, 163
Green-Tomato Sauce, 164
Hot Tomato Toddies, 66
Italian Tomato-Herb Bread, 203
Meatless Tomato Sauce, 171
Onions Stuffed with Tempeh, Tomatoes, and Peppers, 183
Salt-Free Southern Italian Pasta Sauce, 162-63
Salt-Free Tomato Sauce with Mushrooms, 161
Tomato-Cilantro Soup, 124-25
Tomato and Green-Olive Sauce, 162
Tomato-Tarragon Dressing, 81
Triglycerides, 5

U
Unsaturated fats, 10

V
Vegetables, 40-43, 51, 75-77, 103-7. *See also specific vegetables*
Caper and Garlic Dip with Fresh Vegetables, 56-57
Chinese Supper Stir-Fry, 173
Creamy Polenta with Roasted Vegetables, 147
Grilled Vegetables en Papillote, 70
Harvest Salad, 68-69
Indian Rice Pilaf with Vegetables, 144-45
John's Special Sauce for Vegetables, 188
Miniature Stuffed Vegetables, 58-59
Miso Marinade for Vegetables, 87
Refrigerator Pickled Vegetables, 56
Tahini Creamed Vegetable Soup, 116-17
Thai Noodle and Vegetable Salad, 160
Vegetable Breakfast Scramble, 176
Vegetable Stock, 113
Warm Chopped-Vegetable Salad, 92-93
Vegetarians, cholesterol and, 3
Very low-density lipoproteins (VLDLs), 5
Vinegars, 29-31
VLDL cholesterol, 5

W

Walnuts. *See also* Nuts
    Orange Salad with Walnuts, 89
    Red and Green Pasta with Walnut Sauce, 158
    Walnut Poteca, 198
Weight control, cholesterol and, 11
Weight loss, 22-24
Wheat berries
    sprouted, 86, 213
    Sprouted Bean Burgers, 144
    Wheat Berry and Tempeh Salad with Curry
        Dressing, 181
Whipped cream
    substitutes for, 27
    Tofu Whipped Cream, 229
White bread crumbs, substitutes for, 27
White flour, substitutes for, 27

Whole grains, 35-38, 139-41. *See also specific grains*
Whole wheat, 38, 141. *See also* Breads; Wheat berries
    pastry flour, 223-24
Wild rice
    Spinach and Wild Rice Soup, 124
    Wild Rice with Mushrooms and Pecans, 149
Wines, 33-34

Y

Yeast, 33, 191-97
Yeasted breads, 191-212

Z

Zucchini
    Ratatouille Salad in Lettuce Cups, 97